STRATEGIC MANAGEMENT IN ORGANISATIONAL BEHAVIOUR AND DEVELOPMENT

Dr. Sanjay Bhattacharya

M.A. (SW), M.Phil., PGDLLIR, PGDHRD, LL.B., Ph.D.

People and Culture Professional,
World Vision India.
Ex-Assistant Professor of Human Resource Management,
Department of Social Work,
BSSS, Bhopal (India).

Himalaya Publishing House

MUMBAI • NEW DELHI • NAGPUR • BENGALURU • HYDERABAD • CHENNAI • PUNE • LUCKNOW • AHMEDABAD • ERNAKULAM • BHUBANESWAR • INDORE • KOLKATA • GUWAHATI

First Edition: 2013

Published by : Mrs. Meena Pandey for **Himalaya Publishing House Pvt. Ltd.,**
"Ramdoot", Dr. Bhalerao Marg, Girgaon, **Mumbai - 400 004.**
Phone: 022-23860170/23863863, Fax: 022-23877178
E-mail: himpub@vsnl.com; Website: www.himpub.com

Branch Offices :

New Delhi : 'Pooja Apartments', 4-B, Murari Lal Street, Ansari Road, Darya Ganj, New Delhi - 110 002. Phone: 011-23270392, 23278631; Fax: 011-23256286

Nagpur : Kundanlal Chandak Industrial Estate, Ghat Road, Nagpur - 440 018. Phone: 0712-2738731, 3296733; Telefax: 0712-2721215

Bengaluru : No. 16/1 (Old 12/1), 1st Floor, Next to Hotel Highlands, Madhava Nagar, Race Course Road, Bengaluru - 560 001. Phone: 080-32919385; Telefax: 080-22286611

Hyderabad : No. 3-4-184, Lingampally, Besides Raghavendra Swamy Matham, Kachiguda, Hyderabad - 500 027. Phone: 040-27560041, 27550139; Mobile: 09390905282

Chennai : No.8/2, Madley 2nd Street, Ground Floor, T. Nagar, Chennai - 600 017. Mobile: 09345345055

Pune : First Floor, 'Laksha' Apartment, No. 527, Mehunpura, Shaniwarpeth (Near Prabhat Theatre), Pune - 411 030. Phone: 020-24496323/24496333; Mobile: 09370579333

Lucknow : House No 731, Shekhupura Colony, Near B.D. Convent School, Aliganj, Lucknow - 226 022. Mobile: 09307501549

Ahmedabad : 114, 'SHAIL', 1st Floor, Opp. Madhu Sudan House, C.G. Road, Navrang Pura, Ahmedabad - 380 009. Phone: 079-26560126; Mobile: 09377088847

Ernakulam : 39/176 (New No: 60/251) 1st Floor, Karikkamuri Road, Ernakulam, Kochi - 682011, Phone: 0484-2378012, 2378016; Mobile: 09344199799

Bhubaneswar : 5 Station Square, Bhubaneswar - 751 001 (Odisha). Phone: 0674-2532129, Mobile: 09338746007

Indore : Kesardeep Avenue Extension, 73, Narayan Bagh, Flat No. 302, IIIrd Floor, Near Humpty Dumpty School, Indore - 452 007 (M.P.). Mobile: 09301386468

Kolkata : 108/4, Beliaghata Main Road, Near ID Hospital, Opp. SBI Bank, Kolkata- 700 010, Phone: 033-32449649, Mobile: 09883055590, 07439040301

Guwahati : House No. 15, Behind Pragjyotish College, Near Sharma Printing Press, P.O. Bharalumukh, Guwahati - 781009, (Assam). Mobile: 09883055590, 09883055536

DTP by : HPH Editorial Office, Bhandup (Nitin Gode)

Printed at : Shri Krishna offset Press Delhi-93 On behalf of HPH.

This book is dedicated to

my admiring daughter

Reena Sara Sanjay

(The spout of blaze)

Foreword

Management of People in organisation and channelising it into correct direction has become important. Due to scientific advancement it has become more challenging. Social obligations have increased and everybody wants to catch up with next strata of lifestyle. The traditional ways of managing organisation in fact have diminished. Redesigning of work and organisational structure, have become the order of the day. Many individuals are overwhelmed by the idea of developing strategies, but it can be a fun and reviving process.

It is greatly satisfying to note that Dr. Sanjay Bhattacharya is bringing out a text-book that contains discussions on Strategic Management in context to Organisational Behaviour and Development. This is certainly a welcome initiative. The various chapters of this book are presented in the hope that the tentative explorations contained in its pages will help readers to examine new issues, to examine old issues in new ways, and challenge many of these issues raised for the accepted ways of doing things in the best interest of Organisation and its people. I am confident that this book will join the corpus of literature on 'Human Resource Management and Practice' in adding to the knowledge of those involved in managing people and developing organisational culture by examining the organisation's critical issues and choosing the best approaches for the organisation.

Prof. (Dr.) James Thomas

MS, M.Ch. (Thor), MNASMS, Ph.D., FICS, FACS, FICC, FACC.

Vice Chancellor and Prof. of Cardiac Surgery,

Padmashree Dr. D Y Patil University, Mumbai, (India)

30th April, 2012

Preface

The fast paced changes that are taking place in the corporate world makes it is important to realise the dynamism of people and talent to manage people and develop culture leading to collective innovativeness. To add value, the process of people management must deliver business results. It needs to develop the right mix of people in terms of uniqueness and competencies according to business strategy and desired business outcome. A systemic approach needs to be adopted to drive human capital investment through learning and to ensure learning transfer. A corporate wide monitoring mechanism needs to be set up in order to document results and to ascertain performance support.

Whether an organisation is large, medium, or small business set up, the success of a business depends upon the efficiency and effectiveness of the employees working in its organisation. Hence, a coherent as well as strategic approach is inevitable for the successful coordination and performance of employees working in an organisation. Here comes the importance of Human Resource Management (HRM) in an organisation. It is a discipline of management that deals with the activities that are related to people in the organisation, and above all providing proper guidance to them. It includes creation of work plans, supervision, resolution of conflicts, dealing with issues regarding termination, and day-to-day administration of human resources. An effective HR management is staple for the maintenance of a healthy relationship between staff and board members, effective communication, and minimised costs. Above all, the prime purpose of organisation management is to create a favourable working condition for employees, through effective supervision, adequate appreciation and freedom, effective tools to aid work, good pay and benefits, and encouragement to face challenges.

The book on 'Strategic Management in Organisational Behaviour and Development' contains 12 chapters. Chapter 1 – Strategic Management deals with various approaches and strategic planning in organisation. Chapter 2 – Management By Objectives deals with effectiveness of MBO in an organisational system. Chapter 3 – Human Behaviour in Organisation deals with the application of Organisational Behaviour in performance. Chapter 4 – Organisational Development deals with its intervention strategies. Chapter 5 – Change Management deals with change management strategies. Chapter 6 – Organisational Culture and Climate deals with the understanding of organisational culture and climate and its relationship with work. Chapter 7 – Conflict Management deals with conflict handling models. Chapter 8 – Team Building deals with team building interventions in an organisation. Chapter 9 – Organisational Effectiveness deals with models of organisational effectiveness. Chapter 10 – Organisational Stress Management deals with strategies and model of managing organisational stress. Chapter 11 – Learning

Organisation deals with creating a learning organisation and various models. Chapter 12 – SWOT Analysis deals with its utility in strategy formulation.

I have tried to write this book in simple language so that it is interesting to read and understand. Concepts have been explained with the help of flow charts. Review discussions at the end of the chapters and incorporation of case studies at the end have been aimed at absorption by the readers. This book has been thoroughly prepared in terms of contents and presentation of subject matter. This book is intended for a wider readership. An attempt has been made to incorporate the contents from latest curriculum of various universities across the country. It is not only useful to scholars of HRM but also for the professionals who are involved in developing and implementing organisational strategies.

I do wish that this book would enrich the readers and meet the requirement of students, academicians, professionals, and people who are interested to know the wide-spread understanding of managing people and culture in organisation.

Dr. Sanjay Bhattacharya
E-mail: mail2drsanjay@yahoo.co.in

'Blessed Villa'
3- Buddha, Chinar Fortune City,
Hoshangabad Road,
Bhopal-462026(INDIA)

15th April 2012

Acknowledgements

Any textbook is a set project and it would be unfair, if I don't recognise the support rendered by them in completing this text on 'Strategic Management in Organisational Behaviour and Development'.

First of all, I lift up my heart to the Almighty whose guidance is constantly a light of lamp for my pathway.

In the process of writing this book I have referred many books, papers, and cases of various eminent and distinguished writers. Without their literature, the book would not have seen the light of the day. I have tried to acknowledge their contribution wherever possible. Notwithstanding the above, I would like to convey my deep gratitude to each one of them including those whose names do not appear. I do express my deep appreciation to a large number of my associates and well-wishers who have encouraged me in this scholarly pursuit. In particular, I am obliged to Dr. Jayakumar Christian, National Director, World Vision India; Mr. John Selvaraj, Associate Director, World Vision India; Prof. V.P. Singh, former Director, Crescent Institute of Management, Bhopal; Dr. S.R. Billora, former Reader, Institute of Open and Distance Education, Barkatullah University, Bhopal; Prof. Gracious Thomas, Director School of Social Work, IGNOU, New Delhi; and Mr. Sarvesh Agnihothri, Librarian, BSSS, Bhopal; for their whole-hearted concern and priceless backing in carrying out this project, and as such I express my recognition to them.

I owe a bottomless sense of gratitude to my family members especially my loving father, Mr. Santhosh Bhattacharya for his invariable support, backup, and inspiration that has been a source of insight to complete this book with full passion. I am appreciative to my wife Mrs. Renu Sanjay for her sensible cooperation in typing out my manuscript and it has been of great value to me.

I am grateful to Himalaya Publishing House (Pvt) Ltd.,Mumbai for having uncovered interest in bringing out this book.

I do wish that this book supplemented the readers with a wide ranging understanding and information about the area under discussion. I would welcome to those who come out with practical suggestions and shall be duly acknowledged.

Bhopal
15th April, 2012

Dr. Sanjay Bhattacharya
E-mail: mail2drsanjay@yahoo.co.in

Contents

1. Strategic Management **1-20**
Introduction, Definition of Strategic Management, The Strategic Approach, Benefits of Strategic Management, Levels of Strategies, Process of Strategic Management, Interaction of Basic Elements of Strategic Management, Strategic Planning, Difference between Strategic Planning and Long Range Planning, Developing HRM Strategy, McKinsey's 7S Framework, MacMillan Matrix, BCG Matrix Model, Strategic Thinking and Strategic Management

2. Management By Objectives **21-32**
Introduction, Benefits of Well Defined Objectives, Definition of Objectives, Major and Derivative Objectives, Time Dimension of Objectives, Hierarchy of Objectives, Multiplicity of Objectives, Essential Criteria for Effective Objectives, MBO Concept, Benefits of MBO, Essentials of MBO, The Process of MBO, Limitations of MBO, Making MBO Effective.

3. Human Behaviour in Organisation **33-58**
Introduction, Personality, Attitudes, Johari Window, Organisational Behaviour, Models of OB, Motives, Morale, Motivation,

4. Organisational Development **59-76**
Introduction, Need for Organisational Development, Steps in Organisational Development, Organisational Development Interventions, Ethics in Organisational Development, Organisational Development Values, Marvin Weisbord Six-Box Model (Weisbord's Model).

5. Change Management **77-90**
Introduction, Nature of Organisational Change, Types of Organisational Change, Levels of Organisational Change, Essentials of Organisational Change, Reasons for Organisational Change, Resistance to Organisational Change, Why Change Projects Fail?, Change Management, Importance of Change Management, Change Management Strategies, Factors Influencing Selection of Change Strategy, Three Phases of Change Strategy, Principles of Change Management, Steps Involved in Change Management.

6. Organisational Culture and Climate **91-103**
Introduction, Understanding Organisational Culture, Understanding Organisational Climate, Organisational Culture, Characteristics of Organisational Culture, Uniformity of Culture, Improving Organisational Culture, Components of Culture, Developing Organisational Culture, Guidelines for Developing Culture, How Culture Affects Work?, Organisational Climate, Meaning of Organisational Climate, Characteristics of Organisational Climate, Factors affecting Organisational Climate, Changing Organisational Climate.

7. Conflict Management **104-119**
Introduction, Meaning of Conflict, Types of Organisational Conflict, Sources of Conflict, Levels of Conflict, Functional Features of Conflict, Dysfunctional Features of Conflict, Managing Organisational Conflicts, Avoidance of Conflict, Competency in Resolving Tough Conflict, Pondy's Conflict Episode Process,

Thomas-Kilmann Conflict Handling Model, Role Conflict, Role Ambiguity, and Role Analysis.

8. Team Building 120-135
Introduction, Essentials of Successful Team, Types of Teams, Stages of Team Development, Belbin Team Roles, Principles of Effective Team, Team building Procedure, Purpose of Team building, Selection of Key Subordinates in Team building, Team building Interventions, Managing Team building Activities.

9. Organisational Effectiveness 136-156
Introduction, Interpersonal Relationship, Transactional Analysis, Group Dynamics, Formal and Informal Organisation, Human Resource Development System, Organisational Efficiency and Effectiveness, Organisational Effectiveness Model, Likert's Model of Organisational Effectiveness, Factors Affecting Organisational Effectiveness, Role of Human Resource Professional in Organisational Effectiveness.

10. Organisational Stress Management 157-169
Introduction, Stress and Job Performance, Stress Factors, Consequences of Stress, Organisational Development and Stress Management, Organisational Stress Management Strategies, Organisational Development Intervention Stress Management (ODISM) – Model, Definition of Organisational Stress Management, Analysis of Definition, Work Life Balance.

11. Learning Organisation 170-182
Introduction, Definition of Learning Organisation, Need of Learning Organisation, Creating a Learning Organisation, Benefits of Learning Organisation, Levels of Learning, Learning Models, Organisational Learning and Learning Organisation, Obstacles of Learning Organisation.

12. SWOT Analysis 183-192
Introduction, SWOT Analysis–What to look for?, Tool for Strategy Formulation, Strategic Use of SWOT.

Case Studies 193-216
Salary Revision, Formation of the Union, Pay Package: Seniors v/s. Juniors, Leadership Style – After Promotion, Leadership and Work Behaviour, Selection, Appraisal, and Training, Foreign Business Partner, Ego and Teamwork, Stress Management, Vision, Microsoft's Workaholic Culture, Career Development as a Personal Responsibility, San Diego Zoo's Team Approach, The First-level Supervisors, Relevance of Theoretical Concepts.

Bibliography 217-220

CHAPTER 1

STRATEGIC MANAGEMENT

After studying this chapter, you should be able to:

- Comprehend strategic management.
- Be familiar with strategic approach and benefits of strategic management.
- Be acquainted with levels of strategic management.
- Identify process of strategic management.
- Differentiate between strategic planning and long range planning.
- Develop HRM strategy.
- Be acquainted with McKinsey's 7S framework.
- Be familiar with MacMillan matrix.
- Discern strategic thinking and strategic planning.

Introduction

Strategic management is a particular course of action that is meant to achieve a corporate goal. It is really significant in defining and setting up the organisation's mission, goals, and procedures. Generally, the owners and the founders of the company take the first step in creating a strategic management process. This process is responsible for carrying out several functions such as providing direction and guidance to the employees, setting up measurable goals and a time-span to achieve them, and designating duties to all corporate personnel. Marketing and sales projections are the most important elements in a conventional strategic plan which also includes the steps to assess the accomplishments of every department. Strategic management can be used to determine mission, vision, values, goals, objectives, roles and responsibilities, timelines, etc.

Strategic management can be defined as 'the art and science of formulating, implementing and evaluating cross-functional decisions that enable an organisation to achieve its objective'.

Before we further discuss strategic management, we should know key terms:

1. Vision
2. Mission
3. Environment Scanning (SWOT Analysis)
4. Objective
5. Policies
6. Strategies

1. Vision: Every organisation has its own vision which answers the question, what do we want to become? Developing a vision statement is often considered the first step in strategic planning, preceding strategic management even development of a mission statement. For example; vision statement of World Vision – an international humanitarian organisation is as follows: '*Our vision for every child, life in all its fullness; our prayer for every heart, the will to make it so*'.

2. Mission: It is enduring statement of purpose that distinguishes one business from other similar organisations. A mission statement identifies the scope of an organisation's operations in product and market terms. It describes the values and priorities of an organisation. Every organisation has a mission statement which is the primary reason for running the business. The mission statement should mainly concentrate on the ambitions and purposes of the organisation. Defining the mission statement is the first step for initialising a strategic management process, and all other work procedures are a part of devising a strategic plan. The organisational goals need to be set up after the mission is determined. The goals include fiscal anticipations which strongly emphasises on sales growth, profit levels, customer retention and attraction, and expenditure factors. The goals set up in the strategic planning process are required to be measurable and achievable, and effective schedules should be put into practice to review every aspect of the goals.

3. Environment Scanning: It is the process of conducting research and gathering and assimilating external and internal information. It is the external and internal analysis of environment of the organisation. It is also called SWOT analysis. External analysis helps to know opportunities and threats of the organisation and internal analysis helps to know the strength and weakness of the organisation.

4. Objective: Objectives can be defined as specific results that an organisation seeks to achieve in pursuing its basic mission. It is essential for organisational successes because they state direction, aid in evaluation, create synergy, reveal priorities, focus coordination and provide a basis for effective planning, organising, motivating and controlling activities. Objectives should be challenging, measurable, consistent, reasonable and clear. Objectives can be long-term and short-term.

5. Policies: Policies are the means by which annual objectives will be achieved. Policies include guidelines, rules, and procedures established to support efforts to achieve stated objectives. It can be established at the corporate level and apply to an entire organisation.

6. Strategies: Strategies are the means by which objectives will be achieved. Business strategies may includes geographic expansion, diversification, acquisition, product development, market penetration, retrenchment, divestiture, liquidation, and joint venture. Strategies are potential actions that requires top management decisions and large amounts of the organisational resources.

Definition of Strategic Management

Strategic management is the on-going process of formulating, implementing, and controlling broad plans that guide the organisation in achieving the strategic goals given in its internal and external environment.

Interpretation

- **On-going process:** Strategic management is an on-going process which is in existence throughout the life of organisation.
- **Shaping broad plans:** First, it is an on-going process in which broad plans are firstly formulated than implementing and finally controlled.
- **Strategic goals:** Strategic goals are those which are set by top management. The broad plans are made in achieving the goals.
- **Internal and external environment:** Internal and external environment generally set the goals. External environment force internal environment to set the goals and guide them to achieve the goals.

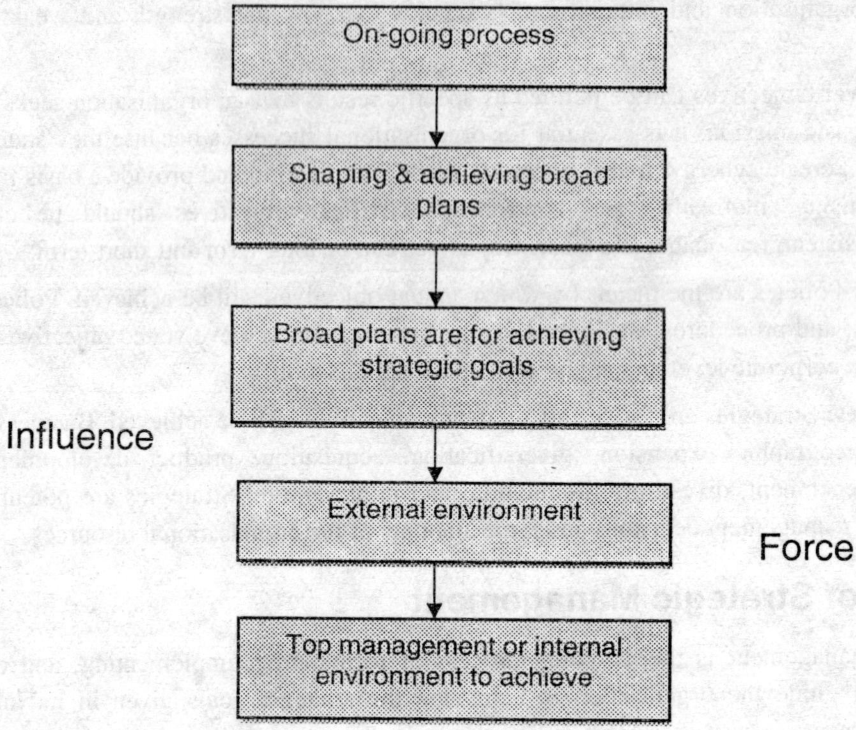

Fig.1.1. Strategic Management

The Strategic Approach

The strategic approach mainly consists of four main elements:

1. The strategic approach is oriented towards the future. It recognises that the environment will change. It is a long range orientation, one that tries to anticipate events rather than simply react as they occur. The approach leads the manager to ask where his/her organisation wants to be after a certain period, what it will need to get to where it wants, and how to develop strategies and the means to get there, and finally, how to manage those strategies to achieve the organisation's goals and objectives. It is recognised that the future cannot be controlled, but the argument can be made that by anticipating the future, organisations can help to shape and modify the impact of environmental change.
2. The strategic approach has an external emphasis. It takes into account several components of the external environment, including technology, politics, economics and the social dimension. Strategic thinking recognises that each of these can either constrain or facilitate an organisation as it seeks to implement policy. Politics will determine the policies that are to be implemented, economics will determine the organisation's level of resources, and social factors might well determine who the organisation's beneficiaries will be. In particular, strategic thinking recognises and emphatically takes into account politics and the exercise of

political authority. Managers are not free to do anything they decide. Managers must be sensitive to the needs and respond to demands of constituents over whom they have little or no control. Among those constituents, political actors are perhaps the most important.

3. The strategic approach concentrates on assuring a good fit between the environment and the organisation (including its mission and objectives, strategies, structures, and resources) and attempts to anticipate what will be required to assure continued fit. Under conditions of rapid political, economic and social change, strategies can quickly become outmoded or no longer serve useful purposes; or the resources traditionally required by the organisation to produce its goods and services may suddenly become unavailable. The strategic approach recognises that to maintain a close fit with the environment, the different elements of the organisation will need to be continuously reassessed and modified as the environment evolves.
4. The strategic approach is a process. It is continuous and recognises the need to be open to changing goals and activities in light of shifting circumstances within the environment. It is a process that requires monitoring and review mechanisms capable of feeding information to managers continuously. Strategic management or planning are not one-shot approaches, they are on-going.

When all taken together these attitudes and behaviours are really a way of approaching or thinking about how to manage or how to implement policy change. Strategic management (or planning) is not something that can be applied only once and then forgotten about or ignored. In that sense it is more than a tool; it is a mental framework.

Benefits of Strategic Management

Strategic management helps in proactively shaping organisation's future, initiate and influence actions and formulates better strategies (systematic, logical, rational approach). Some of the major benefits of strategic management are broadly classified as financial and non-financial as follows:

Financial benefits includes:

- Improved productivity
- Improved sales
- Improved profitability

Non-financial benefits includes:

- Increased employee productivity.
- Improved understanding of competitors strategies.
- Greater awareness of external threats.
- Understanding of performance reward relationships.
- Better problem-avoidance.
- Lesser resistance to change.

Levels of Strategies

In strategic planning it is critical to formally consider how your organisation will accomplish its goals. The answer to this question is a strategy. There are a variety of formal definitions for strategies, but everyone fundamentally agrees that a strategy is the answer to the question, 'How'? 'strategies are simply a set of actions that enable an organisation to achieve results'.

Essentially, there are three different categories of strategies: organisational or corporate, programmatic or business, and functional. The difference among the categories is the focus of the strategy: Organisational strategy outlines the planned avenue for organisational development (e.g., collaborations, earned income, selection of businesses, mergers, etc.). Programmatic strategy addresses how to develop, manage, and deliver programs (e.g., market a pre - natal care service to disadvantaged expectant mothers by providing information and intake services in welfare centres). Functional strategies articulate how to manage administration and support needs that impact the organisation's efficiency and effectiveness, (e.g., develop a financial system that provides accurate information using a cash accrual method).

There are three levels of strategies:

1. **Corporate Strategy:** It describes a company's overall direction towards growth and stability by managing business and product-lines.
2. **Business Strategy:** Usually occurs at business unit or product level emphasising the improvement of competitive position of a firm's products or services in an industry or market segment served by that business unit. Business strategy falls in the realm of corporate strategy.
3. **Functional Strategy:** It is the approach taken by a functional area to achieve corporate and business unit objectives and strategies by maximising the resource productivity. It is concerned with developing and nurturing a distinctive competence to provide the firm with a competitive advantage.

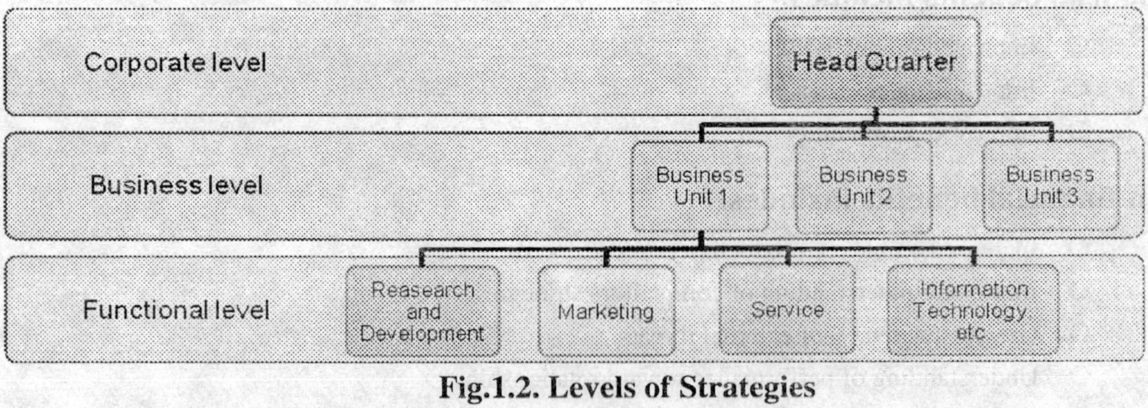

Fig.1.2. Levels of Strategies

Over time, businesses often diversify into different areas; perhaps they develop a new type of product or move into a number of different geographical areas, each of which may have the need for a slightly different type of management. Sometimes, these businesses are related to one another, sometimes they are not. Sometimes, they are separate legal entities, sometimes not. But when an organisation has a range of different types of business within its portfolio, its managers have to take decisions about how these businesses work together, and how many and what sort of businesses should be in its portfolio. These are corporate level strategy.

Process of Strategic Management

Strategy development follows the creation and affirmation of the organisation's purpose statement, environmental and program data collection and analysis, and identification of critical issues. It is critical that strategy development follow these steps because the information gathered and decisions made in these phases are the foundation for strategy creation and selection. Each of these steps provides the following: The purpose statement, the statement of the organisation's ultimate goal, provides the direction to which the strategies should ultimately lead.

External market data and program evaluation results provide critical data to support strategy development. Without this information and insight, the organisation's strategies will not be in alignment with or effective in the marketplace. The critical issues list serves as the specific focus and framework for the activities of the organisation and the pattern of these activities (developing and selecting the strategies).Strategic management consists of four basic elements:

1. Environmental Scanning.
2. Strategy Formulation.
3. Strategy Implementation.
4. Evaluation and Control.

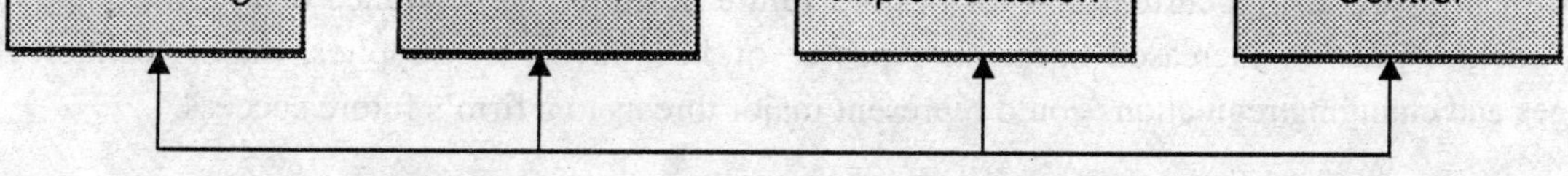

Fig.1.3. Basic Elements of Strategic Management

Interaction of Basic Elements of Strategic Management

1. Environmental Scanning

It is the monitoring, evaluation, and disseminating of information from the external and internal environments to key people within the corporation. Its purpose is to identify strategic factors with those external and internal elements that will determine the future of the corporation.

The external environment consists of variable (Opportunities and Threats) that are outside the organisation and not typically with the short-term control of top management. These variables are from the context within which the corporation exists.

The internal environment of a corporation consists of variable (Strengths and Weaknesses) that are within the organisation itself and are management. These variables are from the context in which work is done. They include the corporation's structure, culture, and resources. The simplest way to conduct environmental scanning is through SWOT analysis.

SWOT Analysis: It is an acronym for the internal strengths and weaknesses of a business and environmental opportunities and threats facing that business. SWOT analysis is a systematic identification of these factors and the strategy that reflects the best match between them. It is based on the logic that an effective strategy maximises a business's strengths and opportunities but at the same time minimise its weaknesses and threats. This simple assumption, if accurately applied, has powerful implications.

Strengths: Strength is a resource, skill or other advantage relative to competitors and the needs of market, a firm serves or anticipates serving. Strength is a distinctive competence that gives the firm a comparative advantage in the marketplace.

Weaknesses: Weaknesses is a limitation or deficiency in resources, skills and capabilities that seriously impedes effective performance. Facilities, financial resources, management capabilities marketing skills and brand image could be sources of weakness.

Opportunities: An opportunity is a major favourable situation in the firm's environment. Key trends represent one source of opportunity. Identification of a previously overlooked market segment, change in competitive or regulatory circumstances, technological changes, and improved buyer or supplier relationships could represent opportunities for the firm.

Threats: Threat is a major unfavourable situation in the firm's environment. It is a key impediment to the firm's current and for desired future position. The entrance of a new competitor, show market growth, increased bargaining power of key buyers or supplier, major technologies changes and changing regulations could represent major threats to a firm's future success.

Usefulness of SWOT Analysis

SWOT analysis helps in narrowing the choice of alternatives and selecting a strategy. The most common application provides a logical framework guiding systematic discussions of the business's situation, alternative strategies and ultimately the choice of strategy. What one manager sees as an opportunity, another may see as a potential threat.

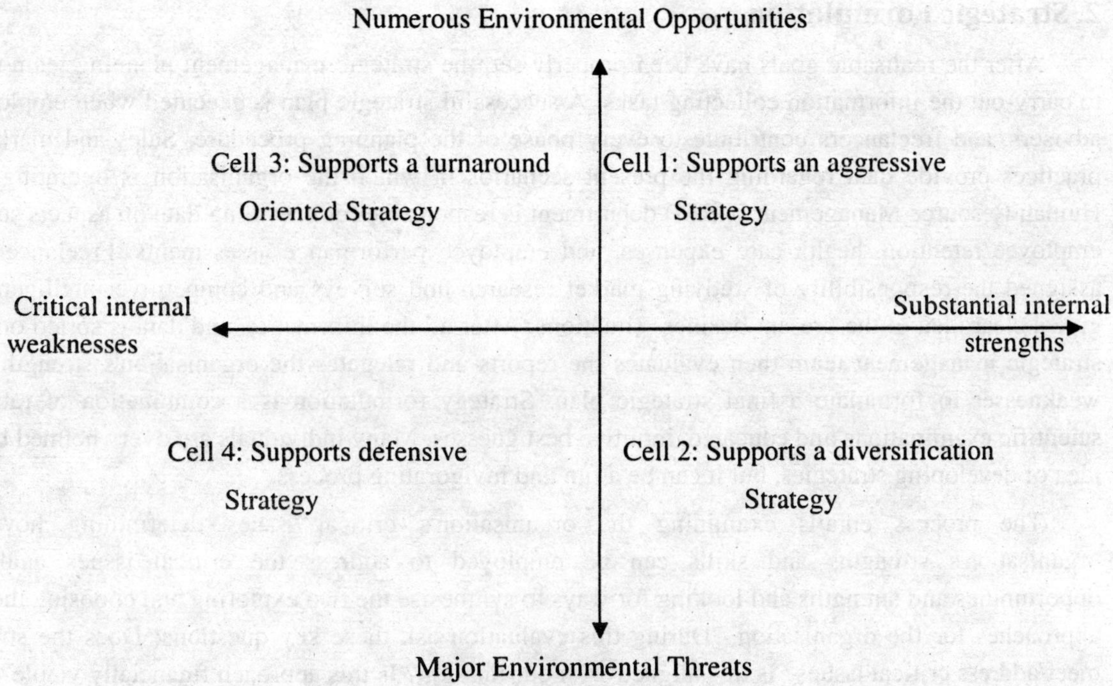

Fig.1.4. SWOT Analysis

A second application of SWOT analysis is that the key external opportunities and threats are systematically compared to internal strengths and weaknesses in a structured approach. The objective is identification of one of four distinct patterns in the match between the firm's internal and external situation. The four cells in figure represent these patterns.

Cell 1 is the most favourable sit situation, the firm several environmental opportunities and has numerous strengths that encourage pursuit of such opportunities. This condition suggests growth oriented strategies to exploit the favourable match.

Cell 2 a firm with key strengths faces an unfavourable environment. In this situation, strategies would use current strengths to build long-term opportunities in other products/markets.

Cell 3 faces impressive market opportunity but is constrained by several internal weaknesses. Businesses in this predicament are like the question marks in the Boston Consulting Group (BCG) matrix. The focus of strategy for such firms is eliminating internal weaknesses to more effectively pursue market opportunity.

Cell 4 is the least favourable situation, with the firm facing major environmental threats from a position of relative weakness. This condition clearly calls for strategies that reduce or redirect involvement in the product markets examined using SWOT analysis.

2. Strategic Formulation

After the realisable goals have been properly set, the strategic management planning team needs to carry-out the information collecting tasks. A successful strategic plan is executed when employees, advisers, and freelancers contribute to every phase of the planning procedure. Sales and marketing practices provide data regarding the present scenarios in which the organisation is operating. The Human Resource Management (HRM) department is responsible for providing data on aspects such as employee retention, health care expenses, and employee performance assessments. Freelancers are assigned the responsibility of studying market research and surveys and competitive intelligence to give a clear idea of the present business situations. After all the information and data is sorted out, the strategic management team then evaluates the reports and relegates the organisation's strengths and weaknesses to formulate a final strategic plan. Strategy formulation is a combination of rational, scientific examinations and educated, intuitive best guesses. Many individuals are overwhelmed by the idea of developing strategies, but it can be a fun and invigorating process.

The process entails examining the organisation's critical issues determining how the organisation's strengths and skills can be employed to address the critical issues analysing opportunities and strengths and looking for ways to synthesise the two exploring and choosing the best approaches for the organisation. During this evaluation ask these key questions: Does the strategy meet/address critical issues? Is this aligned with our mission? Is this approach financially viable? One effective method of strategy generation is to list critical issues and organisational strengths onto flip charts and then have staff or board members brainstorm possible uses of those strengths or other skills to address the critical issues.

Once the brainstorm session is completed, use a roundtable discussion to investigate and evaluate the possible strategies. Remember to develop a list of alternative strategies to investigate and keep in the contingency planning file. It is important not to discount the ideas that come to people during non-working hours.

Strategic formulation is a combination of three main processes which are as follows:

(i) Performing a situation analysis, self-evaluation and competitor analysis: both internal and external; both micro-environmental and macro-environmental.

(ii) Concurrent with this assessment, objectives are set. These objectives should be parallel to a time-line; some are in the short-term and others on the long-term. This involves crafting vision statements (long-term view of a possible future), mission statements (the role that the organisation gives itself in society), overall corporate objectives (both financial and strategic), strategic business unit objectives (both financial and strategic), and tactical objectives.

(iii) These objectives should, in the light of the situation analysis, suggest a strategic plan. The plan provides the details of how to achieve these objectives.

3. Strategy Implementation

Plans need to be devised and implemented once all the data is readily available. The advertising and marketing processes can now be put into practice. Cutbacks and cost-cutting measures may be executed to maintain and increase the profit levels according to the organisational goals. At this point of time, the company management may also take the decision of introducing new products and services in the market. All factors that increase the profitability of the company should be thought upon by the management, and the strategic leadership should be planned according to different strategies. The managers are required to be given time lines for deliverables, level of expectations, budget parameters, and certain obligations. Strategy implementation requires a firm to establish annual objectives, devise policies, motivating employees and allocate resources so that formulated strategies can be executed. Strategy implementation includes developing strategy supportive culture, creating an effective organisational structure, redirecting marketing efforts, preparing budgets, developing and utilising information system, and linking employee compensation to organisational performance. Strategy implementation is often called the action stage of strategic management. Implementing means mobilising employees and managers in order to put formulated strategies into action. It is often considered to be most difficult stage of strategic management. It requires personal discipline, commitment and sacrifice. Strategy formulated but not implemented serve no useful purpose.

4. Strategy Eva_ation and Control

Efficient strategic thinking and a strategic management plan will always have controls and periodic reviews incorporated into the process. Each stage should be elaborated and then the changes should be made accordingly. The management team needs to keep a detailed record of the allotted deadlines and the required particulars should be presented to the clients or stakeholders. The strategic planning team is required to review the integral strategic management processannually. Business situations, market projections, and technological furtherance demand present and regularly updated strategic planning to enable an organisation to be successful in today's highly competitive environment. The periodic incorporation of the strategic management process is crucial for the smooth running of the company. As a result, companies are giving more importance to the strategic management process implementation.

Strategy evaluation is the final stage in the strategic management process. Management desperately needs to know when particular strategies are not working well; strategy evaluation is the primary means for obtaining this information. All strategies are subject to future modification because external and internal forces are constantly changing. In corporate strategy, Johnson and Scholes present a model in which strategic options are evaluated against three key success criteria:

(i) Suitability (would it work?)

(ii) Feasibility (can it be made to work?)

(iii) Acceptability (will they work it?)

(i) **Suitability:** Suitability deals with the overall rationale of the strategy. The key point to consider is whether the strategy would address the key strategic issues underlined by the organisation's strategic position. Does it make economic sense? Would the organisation obtain economies of scale, economies of scope or experience economy? Would it be suitable in terms of environment and capabilities? Tools that can be used to evaluate suitability include: Ranking strategic options, Decision trees, etc.

(ii) **Feasibility:** Feasibility is concerned with the resources required to implement the strategy that are available, can be developed or obtained. Resources include funding, people, time, and information. Tools that can be used to evaluate feasibility include: cash flow analysis and forecasting break-even analysis, resource deployment analysis, etc.

(iii) **Acceptability:** Acceptability is concerned with the expectations of the identified stakeholders (mainly shareholders, employees and customers) with the expected performance outcomes, which can be return, risk and stakeholder reactions. Return deals with the benefits expected by the stakeholders (financial and non-financial). For example, shareholders would expect the increase of their wealth, employees would expect improvement in their careers, and customers would expect better value for money.

Strategic Planning

Strategic planning is a management tool. As with any management tool, it is used for one purpose only: to help an organisation do a better job – to focus its energy, to ensure that members of the organisation are working towards the same goals, to assess and adjust the organisation's direction in response to a changing environment. In short, strategic planning is a disciplined effort to produce fundamental decisions and actions that shape and guide what an organisation is, what it does, and why it does it, with a focus on the future. A word-by-word dissection of this definition provides the key elements that underlie the meaning and success of a strategic planning process: The process is strategic because it involves preparing the best way to respond to the circumstances of the organisation's environment, whether or not its circumstances are known in advance; non-profits often must respond to dynamic and even hostile environments. Being strategic means being clear about the organisation's objectives, and aware of the organisation's resources, and incorporating both into being consciously responsive to a dynamic environment.

The process is about planning because it involves intentionally setting goals (i.e., choosing a desired future) and developing an approach to achieving those goals. The process is disciplined in that it calls for a certain order and pattern to keep it focused and productive. The process raises a sequence of questions that helps planners examine experience, test assumptions, gather and incorporate information about the present, and anticipate the environment in which the organisation will be working in the future. It is about fundamental decisions and actions because choices must be made in order to answer the sequence of questions mentioned above. The plan is ultimately no more, and no less, than a set of decisions about what to do, why to do it, and how to do it. Because it is impossible to do everything that needs to be done in this world, strategic planning implies that some organisational decisions and actions are more important than others – and that much of the strategy lies in making the tough decisions about what is most important to achieving the organisational success. The strategic planning can be complex, challenging, and even messy, but it is always defined by the basic ideas outlined above – and you can always return to these basics for insight into your own strategic planning process.

Everything said above to describe what strategic planning is can also provide an understanding of what it is not. For example, it is about fundamental decisions and actions, but it does not attempt to make future decisions (Steiner, 1979). Strategic planning involves anticipating the future environment, but the decisions are made in the present. This means that over time, the organisation must stay abreast of changes in order to make the best decisions it can at any given point – it must manage, as well as plan, strategically. Strategic planning has also been described as a tool – but it is not a substitute for the exercise of judgement by leadership. Ultimately, the leaders of any enterprise need to sit back and ask, and answer, 'What are the most important issues to respond to'? and 'How shall we respond'? Just as the hammer does not create the bookshelf, so the data analysis and decision-making tools of strategic planning do not make the organisation work – they can only support the intuition, reasoning skills, and judgement that people bring to their organisation.

Finally, strategic planning, though described as disciplined, does not typically flow smoothly from one step to the next. It is a creative process, and the fresh insight arrived at today might very well alter the decision made yesterday. Inevitably the process moves forward and back several times before arriving at the final set of decisions.

Difference between Strategic Planning and Long Range Planning

Although many use these terms interchangeably, strategic planning and long range planning differ in their emphasis on the 'assumed' environment. Long range planning is generally considered to mean the development of a plan for accomplishing a goal or set of goals over a period of several years, with the assumption that current knowledge about future conditions is sufficiently reliable to ensure the plan's reliability over the duration of its implementation. In the late 1950s and early 1960s for example, the US economy was relatively stable and somewhat predictable, and, therefore, long range planning was both fashionable and useful. On the other hand, strategic planning assumes that an organisation must be responsive to a dynamic, changing environment (not the more stable environment assumed for long range planning).

Certainly a common assumption has emerged in the non-profit sector that the environment is indeed changeable, often in unpredictable ways. Strategic planning, then, stresses the importance of making decisions that will ensure the organisation's ability to successfully respond to changes in the environment.

Developing HRM Strategy

Being a part of the dynamic environment with rapid changes organisations are required to develop more focused and coherent approach to managing people. Now it is the real time to understand its human power and to convert it into human capital.

For the development of the strategy the two issues are important to study and analyse, these are:

1. What kinds of people do you need to manage and run your business to meet your strategic business objectives?
2. What kind of the people programs and initiatives must be designed and implemented to attract, develop, and retain staff to compete effectively?

Now to overcome and to answer these two questions we are having the following dimensions:

- *Culture:* the beliefs, values, norms, and management style of the organisation
- *Organisation:* the structure, job roles, and reporting lines of the organisation
- *People:* the skill levels, staff potential, and management capability
- *Human resources systems:* the people focused mechanisms which deliver the strategy – employee selection, communications, training, rewards, career development, etc.

Normally, in managing the people element of their business managers will only focus on one or two dimensions and neglect to deal with the others, and then fail to develop the human power. This will result in overall inefficiency. What is required is a strategic perspective aimed at identifying the relationship between all four dimensions. If you require an organisation which really values quality and service you not only have to retrain staff, you must also review the organisation, reward, and appraisal and communications systems. Here the rewarding becomes the real problem which leads to dissatisfaction and hence the lower productivity.

There are seven steps to developing a human resource strategy and the active involvement of senior line managers should be sought throughout the approach.

Step 1: Study the whole business picture

- Highlight the key driving forces of business. What are they?
- What are the implications of the driving forces for the people side of business?
- What is the fundamental people contribution to bottom line business performance?

Step 2: Develop a mission statement

Do not be put off by negative reactions to the words or references to idealistic statements – it is the actual process of thinking through the issues in a formal and explicit manner that is important.

- What is the contribution of people?

Step 3: Conduct a SWOT analysis of the organisation

Focus on the internal strengths and weaknesses of the people side of the business.

- Consider the current skill and capability issues.

Vigorously research the external business and market environment. Highlight the opportunities and threats relating to the people side of the business.

- What impact will/might they have on business performance?
- Consider skill shortages?
- The impact of new technology on staffing levels?

From this analysis we then need to review the capability of personnel department. Complete a SWOT analysis of the department – consider in detail the department's current areas of operation, the service levels, and competences of personnel staff.

Step 4: Conduct a detailed human resources analysis

Concentrate on the organisation's COPS (culture, organisation, people, and HR systems)

- Consider: Where we are? Where do we want to be?
- Study the gaps between reality of where we are now and where we want to be?

Step 5: Determine critical people issues

- Identify the critical people issues namely those that must be addressed. Those which have key impact on the delivery of business strategy.
- Prioritise the critical people issues. What will happen if we fail to address them?

Step 6: Develop consequences and solutions

For each critical issue highlight the options for managerial action generate, elaborate and create – don't go for the obvious. This is an important step as frequently people jump for the known rather than challenge existing assumptions about the way things have been done in the past. Think about the consequences of taking various courses of action.

Once the process is over it should then be possible to translate the action plan into broad objectives. These will need to be broken down into the specialist HR Systems areas of:

- Employee training and development
- Management development
- Organisational development
- Performance appraisal
- Employee reward
- Employee selection and recruitment
- Manpower planning
- Communication

Develop action plan around the critical issues. Set targets and dates for the accomplishment of the key objectives.

Step 7: Implementation and evaluation of the action plans

The ultimate purpose of developing a human resource strategy is to ensure that the objectives set are mutually supportive so that the reward and payment systems are integrated with employee training and career development plans.

There is very little value or benefit in training people if it is only to frustrate them through a failure to provide ample career and development opportunities.

McKinsey's 7S Framework

It is all very well devising a strategy, but we have to be able to implement it if it is to do any good. The 7S Framework first appeared in *'The Art of Japanese Management'* by Richard Pascale and Anthony Athos in 1981. They had been looking at how Japanese industry had been so successful, at around the same time that Tom Peters and Robert Waterman were exploring what made a company excellent. The 7S model was born at a meeting of the four authors in 1978. It went on to appear in 'In Search of Excellence' by Peters and Waterman, and was taken up as a basic tool by the global management consultancy McKinsey. It is sometimes known as the McKinsey's 7S model.

The seven factors are:

Strategy	A set of actions that you start with and must maintain
Structure	How people and tasks/work are organised
Systems	All the processes and information flows that link the organisation together
Style	How managers behave
Staff	How you develop managers (current and future)
Super ordinate Goals	Longer-term vision, and all that values stuff, that shapes the destiny of the organisation
Skills	Dominant attributes or capabilities that exist in the organisation

Managers, they said, need to take account of all seven of the factors to be sure of successful implementation of a strategy – large or small. They're all interdependent, so if you fail to pay proper attention to one of them, it can bring the others crashing down around you. Oh, and the relative importance of each factor will vary over time, and you can't always tell how that's changing. Like a lot of these models, there's a good dose of common sense in here, but the 7S Framework is useful way of checking that you've covered all the bases.

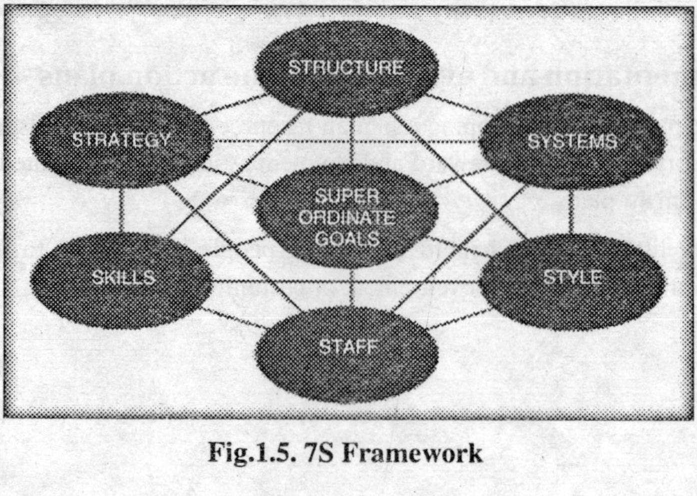

Fig.1.5. 7S Framework

There's a lot more to the 7S Framework of course, especially how we apply it in practice. It may appear as an outmoded concept in today's environment of 'constant change and learning', but the basic principle that we have got to watch a lot of factors all the time as we implement any strategy still applies.

MacMillan Matrix

This strategy grid, developed by Dr. Ian MacMillan, is specifically designed to assist non-profit organisations to formulate organisational strategies. There are three assumptions underlying this approach: the need for resources is essentially competitive and all agencies wanting to survive must acknowledge this dynamics given that resources are scarce, there is no room for direct duplication of services to a single constituency – this is wasteful and inefficient mediocre or low quality service to a large client population and is less preferable to delivering higher quality services to a more focused population. These assumptions have implications that are difficult and painful for many organisations and individuals. It might mean terminating some programs to improve core services and competencies, giving programs and clients to more efficient, effective agencies, or competing aggressively with those programs that are less effective or efficient. MacMillan's matrix examines four program dimensions that guide placement on the strategy grid and indicate implied strategies as discussed below:

1. **Alignment with Mission Statement:** Services or programs that are not in alignment with the organisational mission, unable to draw on existing organisational skills or knowledge, unable to share resources, and/or unable to coordinate activities across programs should be divested.
2. **Competitive Position:** Competitive position addresses the degree to which the organisation has a stronger capability and potential to fund the program and serve the client base than the competitive agencies.
3. **Program Attractiveness:** Program attractiveness is the complexity associated with managing a program. Programs that have low client resistance, a growing client base, easy exit barriers, and stable financial resources are considered simple or 'easy to administer'. The level of program attractiveness also includes an economic perspective or a review of current and future resource investments.
4. **Alternative Coverage:** Alternative coverage is the number of other organisations attempting to deliver or succeeding in delivering a similar program in the same region to similar constituents.

The MacMillan Matrix provides ten cells to place programs that have been reviewed in terms of these four dimensions. Each cell is assigned a strategy that directs the future of the program (s) listed in the cell, (e.g., aggressive competition, joint venture, orderly divestment, etc.). One cell of the matrix, 'Soul of the Agency', requires additional explanation. These are the difficult programs for which the organisation is often the clients' 'last, best hope'. Management must find ways to use the programs in other cells to develop, piggyback, subsidise, leverage, promote, or otherwise support the programs in this category.

BCG Matrix Model

In the early 1970s the Boston Consulting Group developed a model for managing a model for managing a portfolio of different business (or major product-line). The BCG Matrix displays the various business units on a graph of the market growth rate and market share relative to competitors.

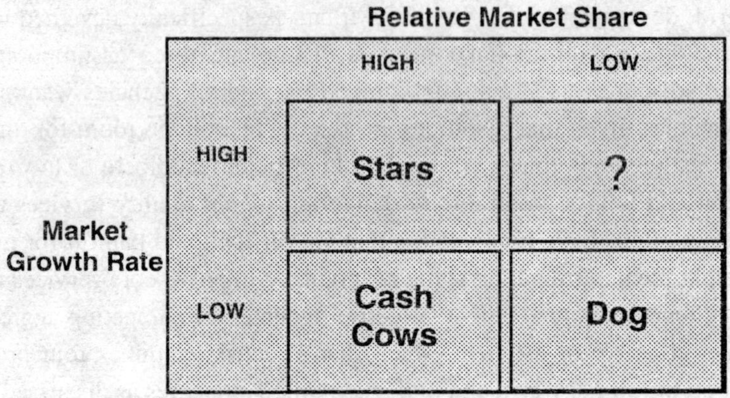

Fig.1.6. BCG Matrix Model

Resources are allocated to business units according to where they are situated on grid as follows:

- *Cash cows:* A business unit that has a large market share in a mature industry, show growing industry. Cash cows require little investment and generate cash that can be used to invest in other business units.
- *Stars:* A business unit that has a large market share in a growing industry. Stars may generate cash, but because the market is growing rapidly they require investment to maintain their lead. If successful as star will become a cash when it industry matures.
- *Question mark:* A business unit that has a small market share in a high growth market. There business units require resources to grow market share, but whether they will succeed or not is unknown.
- *Dog:* A business unit that has a small market share in a mature industry. A dog may not require substantial cash, but it ties up capital that could better be deployed elsewhere. Unless a dog has some other strategic purpose, it should be liquidated if there is little prospect for it to gain market share.

The BCG Matrix provides a framework for allocating resources among different business units and allows one to compare many business units at a glance.

Strategic Thinking and Strategic Management

Strategic planning is only useful if it supports strategic thinking and leads to strategic management – the basis for an effective organisation. Strategic thinking means asking, 'Are we doing the right thing'? Perhaps, more precisely, it means making that assessment using three key requirements about strategic thinking: a definite purpose is in mind; an understanding of the environment, particularly of the forces that affect or impede the fulfilment of that purpose; and creativity in developing effective responses to those forces. It follows, then, that strategic management is the application of strategic thinking to the job of leading an organisation.

Dr. Jagdish Sheth, a respected authority on marketing and strategic planning, provides the following framework for understanding strategic management: continually asking the question, 'Are we doing the right thing'? It entails attention to the 'big picture' and the willingness to adapt to changing circumstances, and consists of the following three elements: formulation of the organisation's future mission in light of changing external factors such as regulation, competition, technology, and customers development of a competitive strategy to achieve the mission creation of an organisational structure which will deploy resources to successfully carry-out its competitive strategy. Strategic management is adaptive and keeps an organisation relevant. In these dynamic times it is more likely to succeed than the traditional approach of 'if it is not broken, do not fix it'.

'Strategic management is an on-going process that evaluates and controls the business and the industries in which the company is involved; assesses its competitors and sets goals and strategies to meet all existing and potential competitors; and then reassesses each strategy annually or quarterly [i.e., regularly] to determine how it has been implemented and whether it has succeeded or needs replacement by a new strategy to meet changed circumstances, new technology, new competitors, a new economic environment or a new social, financial, or political environment.' (Lamb, 1984)

Strategic management is a field that deals with the major intended and emergent initiatives taken by general manager on behalf of owners, involving utilisation of resources, to enhance the performance of organisations in their external environments. It entails specifying the organisation's mission, vision and objectives, developing policies and plans, often in terms of projects and programs, which are designed to achieve these objectives, and then allocating resources to implement the policies and plans, projects and programs. A balanced scorecard is often used to evaluate the overall performance of the business and its progress towards objectives. Recent studies and leading management theorists have advocated that strategy needs to start with stakeholders expectations and use a modified balanced scorecard which includes all stakeholders. Strategic management is a level of managerial activity under setting goals and over tactics. Strategic management provides overall direction to the enterprise and is closely related to the field of organisational studies. In the field of business administration it is useful to talk about 'strategic alignment' between the organisation and its environment or 'strategic consistency'. According to Arieu (2007), 'there is strategic consistency when the actions of an organisation are consistent with the expectations of management, and these in turn are with the market and the context'. Strategic management includes not only the management team but can also include the Board of Directors and other stakeholders of the organisation. It depends on the organisational structure.

Review Discussions

1. Define strategic management and explain its approaches in context of business organisation.
2. Discuss various levels of strategies of an organisation.
3. What are the stages of strategic management?
4. 'Strategic Planning is a tool to focus energy in achieving organisational goals', enumerate this statement.
5. Explain BCG Matrix model.
6. Discuss MacMillan Matrix.
7. Critically explain McKinsey's 7S Framework.
8. What are the steps of developing strategies for human resource management?

♣♣♣♣♣♣

CHAPTER 2

MANAGEMENT BY OBJECTIVES

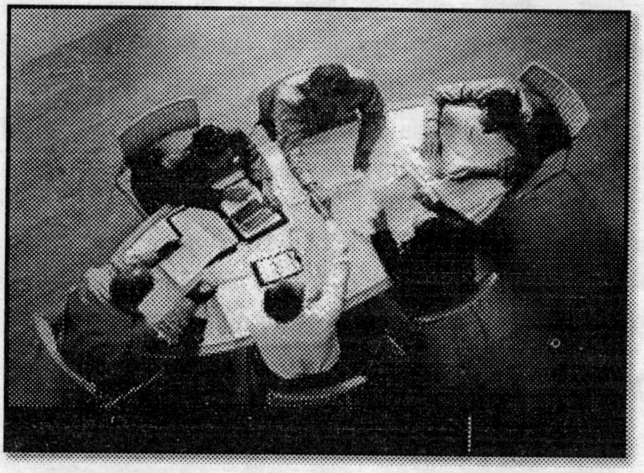

After studying this chapter, you should be able to:

- Understand Management By Objectives concept and benefits of well defined objectives.
- Define objectives.
- Know major and derivative objectives.
- Make out time dimension of objectives.
- Identify hierarchy of objectives.
- Spot multiplicity of objectives.
- Be acquainted with essential criteria of effective objectives.
- Be on familiar terms with benefits, essentials, process, and limitations of Management By Objectives.
- Recognise making Management By Objectives effective.

Introduction

Every rational human activity must have certain clear-cut objectives or goal. A manager, before performing the managerial functions, must ask: what are objectives of the activity she/he is going to manage? The answer to this question will serve many functions. The objective provides orientation by depicting a future state of affairs which the organisation strives to achieve. They set down guidelines for group activity. Objectives constitute a source of legitimacy which justifies the activities of the organisation and indeed its very existence. Moreover, objectives serve as standards for assessing the success of the organisation from deviating from the route they have set for themselves.

Management By Objectives (MBO) is a massive change program. It calls for fundamental changes in the style, attitude, and behaviour of most managers. Principally, the changes required by MBO in a Manager are that she/he should cultivate a participative style of management and develop in one self a result-oriented attitude. A MBO manager should learn to share power and information so that a helping relationship becomes possible between him/her and the people who report to him/her. These qualities do not develop overnight. A system demanding such massive changes in people can only be successful if the organisation is prepared for it and gets committed to it.

Benefits of Well Defined Objectives

The accomplishment of objectives is necessary for the survival of any business enterprise. The management must specify the objectives in all areas on which the survival of the business depends. Well-defined objectives in major areas of the business will achieve the following benefits:

1. Unity of Directions

All manager at various levels make plan of their own planning may lose its consistency unless various plans have the same focus of action.

2. Means of Decentralisation

A large number of managers share their managerial work with appropriate authority and capacity for independent decision. This may lead to disintegration in place of decentralisation unless there is a common goal. The objectives guide to coordinate and remove conflicts or misunderstandings between various individuals.

3. Stimulates Motivation

Objectives fit individual of control by clarifying the contribution of each job as well as each unit.

4. Basis of Control

Objectives provide the basis of control by clarifying the contribution of each job as well as each unit.

5. Better Communication

Objectives lead to improved communication and organisational structure which help in locating problem areas.

6. Better Co-ordination

Objectives facilitate coordination of efforts and resources of the enterprise by providing unity of direction. Objectives force managers to think in terms of results.

7. Higher Productivity

Managing by objectives leads to increased productivity because often management concentrates their energies on unimportant matters.

Definition of Objectives

According to Louis Allen, 'Objectives are goal established to guide the efforts of the company and each of its components'. An objective has no meaning unless it relate to certain well defined objectives or goals. Objectives are not only useful in planning but also in other managerial functions like organising, directing, and controlling. They are important in decision making in any area of business. Clear-cut objectives encourage constancy in decision making in the long run.

Objectives are the ends towards which the activities of an enterprise are directed. They provide directions to various activities of the enterprise. They depict a future state of affair which an organisation strives to realise. They lay down guidelines for various activities and also constitute a source of legitimacy which justifies various activities of an organisation and also its very existence. Objectives serve as benchmark for people working in the organisation and the overall effectiveness and efficiency of the organisation.

Major and Derivative Objectives

Generally, big enterprises have both major and derivative objectives. Major objectives are set up for the entire organisation. They are broader in scope and are applicable throughout the enterprise. They are also known as primary objectives of the enterprise. Derivative objectives are derived from the major objectives in order to contribute to the major goals of the enterprise. They are also known as departmental objectives and are subsidiary to the main objectives of the enterprise.

Time Dimension of Objectives

Since a business enterprise is a continuous entity, it must have both long range, as were as short range objectives. Short range objectives are set up for a short period of time, say up to one year, and long range objectives are to be followed in the long run. As a matter of fact, short range objectives are devised to achieve the long range objectives of the enterprise. They are more specific as compared to the long range objectives.

Hierarchy of Objectives

The objectives of a company can be structured into a hierarchy. The objectives at the lower levels are the mean for the higher levels. For example, a company may have the overall objectives at the highest level to earn a fair rate of return by manufacturing and marketing specialised machine tools. If we go down the hierarchy, we shall find that the major objectives followed by different departments focuses on creating the form of specialised machine tools. At the next level, there may be intermediate objectives concerned with manufacturing and assembling the major components. At the lowest level, the objectives of the individuals consist of performing the detailed work on subcomponent posts. This example illustrates the fact that objectives at various levels in a company are integrated and follow an logical sequence as reflected by its organisational chart. Each operation has a specific objective, which must contribute to the overall objectives. The objectives at the top level provides the basis for setting the objectives at the second lével which in turn becomes the basis for objectives at the third level and so on. In other words, the goal at the fourth level is a mean for the third level and so on.

Multiplicity of Objectives

It is wrong to presume that there can be only one objective of an organisation. Peter Drucker has exposed that fallacy of single objectives. Much of today's lively discussion of management by objectives is concerned with the search for the one right objective. This search is likely to be as unproductive as the quest for their philosopher's stone: it does harm and misdirects. To manage a business is to balance a variety of needs and goals. And this requires multiple objectives.

Peter Drucker suggested eight areas in which objective must be set. They are – Marketing, Innovation, Human Organisation, Financial Resource, Physical Resource, Productivity, Social Responsibility, and Profit Requirement.

Koontz and O'Donnell are also of the view that broad major enterprise objectives are normally multiple. A business might include among its overall objectives a certain rate of profit and return on investment, emphasis on research to develop a continuous flow of proprietary products, developing publicly held stock ownership; financing primarily by earning; distributing products in foreign markets; assuring competitive prices for superior products; achieving a dominant positioning of an industry; and adhering in all respects, to the values of our society. Objectives in key areas enable the management:

1. To organise and explain the whole range of business phenomena,
2. To test the objectives in actual experience,
3. To predict behaviour,
4. To appraise the soundness of decision while they are still being made, and
5. To set managers on all levels and analyse their own experience, as a result to improve their performance.

Essential Criteria for Effective Objectives

Peter Drucker has given the following guidelines regarding the objectives of a business organization:

1. Objectivés must be derived from what our business is, what it will be and what it should be. They are not obstruction. They are the action commitments through which the mission of

business is to be carried out against which performance is to be measured. Objective, in other words, are the fundamental strategy of a business.

2. Objectives must be operational. They must be capable of being converted into specific targets and assignments. They must also be capable of becoming the basis, as well as the motivation, for work and achievements.
3. Objectives must make possible concentration of resources and efforts. They must win out the fundamentals among the goals of a business so that the key resource of men, money, and physical resource can be concentrated. They must therefore, be selective rather than encompassing everything.
4. There must be multiple objectives rather than single objective.
5. Objectives are needed in all areas on which the survival of the business depends. The specific targets in any area in which objectives are needed are the same for all businesses, and depends on the same factors for their survival.

MBO Concept

Management by objectives, lays emphasis on result-oriented and participative style, is basically a simple approach to management. Successful managers all over the world, whether in industry, defence, government, or educational institutions have unconsciously practiced the essence of management by objectives.

The concept of management by objectives was introduced by Peter Drucker in 1954 and later developed by various writers like John Humble, Prof. Reddin, George Odirone, Edwards Schleh, and Douglas McGregor. It is significant to note that even many years before 1954 objectives were emphasised by classical management's writer like Rayol, Urwrick, and Barnard. Peter Drucker believes that what the business enterprise needs is a principle of management that will give full scope to individual strength and responsibilities and at the same time give common direction to vision and efforts to establish teamwork and harmonise the goal of the individual with the common organisational goals. The only principle that can do this is the management by objectives. Peter Drucker emphasise that objectives are needed in every area where performance and results directly and vitally affect the survival and prosperity of the business. The performance that is expected of the manager must be derived from the performance goals of the business, the result must be measured by the contribution they make to the success of the enterprise. This in terms requires management by objectives and control by self-control. 'Management by objectives' was called work planning in General Electric Company U.S.A. General Electric Company laid out the elements of managing by objectives in its extensive planning for reorganisational program in 1954. Its manual pointed out that decentralisation of managerial decision making requires, that objective goals and objective measurements of progress towards these goals be substituted for objective appraisals and personal supervision. Through a program of objectives measurements, managers will be equipped to focus attention on the relevant trends on the future.

In recent years, management by objectives has become a philosophy of managing in many enterprises and it has come to be recognised as the most dynamic existing thinking in the area of management. John Humble define managing by objectives as a dynamic system which integrates the company's need to achieve its goals for profit and growth with manager's need to contribute and develop him/herself. According to George Odirone, the system of management by objectives can be described as a process, whereby the superior and subordinate managers of an organisation jointly identify its common goals, define each individual's major areas of responsibility in terms of expected results and use these measures as guides for operating that unit and assessing the contribution of each of its members. Odirone also stressed that MBO is not merely a set of rules, a series of procedures or even a set method of managing, but it is a way of thinking about management.

Management by objectives is also known as management by results and goals setting approach. Dale McConvey has preferred the term as management by results and has defined it as an approach to management planning and evaluation in which specific targets for a year, or some length of time are established for each manager, on the basis of the results which each must achieve if the overall objectives of the company are to be realised. At the end of this period, the actual results achieved are measured against the original goals, i.e., against the expected results which each manager is responsible for achieving. Management by objectives becomes comprehensive management planning and control technique and is bound to affect the entire organisational structure, culture, and style. In management by objectives the whole emphasis is on attainment of the common objectives through the role played by the management. Management by objectives is not merely a set of rules, a series of procedures or even a set method of managing, but is a particular way of thinking about management.

Management by objectives is a system which makes the organisation function more effectively by bringing about more vitality and personal involvement of the people in the hierarchy. Management by objectives provides for the maintenance and orderly growth of the organisation by means of a system of what is expected of everyone involved and measurement of what is actually achieved. It lays emphasis on the policy and achievement rather than personality. As a system, it is especially applicable to professional and managerial employees. It can extend as far down as first line supervisors and also cover many staff and technical positions.

Benefits of MBO

Management by objectives calls for regulating the entire process of management in terms of meaningful, specific, and variable objectives at different levels of hierarchy. Management by objectives moulds planning, directing, and controlling in a number of ways. It stimulates meaningful action for better performance and higher accomplishment. It is closely associated with the concepts of decentralisation because decentralisation cannot work without the support of management by objectives. Thus, management by objectives is being increasingly recognised not merely as a philosophy of management, but also as a system, which aims at synchronising the objectives of the individuals with the objectives of the organisation. When applied consciously and systematically, it helps to overcome many of the chronic problems of managing managers and professionals. It helps in:

1. Improvement in productivity due to the fact that management team concentrates on the important task of reducing costs and harnessing opportunities rather than dissipating energies on less important matters.
2. A greater sense of identification by the management team with the objectives of the enterprise where in control are reckoned as tools of 'self-controls' rather than devices to be used against managers.
3. Improved communication and organisational structure, which helps in locating weak and problem areas.
4. Serving as a device for organisational control and integration.
5. Providing a realistic means of analysing training needs and opportunities for growth on the basis of measurement of performance against accepted standards.
6. Measuring the true contributions of managerial and professional personal.
7. Defining the common goals of people and organisations and measuring individual contribution to them.
8. Enhancing possibility of coordinated efforts and teamwork.
9. Providing solutions to the key problems and defining major areas of responsibility for each person in the organisation including joint or shared responsibilities.
10. Gearing the organisation for achieving the desired results.
11. By eliminating the needs for people to change their personalities, as well, for appraising people on the basis of their personality traits.
12. By providing a means to determine each manager's span of control.
13. By offering an answer to the key question of salary administration.
14. By aiding and identifying potential for advancement and also finding out promotable people within the organisation.

Essentials of MBO

Management by objectives enable the managerial core of the organisation to introduce a workable management system offering solutions to the problems like organisational development and individual motivation. The discipline of management by objectives makes each individual, output-centered, result-oriented, result-committed, and achievement motivated. The requirements of its success are:

1. Improved morale and sense of involvement.
2. Recognition of abilities.
3. Effective development of managerial skills.
4. Isolation of problems affecting performance.
5. Improved delegation.
6. Effective communication.

7. Emphasis on profit making.
8. Generation of environment of managerial self-development.
9. Better understanding between the subordinate and the superior.
10. Better information control.
11. Better succession planning based on measured past performance.

The Process of MBO

The process of MBO revolves around the setting up of organisational goals and goals of various division and subdivisions. It is a never-ending process. The continuous nature of the process of MBO not only answer sustained concentration of efforts towards organisational objectives, but also helps in modifying objectives to suits the changed situation. The Procces of MBO are described as under:

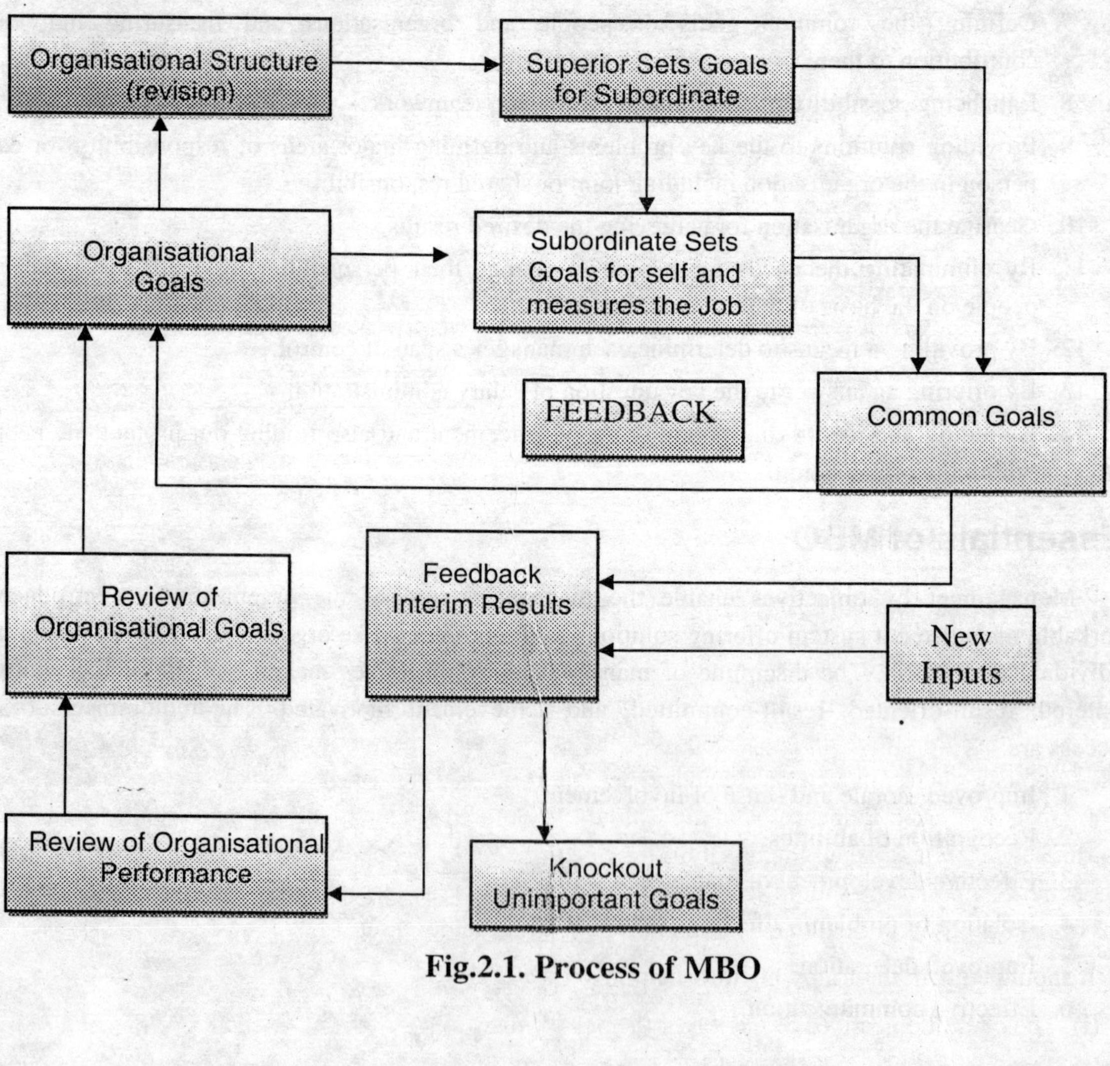

Fig.2.1. Process of MBO

Steps in MBO

Management By Objectives system comprises the following essential steps:

1. Setting of Objectives

The first step while installing the system of 'Management By Objectives' in an organisation is to establish veritable objectives for various positions at various levels. Formulating goal, discussing them with subordinates and providing feedback based on these goals will do more to make the program work. In order to set objectives of the enterprise, a detailed assessment has to be made of the various resources at its disposals. A market survey must be conducted to know what types of goods and services are required by the community. Proper forecasts should be made to estimate the demand and the business conditions in the country. This detailed analysis would lead to highlighting of desirable objectives, both long range and short range. An attempt should be made to set specific goals in various key areas on which the survival and growth of the business depends. These are the objectives which the top management will tend to achieve.

The major activities of every enterprise are divided on some basis of departmentalisation; the top management must determine the objectives of every department. At this stage, the top management should discuss the objectives with their departmental managers so that a statement of agreed objectives may be evolved. Each department sets its both long range and short range objectives with the approval of top management. This process of setting objectives is reported at lower levels of management. At each level, objectives are set in verifiable units so that performance of every department and individual may be reviewed after the end of a particular period. Once this process is complete, there will exist a meeting of minds of each superior and his/her subordinates as to what is to be accomplished and why it is to be accomplished.

2. Revision of Organisational Structure

When the goals for each individual are reset under MBO, there is a considerable change in the job description of various positions. This may call for a revision of the existing organisational structure. The organisational charts and manuals should be suitably amended to depict the change brought by the introduction of management by objectives. The job description of various jobs must clearly lay down the relationship with other job positions in the organisation.

3. Establishing Check Points

Management by objectives ensures periodic meetings between the superior and the subordinates to review the progress towards the accomplishment of target of the subordinates. For this, the superior must establish check points or standards of performance for evaluating the progress of the performance of the subordinate. Evaluation should be defined quantitatively as far as possible and the subordinates must understand them fully. This practice should be followed by every superior for each of its subordinates and it should lead to key result analysis, as targets and goals are represented in terms of results. The key result analysis should be reduced into writing.

It should contain the following information:

(i) The overall objectives of the job of the subordinate.

(ii) The key results achieved to fulfil the objectives.

(iii) The long-term and short-term priorities of tasks.

(iv) The scope and extent of assistance one may expect from the superior and related departmental managers and the assistance she/he must extend to other departments.

(v) The nature of information and reports she/he will receive to carry-out self-evaluation.

(vi) The standard by which his/her performance shall be evaluated.

4. Appraisal of Performance

While informal performance appraisal of a subordinate is done by the immediate superior almost everyday, formal appraisal at periodic intervals, needs to ensure that a thorough appraisal of performance is being done at least once or twice a year when the achievements are carefully analysed against the background of prevailing circumstances and given objectives. The design and format of the performance review form will depend on the nature of the enterprise. The important benefit of MBO is that it does away with the judgemental role of the supervisor. The performance of every individual is evaluated in terms of the standards or end-results clearly agreed by the superior and the subordinate. Whenever MBO has been introduced, it has led to greater satisfaction, more agreement, greater comfort, and less tension and hostility between the superiors and the subordinates. Under MBO, the superior does not evaluate the individual concerned but his/her performance in terms of the standards set in advance. Moreover, the performance review is aimed to assist the subordinate to improve his/her performance in the future. It also helps in setting goals for the next period.

The continuous nature of management by objectives not only ensures sustained concentration of effort but also flexibility in adapting objectives to suit changing environment.

Limitations of MBO

The limitations which make the implementation of MBO difficult are discussed as follows:

1. Poor planning

One of the major weaknesses often seen in MBO is poor planning of the program prior to implementation. Implementation personnel must be well trained. They must know how to involve all levels of management and obtain their support.

2. Lack of training

There is generally lack of training and knowledge on the part of the supervisor in implementing the program. Many are prone to sit down with the subordinate, dictate their goals and targets with no input permitted from the subordinate, and then demand that they be met in a specific time. Whether they are realistic goals or not does not enter the picture. No consideration is given to any outside factors or influence. In this type of environment, there can't be two-way communication because of the outer imposed objectives. This stab at MBO will destroy morale initiative and good results faster than anything else in the enterprise. Therefore, there must be proper training and orientation of the personnel responsible for implementation of MBO program.

3. Lack of follow-up

Lack of follow-up by the superior at the appropriate time is another hurdle in the successful implementation of MBO. In the practice, superiors have many things to do. It is most easy to procrastinate. The superior must get along with the subordinates and they must be prepared to tell the boss exactly what has been accomplished and how. If the superiors delays the meeting, the subordinate will think it is just one of those management program which just happens formally at the initial stage and has now gone down to the drain. This problem may also be due to instability of personnel in top position which becomes a barrier to the success of MBO. People who are not sure of their own positions, are likely to be committed and the concept of MBO goes out of the organisation with the departure of the concerned personnel. Consequently the job efforts of subordinates probably will be relaxed since the superior does not appear to attach much importance to a review of results. Needless to say, this may affect their performance in a negative way.

4. Inflexibility

Management by objectives may tend to introduce inflexibility in the organisation. Since goals are set after every six months or one year, the superior may not like to modify them in between because of fear of resistance from the subordinates. They may be required to revise the goals at lower levels to achieve the long range objectives of the enterprise. The managers give more emphasis on goal setting. But they should remember that they are also to perform other functions of management like organising, directing, controlling, etc.

Making MBO Effective

Despite various difficulties and shortcomings in management by objectives, it is an effective way of managing as it emphasises in practice the setting of objectives as the logic of planning and control. In order to achieve all the advantages of managing by objectives, it is essential that it should start at the top of the organisation. The active participation of top management in this program is essential for its implementation. If the top managers uses the objectives as an instrument for managing subordinates, this practice will also be followed constructively in the organisation.

It is essential that goals should be set in participation with the subordinate. There should be face-to-face communication between the superior and the subordinates for setting the goals, discussing the subordinates' problem, and for reviewing the performance. Thus, there must be effective two way communication in the organisation. Moreover, a greater degree of decentralisation of authority is required for the success of the MBO. The subordinates, who have accepted the challenging assignment along with the superior, must be given the adequate authority to accomplish their goals. MBO will not work if the manager is not willing to delegate sufficient authority to the subordinates as the subordinate will not be willing to accept new assignments and they will resist the setting of specific goals.

Management by objectives is an approach to management planning and evolution in which specific targets for a certain period of time are established for and by each manager. Their objectives are made to interconnect with the overall goals of the organisations. These established goals then become benchmarks for managerial and organisational measurement. It is a systems approach to managing and directing the organisation and determines where they want to take up the organisation. It is a process of encouraging the personnel to contribute their maximum for achieving the overall goal of the organisation. MBO is an evaluation mechanism and is also known as appraisal by result.

Review Discussions

1. Describe management by objectives and what are its important steps?
2. 'MBO may collapse in an organisation', what are the factors responsible for this and how it can be made effective in a management system?
3. Discuss the MBO process and its prerequisites for success.

♣♣♣♣♣♣

CHAPTER 3

HUMAN BEHAVIOUR IN ORGANISATION

After studying this chapter, you should be able to:

- Understand human personality.
- Know attitudes.
- Comprehend Organisational Behaviour.
- Be acquainted with Johari Window.
- Comprehend motives, morale, and motivation

Introduction

People have much in common (they become excited on achievement or they are grieved by the loss of a loved one) but each person in the world is also individually different. Each one is different from others, in many ways, just as each of our fingerprints is different, and these differences are usually substantial rather than meaningless. The idea of individual differences comes originally from psychology from the day of birth. Each person is unique, and individual experiences often make people even more different. Individual differences mean that management can get the greatest motivation among employees by treating them differently.

A group is powerless until individuals act therein and following aspects are to be taken into consideration while treating individuals within the organization:

Whole person: Although some organisations may wish they could employ only a person's skill or brain, all that they can employ is a whole person, rather than certain separate part of an individual. Different human traits may be separately studied, but in the final analysis they are all part of one system making up a whole person. A skill does not exist apart from background or knowledge. Home life is not totally separable from work life, and with emotional conditions people functions as total human beings. For example, a supervisor wanted worker to work overtime on night on a rush report. The worker had the necessary knowledge and skill for the job and he also wanted the overtime pay. However, from his point of view a social obligation made it impossible for him to work that night. The day was his tenth wedding anniversary, and an anniversary party was scheduled with a few friends at his house. This anniversary was important to him, so his supervisor had to consider his needs as a whole person, not just a worker.

When management practices organisational behaviour, it is trying to develop a better employee, but also it wants to develop a better person in terms of growth and fulfillment. Research suggests that jobs do shape people and its effects on the whole person. Employees belong to many organisations other than their employer play many roles outside the firm. If the whole person can be improved, then benefits will extend beyond the firm into the larger society in which each employee lives.

Caused behaviour: Normal behaviors have certain causes. These may relate to a person's needs and for the consequences that results from acts. To an outside observer a person's needs may be illusory or unrealistic. This fact leaves management with two basic ways to motivate people. It can show them how certain actions will increase their need fulfilment, or it can threaten them by decreased need fulfilment unless they follow a required course of action. Clearly a path toward increased need fulfilment is the better approach. Motivation is essential to the operation of organisations no matter how much machinery and equipment an organisation has cannot be put to use until they are released and guided by people who have been motivated.

Value of the person: This concept is more of an ethical philosophy than a scientific conclusion. It confirms that people are to be treated differently from other factors of production because they are of a higher order in the universe. It recognises that because people are of higher order, they want to be treated with respect and dignity and should be treated this way. Every job, however simple, entitles the people who do it to get proper respect and recognition of their unique aspirations and abilities. The concept of human dignity rejects the old idea of using employees as economic tools. Ethical philosophy is reflected in the conscience of humankind confirmed by the experience of people in all ages. It has to do with the consequences of our acts to ourselves and to others. It recognises that life has an overall purpose and accepts in the inner integrity of each individual. Since organisational behaviour always involves people, ethical philosophy is involved in one way or another. In each action; human decisions cannot, and should not be made apart from values.

Personality

The term 'personality' is derived from the Latin term *per sona* which means to 'speak through'. Common usage of the word 'personality' specifies the role which the person (actor) displays to the public. Because of differences in personality, individual differ in their manner of responding to different situations. In psychological term 'personality' is interpreted in different ways by different theorists. For example, Carl Rogers views personality in term of self, an organised, permanent, subjectivity perceived entity which is at the very heart of all our experiences.

According to Gordon Allport, personality is the dynamic organisation within the individual of those psychological systems that determine his/her unique adjustment to his/her environment. In the words of Floyd L. Ruch, 'Personality includes external appearance and behaviour, inner awareness of self as a permanent organising force and the particular pattern or organisation of measurable traits, both inner and outer'.

Attributes of Personality

Attributes of personality may be broadly classified as individual and social. They are discussed as below:

1. Individual Attributes

Individual attributes, for the most part, are that part of our personality that cannot be altered much. We cannot become more intelligent, but we can become more educated. We cannot become more attentive, or less impatient, or more optimistic. These are physical characteristics that are determined by our brain structure and our body chemistry. Drugs such as alcohol, tobacco, caffeine, etc., can affect our brain chemistry and our personality. Some changes are reversible, but others are permanent and may result in addiction, flashbacks, hallucinations, and other abnormal conditions. Strokes and head injuries can also cause personality changes.

- **Achievement attitudes:** Degree of motivation towards goals.
- **Emotional temperament**: Emotions that rule our lives.
- **Energy level:** The degree of effort that we use in our daily life.
- **Intellectual factor:** Characteristics of our minds.
- **Material attitudes**: How we regard our environment.
- **Maturity:** Our level of experience and wisdom.

- **Philosophical attitudes:** Our preferred ways of thinking.
- **Physical attributes:** How we regard our body.
- **Risk attitudes:** Degree of concern for oneself.
- **Task performance attitudes:** Approaches toward problem-solving.

2. Social Attributes

The social attributes of our personality are formed by our interaction with other people over our lifetime. An individual attribute, such as anger, might be displayed as aggression in a social context. If we are punished or suffer bad consequences from our aggression, we may change our social behaviour in the future. If, on the other hand, we obtain what we want through aggression, threats, and violent behaviour, it may become a way of life for us. By the time we are adults; most of our social attributes are well established and are not easily changed. A person who thinks that another person can be changed does not have a good chance of success. Many marriages fail because the people involved think that they can adjust to incompatible characteristics of the other person or that they can change the other person. This seldom happens. What seems like a little problem before marriage often becomes an irritating, insurmountable problem that erodes the foundation of the relationship.

- **Aggressiveness:** Measure of camaraderie between people.
- **Control attitudes:** Mechanisms by which we influence others.
- **Dependability**: Factors that affect trust in others.
- **Egocentrism**: Selfishness and selfish attitudes.
- **Emotional expression**: Ways of expressing inner feelings towards others.
- **Fairness**: How we judge others.
- **Leadership attributes**: Features that make us standout in a group.
- **Physical appearance**: How we view ourselves physically.
- **Regard for rules:** Obedience for the laws of society.
- **Team spirit**: Attitudes towards working with people.

Development of Personality

A comprehensive definition of personality is given by Fred Luthans. In his words, personality means how a person affects others and how he understands and views himself as well as the pattern of inner and outer measurable traits, and the person-situation interaction. How a person affects others depends upon his physical appearance (such as height, weight, facial features, colour, etc.), and behaviour (such as courteous, friendly, expressive, cooperative, etc.). Thus, personality represents the 'whole person' concept. It includes perception, learning, motivation and more. There are two approaches to development of personality. One approach attempts to identify specific physiological and psychological stages that occur in the development of human personality. The second approach tends to identify the important determinants of personality. The stage approach is theoretical, whereas the determinants based approach is empirical in nature. Many psychologists have contributed to the stage approach. The prominent psychologists include Freud and Erikson.

Freudian Stages

Sigmund Freud propounded psychoanalytic theory of personality which is based on the notion that man is motivated more by unseen forces than by conscious and rational thoughts. This framework contains three aspects, though interrelated but often conflicting. Their brief description is as follows:

1. The Id: The id is the source of psychic energy and seeks immediate gratification for biological or instinctual needs. Freud believed that instincts could be classified under life-instincts and death-instincts. Life-instincts are hunger, thirst, and sex; the energy involved in these is the libido. The id would proceed unchecked to satisfy motives, particularly the sexual relations and pleasures, were it not for channeling activity into acceptable ways by the ego. As an individual matures, he learns to control the id. But even then, it remains a driving force throughout life and an important source of thinking and behaving.

2. The Ego: The ego is the conscious and logical part of the human personality and is associated with the reality principle. While id represents the unconscious part, ego is conscious about the realities of the external environment. The ego keeps the id in check through intellect and reason.

3. The Super Ego: The super ego represents societal and personal norms and serves as an ethical constraint on behaviour. It can best be described on the conscience. The super ego provides norms to ego to determine what is wrong or right. However, a person is not aware of the working of the super ego, and conscience is developed by absorption of cultural values and norms of the society.

Erikson Stages

Erikson criticised the heavy emphasis given by Freud on the sexual and biological factors in the developing personality. He felt that relatively more attention should be given to the social factors. Erikson identified eight stages of life that characterise the unending development of a person. He characterised each stage by a particular conflict that needs to be resolved successfully before a person can move to the next stage. However, these eight stages are not totally separable, and the crises are never fully resolved. Movement between stages is developmental as explained below:

1. Infancy: During the first year of life, a child resolves the basic crises of trust verses mistrust. An infant who is cared for in an affectionate way learns to trust other people. Lack of love and affection results in mistrust. This stage makes a serious impact on a child that influences events for remaining life.

2. Early childhood: In the second and third year of life, a child begins to assert independence. If a child is allowed to control these aspects of life that the child is capable of controlling, a sense of autonomy will develop. If the child encounters constant disapproval by elders a sense of self-doubt and shame is likely to develop.

3. Play age: The four and five-year-old children seek to discover just how much she/he can do. If a child is encouraged to experiment and to achieve reasonable goals, she/he will develop a sense of initiative. If a child is blocked and made to feel capable, she/he will develop a sense of 'guilt and lack of self-confidence'.

4. School age: From ages six to twelve years, a child learns many new skills and develops social abilities. If a child experiences real progress at a rate compatible with his abilities, he or she will develop a sense of enterprise. The reverse situation results in a sense of inferiority.

5. Adolescence: The crisis of the teenage years is to gain a sense of identity rather than to become confused about what you are. While undergoing rapid biological changes, the teen ager is also trying to establish him/her self as socially separate from the parents. The autonomy, initiative and enterprise developed in early stages are very important in helping the teenager to successfully resolve their crisis and prepare for adulthood.

6. Early adulthood: The young adult during the twenties faces the crisis of intimacy versus isolation. The sense of identity developed during the teenage years allows the young adult to begin developing deep and lasting relationships.

7. Adulthood: During this stage, the adults face the crisis of generatively versus self-absorption. Self-absorbed persons never develop and ability to look beyond themselves. They become absorbed in career advancement and maintenance; and they never learn to have concern for future generations, the welfare of organisations to which they belong or the welfare of society as a whole. Generative people see the world as much bigger than themselves. Productivity at work and societal advancement become important to them. Through innovation and creativity, they begin to exert influence that benefits their organisations.

8. Mature adulthood: The person is developed as a highly mature person. She/he has gained a sense of wisdom and prospective that can really guide the younger generations.

Understanding of personality can be of great immense help in the selection of right kinds of people for different jobs. Analysis of an individual's personality will reveal one's strong and weak points. A person may be unfit for a job, but fit for another job as the requirements of both differ. Understanding of personality will also helps in designing training programs for the personnel in the organisation. Personality helps the manager understand why workers behave as they do various incentive schemes could be designed to motivate workers.

Attitudes

Attitude is an internal state of person that is focused on objects, events, and people that can exist in the person's psychological world. An individual's behaviour is also a function of attitudes. An attitude is also a cognitive element. It always remains inside a person. Attitude may be defined as the predisposition of the individual to evaluate some object in a favourable or an unfavourable manner. Every one's psychological world is limited and thus everyone has limited number of attitudes. An attitude is a mental state of readiness, organised through experience, exerting a specific influence upon a person's response to people, objects, and situation with which it is related. In business organisation employees have attitudes related towards environment, job security or uncertainty, prestige of the product or department, and plant location, etc. The individual's attitude towards these factors is indicative of his/her apathy or enthusiasm towards the activities and objectives of the organisation.

Attitudes, Values, and Beliefs

The most pervasive phenomenon of human behaviour is 'attitude'. People at work place have attitudes about lots of topics that are related to them. These attitudes are firmly embedded in a complex psychological structure of beliefs and values. Attitude is a predisposition to respond to a certain sets of facts. Attitude is evaluative statements whether favourable or unfavourable, concerning the objects, people or events.

Attitudes are different from values. Values of a person reveal his/her ideas about what is good or bad, what is right or wrong, or what is desirable or undesirable. They reflect a moral tone. 'Workers should be honest to their work', is a statement of value. The honest workers are good is an evaluative statement and reveals the attitude of the person towards the honest workers. It is to be noted that beliefs are one of the determinants of one's attitudes. A person holds an honest worker to be good because of his/her values that workers should be honest.

Belief reveals what one supposes to be true. It may be about anything. A subordinate may believe his/her superior to be honest. But in fact, the superior may or may not be honest. The attitude of the subordinate towards the superior reveals whether she/he likes or does not like him/her. The positive attitude and the consequent liking may rather make the subordinate condone all the bad qualities in the superior and consider him/her honest.

Attitude is thus a state of one's predispositions toward given aspects of world. They also provide an emotional basis of one's interpersonal relations and identification with others.

Components of Attitude

There are three basic components of an attitude as described below:

1. **Cognitive or informational component:** It involves benefits and values, ideas and other information a person has about the attitude object. For instance, a person seeking a job may learn from newspapers and other people that a particular company is a good pay-master.
2. **Affective or emotional component:** It involves the person's feelings of likes and dislikes towards the attitude object.
3. **Behavioural component:** The tendency of a person to behave in a particular manner towards the attitude object is the behavioural component of an attitude. These components show that an attitude can be considered as a way of thinking, feeling and behaving. For example, if someone has favourable thoughts about his/her supervisor at the job, he would develop feelings of consideration and respect for him/her and, as a result, may like to associate more frequently with him/her.

Characteristics of Attitude

The important characteristics of attitudes are discussed as follows:

1. Attitudes affect behaviour: People have the natural tendency to maintain consistency between two attitudes or attitude and behaviour. Attitudes can lead to intended behaviour if there is no external intervention.

2. Attitudes are invisible: Attitudes constitute a psychological phenomenon which cannot be directly observed. However, we may observe an attitude indirectly through observing it consequences. For example, if a person is highly productive, we may infer that he/she has a positive attitude towards his/her work.

3. Attitudes are acquired: Attitudes are gradually learnt over a period of time. The process of learning attitudes starts right from childhood and continues throughout the life of a person. However, in the beginning, the family members have a greater impact on the attitude of a child. For example, if the family members have a positive attitude towards business and negative towards service, there is a greater likelihood that the child will inculcate similar attitudes towards these objects.

4. Attitudes are pervasive: Attitudes are formed in the process of socialisation and may relate to anything in the world. For example, a person may have positive or negative attitude towards religion, politics, politicians, countries, and so on. At our place of work, we have attitudes towards work, superiors, peers, subordinates, clients, government and its policies, investors, and so on. Thus, there is an endless list of attitude objects.

Development of Attitudes

The development of attitudes is dependent on following factors:

1. Psychological factors: The psychological make-up of a person is made up of his perceptions, ideas, beliefs, values, information, etc. It has a crucial role in determining a person's attitudes. For example, if a person perceives that generally all superiors are exploitative she/he is likely to develop a negative attitude towards his/her superior who in fact may not be exploitative.

2. Family factors: During childhood, a person spends a major part of his/her time in family. Thus, she/he learns from the family members who provide him/her with ready-made attitudes on a variety of issues such as education, work, health, religion, politics, economics, etc. Every family instills or attempts to instill such attitudes among its members as are considered appropriate to its socio-economic status in the society. Therefore, a person from a middle class family may hold a different attitude towards spending than a person from an affluent family. In the later years of life, however, any person whom we admire, respect or fear may have greater influence on our attitudes.

3. Social factors: Societies differ in terms of language, culture, norms, values, beliefs, etc., all of which influence a person's attitudes. For example, people in India in general hold different attitude towards communism than people in China. Similarly, Indians and Americans differ in their attitudes towards religion. Thus, people belonging to a nation develop attitudes which would be in time with the need of the society.

4. Organisational factors: It should be remembered that an employee spends a major part of his/her life in the institution in which she/he works. Thus, organisational factors such as nature of job, factory or office layout, fellow workers, quality of supervision, monetary rewards associated with the job, trade unionism, informal groups, organisation's policies and practices, play an important role in shaping the job attitudes of a person. For example, if a creative person finds the nature of his/her job to be repetitive, dull, boring, and less changing; she/he is likely to develop a negative attitude towards his/her job.

5. Economic factors: A person's attitude towards a host of issues such as pleasure, work, marriage, working with opposite gender, etc., is influenced by economic factors such as his/her economic status in the society, rate of inflation in the economy, government's economic policies, and the country's economic conditions. For example, during the Gulf crises, the Government of India made a big drive to save oil so as to cut the import bill. A big campaign was started to educate people in this regard. It aimed at promoting negative attitude towards pleasure trips and positive attitude towards proper driving and maintenance of vehicles.

6. Political factors: Politics plays a crucial role in the administration of a country. Therefore, political factors such as ideologies of the political parties, political stability and the behaviour of the political leaders greatly affect the attitudes of the people.

Attitudes and Organisational Behaviour

The focus of Organisational Behaviour (OB) is on job-related attitudes of employees. Such attitudes tap positive or negative evaluations that employees hold about certain aspects of their work environment. The behavioural scientists have concentrated on three job-related attitudes as discussed below:

1. Job satisfaction: The term 'job satisfaction' refers to an individual's general attitude towards his job. A person with a high level of job satisfaction holds positive attitude towards the job, while a person who is dissatisfied with his job holds negative attitudes about the job. Job satisfaction is supposed to be an important key to employee's performance.

2. Job involvement: It measures the degree to which a person identifies psychologically with his job and considers his perceived performance level important to his self-worth. Employees with a high level of job involvement strongly identify with and really care about the kind of work they do on their jobs. Such people are reported to have shown lower rates of employee turnover and absenteeism.

3 .Organisational commitment: It is defined as a state in which an employee indentifies with a particular organisation and its goal and wishes to maintain membership in the organisation. High job involvement means identifying with one's specific job, while high organisational commitment means identifying with one's employing organisation.

The research studies demonstrate negative relationships between organisational commitment and both absenteeism and turnover. Infact, studies demonstrate that an individual's level of organisational commitment is a better indicator of turnover than the far more frequently used job satisfaction predictor. Organisational commitment is probably a better predictor because it is a more global and enduring response to the organisation as a whole than is job satisfaction. An employee may be temporarily dissatisfied with his particular job, and not with the organisation. But if she/he is dissatisfied with the organisation, she/he is more likely to find job elsewhere.

Johari Window

Joe Luft and Harry Ingham were researching human personality at the University of California in the 1950s when they devised their Johari Window. Using a form of word derivation normally reserved for suburban house names, they based the title on their two first names. Rather than measuring personality, the Window offers a way of looking at how personality is expressed.

Luft and Ingham observed that there are aspects of our personality that we're open about, and other elements that we keep to ourselves. At the same time, there are things that others see in us that we're not aware of. As a result, we can draw up a four-box grid, which includes a fourth group of traits that are unknown to anyone.

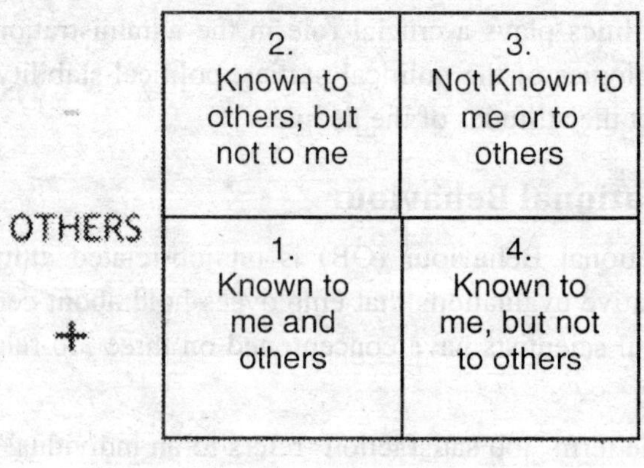

Fig. 3.1. Johari Window

1. **The public area:** Contains things that are openly known and talked about and which may be seen as strengths or weaknesses. This is the self that we choose to share with others
2. **The hidden area:** Contains things that others observe that we don't know about. Again, they could be positive or negative behaviours, and will affect the way that others act towards us.
3. **The unknown area:** Contains things that nobody knows about us – including ourselves. This may be because we've never exposed those areas of our personality, or because they're buried deep in the subconscious.
4. **The private area:** Contains aspects of our self that we know about and keep hidden from others.

The application of the Johari Window comes in opening up the public area, so making the other three areas as small as possible. This is done by regular and honest exchange of feedback, and a willingness to disclose personal feelings. People around you will understand what 'makes us tick', and what we find easy or difficult to do, and can provide appropriate support. And of course we can then do the same for them.

Self-assessment questionnaires can be used to indicate the size of our public window, but any measure is purely subjective.

Organisational Behaviour

Organisational Behaviour (OB) may be defined as a field of study of individuals and groups to know the impact of organisational structure on behaviour within the organisation, in order to workout a solution towards improving organisational effectiveness. The above definition has three main elements; first organisational behaviour is a study of individuals and groups, second, to know the impact of organisational structure on human behaviour, and the third, working out a solution towards improving organisational effectiveness.

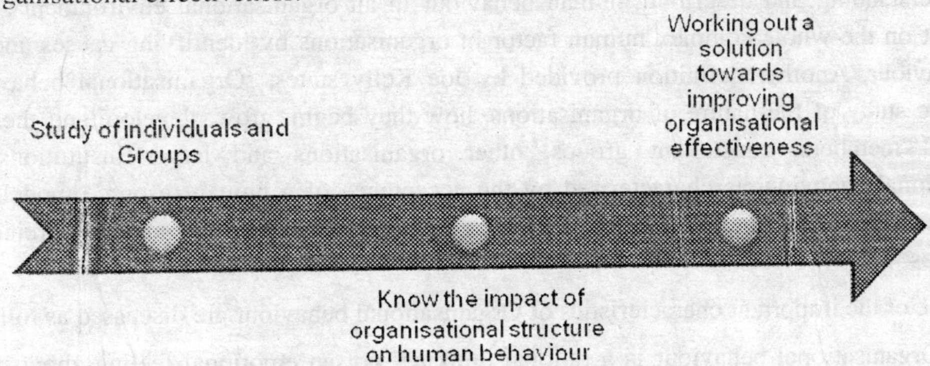

Fig.3.2. Elements of Organisational Behaviour

These factors are interactive in nature and the impact of such behaviour is applied to various systems so that the goals are achieved. The nature of study of organisational behaviour is to establish cause and effect relationship.

OB involves integration of studies undertaken relating to behavioural sciences and is a comprehensive field of study in which individual, group and organisational structure is studied in relation to organisational growth and organisational culture, in an environment where impact of modern technology is great. The aim of the study is to ensure that the human behaviour contributes towards growth of the organisation and greater efficiency is achieved.

Stephen P. Robins defines 'Organisational behaviour as a systematic study of the actions and attitudes that people exhibit within organisations'. It has been observed that we generally form our opinion based on the symptoms of an issue and do not really go to the root cause of the happening. Science of organisational behaviour is applied in nature. Disciplines like psychology, anthropology and political science have contributed in terms of various studies and theories to the field of organisational behaviour. The rules of the work are all different from the rules of play. The uniqueness of rules and the unstable environment of organisations compel managers to study organisational behaviour in predicting human behaviour in the organisational setting by drawing a clear distinction between individual and group behaviour. OB is a study that analyses and explains the behaviour of the workforce acting as individual and as groups in an organisation. It attempts to apply this knowledge in the effective management of human resources in an organisation. OB is a discipline that studies the effect of organisational structure and design, and the changes in the organisational environment on the behaviour of the workforce. It is considered as applied science as it provides theoretical concepts that are applicable to real life situations. The knowledge gained with regard to the OB practices of one organisation may be applied to several other organisations. Thus, OB can be defined as the systematic study and application of human aspects in the management of an organisation.

Characteristics of Organisational Behaviour

According the Keith Davis, 'Organisational behaviour is an academic discipline concerned with understanding and describing human behaviour in an organisational environment'. It seeks to shed light on the whole complex human factor in organisations by identifying causes and effects of that behaviour. Another definition provided by Joe Kelly states, 'Organisational behaviour is the systematic study of the nature of organisations, how they begin, grow, develop, and their effect on individual members, constituent groups, other organisations and larger institutions'. Modern organisational behaviour is characterised by the acceptance of a human resource model. It takes a more positive view of human beings. People are accepted as they are and not prejudged using stereotypes.

Some of the important characteristics of Organisational behaviour are discussed as follows:

1. Organisational behaviour is a rational thinking, not an emotional feeling about people. The major goals of organisational behaviour are to explain and predict human behavioural in organisations. It is action-oriented and goal-directed.
2. Organisational behavioural seeks to balanced human and technical values at work. It seeks to achieve productivity by building and maintaining employee's dignity, growth and satisfaction, rather than at the expense of these values.
3. Organisational behaviour integrates behavioural sciences. Many of its core concepts are borrowed from others fields and discipline like social psychology, sociology, and anthropology, etc.
4. Organisational behaviour is both a science and an art, the knowledge about human behaviour in organisations leans towards being science. Modern organisational behaviour is, at once, empirical, interpretative, and critical. It is an interpretative science in the pursuit of knowledge and meaning. The basic purpose is to make meaningful the facts of organisational life. Modern OB is an optic perspective; a process for looking at events, a way of life. It has empirical facts, and interesting interpretations and powerful paradigms. However it is an inaccurate science to provide specific answers to specific organisational problems. As such

very little can be prescribed to consistently predict relationships between a variable on broad scale. The skills in applying the knowledge clearly leans towards being art.

5. Organisational behaviour exists at multiple like levels. Behaviour occurs at the individual, the group, and the organisational systems levels. Behaviour that is attributable to each of these levels can be both identified and isolated but at the same time these three levels interact with each other and OB-being affected by the behaviour of individuals, group level behaviour is affected by the organisational level phenomena and so on.
6. Organisational behaviour does not exist in vacuum. Organisations are made up of both social and technical components and therefore characterized as social-technical systems. The operational implication of this is that any approach of looking at behaviour must also take into account the technical component of organisation especially such issues as the nature of work and the technology. Organisations at the same time, must take into account the constructs of the working environment, for example, the extent to which the market and the product is changing.

The Role of Organisational Behaviour in Organisational Performance

The place that organisational behaviour occupies in a work system is illustrated by a set of equations.

Let us look first at a worker's ability, it is generally accepted that knowledge and one's skill in applying in a given situation constitute the human trait called 'ability'. This is represented by the equation: ***Knowledge × Skills in a given situation = Ability.***

Ability and Motivation together determine a person's performance in any activity. The importance of organisational behaviour is shown by the equation: ***Ability × Motivation = Human performance.***

Organisational behaviour, as represented by the term 'motivation', is one of due factors in the equation.

Furthermore, organisational behaviour has played a part in motivating workers and enhancing their ability. Thus, organisational behaviour is part and parcel of the whole equation of human performance. Human performance including management and method of operations has to be mixed with resources such as tools, manpower, finance, and materials, to get overall work performance of the organisation, as indicated by the equation: ***Human Performance × Resources = Organisational Performance.***

Learning about organisational behaviour is more than simply storing up facts about people. The field of organisational behaviour is believingly complex. To understand 'Whys' of behaviour, it is necessary to document the organisational factors influencing employees, it is necessary to understand the nature of this soft discipline, and its strengths and weaknesses, etc.

Organisational behaviour offers a number of challenges and opportunities for managers. It helps improve quality and employee productivity by showing managers how to empower their people as well as design and implement change programs. It offers specific insights to improve a manager's people skills. OB recognises differences and helps managers see the value of workforce diversity and practices that may need to be made when managing them in different circumstances. In times of rapid and on-going changes, OB can help managers learn cope in a world of instabilities and declining employee loyalty. Finally, OB can offer managers guidance in creating an ethically healthy work climate.

Models of OB

OB models play a significant role in the management of organisation. Models are the framework of description of how things work and are also known as paradigms. Every model in OB makes certain assumptions regarding the nature of the people working in the organisation. Models of OB not only differ from organization-to-organisation but also from department-to-department within the organisation. The organisational practices are also largely dependent on a manager's personal preferences. Some of the models are discussed as below:

1. Autocratic Model: The basis of this model is power. Under this model, the person who holds power has the authority to demand work from workers. This model was widely popular during the Industrial Revolution. It is based on the assumption that work can only be extracted by means of pushing, directing, and persuading the employees. The model empowers managers with authority which might be used for unfair practices such as suspending the employees for not obeying the orders, giving low pay, etc., such a work environment motivates very few employees to exhibit higher productivity. However, the autocratic model works well under certain conditions, particularly in times of an organisational crisis.

2. Custodial Model: The basis of this model is economic resources with a managerial orientation of money. The employees in turn are oriented towards security, benefits, and dependence on the organisation. The employee need that is met is security. The performance result is passive cooperation. In the custodial model, the emphasis is laid on providing job security. Therefore, employers offer fringe benefits to strengthen the employees' confidence in job security. While this helps in returning the employees, knowing that they are going to get incentives irrespective of their job performance. This might cause the employees to be more laid back in their approach towards work.

3. Supportive Model: The basis of this model is leadership with managerial orientation of support. The employees in turn are oriented towards job performance and participation. The employees' need that is met is status and recognition. The performance result is awakened drives. The supportive model emphasises leadership rather than power or money. Under this approach, leaders promote an environment for the employees to grow while they help in achieving organisation's objectives. Also the support extended by the management motivates the employees to work. The employees are self-motivated to enhance their performance and are not compelled to do so. This model might not be effective for employees whose lower level needs are not satisfied. Nevertheless, the supportive model enhances the relationships between employee and the employer.

4. Collegial Model: The basis of this model is partnership with a managerial orientation of teamwork. The employees in turn are oriented towards responsible behaviour and self-discipline. The employee need that is met is self-actualisation. The performance result is moderate enthusiasm. In the collegial model, employees are self-disciplined, self-satisfied, and have specific goals which motivate them to improve their performance. In this approach, the superior acts more like a leader who leads the way and motivates employees to perform at their best. The term 'collegial' refers to a group of persons working for a common purpose. This model is an extension of the supportive model.

5. SOBC Model: The internal causal factors in an organisation are cognitively oriented, whereas the external environmental factors are behaviour oriented. Therefore, both the approaches have gained considerable importance in the development of the conceptual model of OB. Hence, social learning that incorporates both the approaches is used in the OB. The OB model based on the social learning approach is termed as the SOBC model, where S stands for stimulus, O for organism, B for behaviour, and C for consequence. The S O B C model gives the basic framework rather than a complete explanation of OB.

S: Stimulus is an external environmental variable that depicts the environmental situation, both contextual and organisational.

O: Organism is a cognitive variable that understands organisational participants which link the environmental situation and the resulting organisational behaviour.

B: Represents the organisational behaviour.

C: Consequence is an environmental variable that depicts organisational and group dynamics and the consequences of previous interactions between environmental, personal, and behavioural variables.

Although there are different models, almost no organisation operates exclusively in one. There will usually be a predominate one, with one or more areas overlapping in the other models.

Motives

Motives are the inner drives of an individual. They represent goals directed behaviour of individual. A motive is a cognitive factor which operates in determining one's behaviour towards a goal. Individuals differ in variables which determine the inner drives. The behaviour of an individual to accomplish the goal varies because of inner drives. It is an incentive to act or a reason for doing something or anything that prompted a choice of action. Anything that arouses the individual and directs his or her behaviour towards some goal is called a motive or motive is a factor which influences to do anything because anything we do has a motive behind.

Primary and Secondary Motives

Psychologists generally acknowledge that some of the motives are unlearned and psychological based. These are the primary motives. Although the precedence of primary needs is employed in some motivation theories, there are some situations when these needs are pushed into background. Thus, fasting for a religion or social or political cause or celibacy among priests are the examples. Secondary motives are the results of the increasing social complexity and economic and social developments. These motives are learned and psychologically based. Important among the secondary motives are the motives for power achievements and affiliation.

Hence there are two popular classifications of motives:

1. Primary or biological
2. Secondary or psychosocial

1. Primary Motive: Primary motives also known as biological motives, have a definite physiological basis and are biologically necessary for survival of the individual or species. These arouse the behaviour of the organism in directions that lead to the required change in internal environment. The sources of biological motivational needs include:

- Increase/decrease stimulation (arousal)
- Activate senses (taste, touch, smell, etc.
- Decrease hunger, thirst, discomfort, etc.
- Maintain homeostasis, balance

The biological motives consists of – hunger, thirst, pain, sex, air or need for respiration, fatigue, sleeps, maternal, etc.

2. Secondary Motive: Secondary motives are learned motives and are sometimes known as psycho-sociological motives. They are not physiologically based. These are the causes of the development of a personality. Secondary motives originate during our lifetime. They are acquired and learned through our interaction with people. They are classified in two types which are social and psychological.

(i) Social motives: Social motives are those which motivates us to go out, interact with people and do the things that gives a feeling of pleasure and satisfaction. Social motive evoke unity, love, sympathy, cooperation, coordination, and the formation of a leadership in a group for its existence and survival. Everybody loves to live according to his/her social norms. Social motive helps to imitate positive models, be a part of a group or a valued member, know one's self, communicate, etc.

(ii) Psychological motives: Psychological motives are individualistic in nature as they are related to self esteem, self-security, self-exhibition, self-freedom, and self-assertion. As psychology is the scientific study of an individual's behaviour in relation to his environment, psychological motives are regarded very important in the development of an individual's behavior and personality. Emotions are psychological perspectives and emotions occur as a result of an interaction between perceptions of environmental stimuli, neural/hormonal responses to these perceptions. So, psychological motives are very important because our emotions motivate us to do things. Psychological motives help us in many things like – maintain attention to something interesting or threatening, develop meaning or understanding, increase/decrease cognitive disequilibrium or uncertainty, solve a problem or make a decision, figure something out, eliminate threat or risk secondary or psychosocial motive are important to live a happy life and adequate satisfaction of secondary motives is necessary for mental health to avoid depressions, etc.

Psycho-social or secondary motives contain: need for affiliation, need for approval, need for achievement, need for security, curiosity motive, competence motive, power motive, aggression motive, self-actualisation, etc.

Morale

A moral is a fundamental psychological concept. It revolves around the attitude towards work for the accomplishment of organisational goals. Alexander H. Leighton considers morale as the capacity of group of people to pull together persistently in pursuit of a common purpose. Morale is the degree of enthusiasm and willingness with which the members of a group pull together to achieve group goals. Morale represents a composite of feelings, attitudes, and sentiments that contribute to general feelings of satisfaction. It is the state of mind and spirit affecting willingness to work which, in turn affects organisational and individual objectives It generally refers to '*esprit the corps*' a feeling of enthusiasm, zeal, confidence in individuals or group that they will be able to cope with the tasks assigned to them. Thus, morale is an indicator of attitudes of employees towards their jobs, superiors, and environment. It is the sum total of employees' attitudes, feelings, and sentiments towards these variables. Morale is a by-product of motivation and group relationships in the organisation.

There are three types of morale approach as mentioned below:

1. **Classical approach:** the satisfaction of basic need is the symbol of morale. If the basic needs of the employees are satisfied, their morale will be high.
2. **Psychological approach:** psychological approach emphasises that not only the basic needs but psychological needs also influences the morale of the people.
3. **Social approach:** for a social scientist, the morale is social phenomenon which pulls the men to live in society or group in pursuit of a common goal.

Keeping Employees' Morale Up

Some of the ways of keeping the morale of employees high are:

1. Let the employees express their feelings: We need to let employees express their feelings about the difficulties and changes that are going on. These feelings will only aggravate and turn into anger and resentment or result in employees becoming disengaged. We need not to focus all of our efforts on getting buy-in to the changes we seek. Remember, 'Seek first to understand'. People need to know us, understand their perspective, and their feelings before they will listen to our exhortations.

2. Support constructive criticism: Make it safe for employees to express dissent or criticism without being labeled as not being a 'team player'. If we don't, we will miss out important information and will create a workforce that learns not to care. Give employees as much opportunity as possible to solve problems and take constructive action. Thus, engaging employees in constructive action place a central role in keeping morale up in times of uncertainty and difficulty.

3. Amp up our communication: Make sure employees know what is going on in each step of the way. When people are feeling vulnerable, their tolerance for ambiguity decreases dramatically. To feel safe and secure, they need to know as much as possible about what is going on. Increasing the efficacy of our communication would be most useful.

Morale and Productivity

Productivity increases where morale is high because worker put their heart and soul to achieve the organisational goal. High morale and high productivity are positively correlated.

The following are four possible ways:

1. High morale, high productivity: The cases results in high productivity but only when the workers are motivated in the right spirit and supervision is of right type. There is a circular relationship between morale and productivity. High morale pushes up the productivity and high productivity in turn, pushes up morale and so on.

2. Low morale, low productivity: Morale and productivity both will be lower being lower. In the absence of the proper motivation. Low morale pulls down the productivity and low productivity shrinks the morale of employees.

3. High morale low productivity: This is found in circumstances where the workers are not fully trained and supervisors are not fully competent getting the work done. This is also seen in organisations where supervisors are of the view that workers should not be unhappy.

4. Low morale, high productivity: Low morale and high productivity go together when the management does not cooperate with the workers and disregard the feelings of the workers at work or where management uses penalties and punishments and provides better machines and equipment to carry on the production. Thus, low morale with productivity exists only when management is highly production-oriented.

Indicators of Employees' Morale

For improving workers' performance, managers should provide training for employees, create specific performance goal for workers to strive for, provide performance feedback on a regular and frequent basis, encourage neat and orderly work areas, arrange and increase the number of operations performed by each employee whenever possible, etc. Some of the indicators of employees' morale are discussed as follows:

1. **Creation of whole jobs:** under this, complete jobs are assigned to the workers. Jobs should be enlarged, i.e., the complexity of a job should be increased so that it may appeal to their higher needs.
2. **Job enrichment:** which are intended to motivate the worker rather than to ensure his/her continuing satisfaction with the job she/he performs. Job enrichment opens up for the employee an opportunity for greater recognition, growth, advancement, and responsibility.
3. **Building responsibility into a job:** employees should be encouraged to take responsible risk decisions. This can be done by delegating authority to them.
4. **Modifying the work environment:** this involves the use of teams or work groups.

5. **Flexing working hours:** the introducing flexi-time and flexible working hours so that an employee may have enough time to look after his/her children and family as well as his/her personal affairs.
6. **Job sharing or twinning:** under this system, two workers divide a full-time job between themselves, splitting not only the hours of work but also the salary.

Measurement of Morale

The indicators of morale are the various attitudes and behaviour patterns of employees, which have to be properly and correctly interpreted to determine the kind of organisational climate and culture which prevail at a given time. Since it is an intangible and subjective concept, it cannot be directly measured or evaluated.

John M. Pfiffner has suggested two ways of measuring morale:

1. **Direct Method:** It directs method persons at work are contracted to express their feeling. Morale is measured in terms of the extent of increase or decrease in the profitable. Productivity and other direct benefits, which indicate of high-low morale. The techniques employed in measuring the moral under this method are – Observation techniques, Interview technique (guided interview and unguided interview), Attitude survey, etc.
2. **Indirect Method:** in this method the people at work are not directly approached but in-depth study is made of variations in output, profitability, rate of labour turn-over, absenteeism, number of grievances, and accidents and their severity.

Motivation

Motivation is not a simple concept. It involves a complex combination of individual needs, drives, tensions, discomfort, and expectations. To confound the matter ever further, an individual's needs vary over a period of time. One's value systems evolve continually, and an integral part of that evolution is the motivational process. Motivation theory provides a great deal of insight into the reasons that different individuals exhibit different behavioral patterns in an organisation. It is useful in explaining why the same stimulus works at different times. Motivation may be defined as, giving people incentives that cause them to act in desired ways to lead them to perform in ways that meet the goals of the department and the organisation.

Importance of Motivation

Interest in the topic of motivation in work organisation has escalated a lot in recent years. Several factors appear to account for the prominence of this topic of interest.

1. Researches reveal that managers and organisation cannot avoid a concern with the behavioural requirements of an organisation. Every organisation needs people (in addition to physical and financial resources) in order to function.
2. Motivation as a concept is pervasive and a highly complex activity that effects and is affected by a host of factors in the organisational milieu.

3. Organisational effectiveness becomes to some degree acquisition of management's ability to motivate its employees, to direct at least a reasonable effort towards the goals of the organisation.
4. As technology increases in complexity, machines tend to become necessary, yet they are insufficient vehicles of effective and efficient operations without motivation of employees. In other words, it becomes necessary for an organisation to ensure that it has employees who are capable of using and willing to use the advanced technology to achieve organisational goals.
5. Many organisations are now beginning to pay increasing attention to developing their employees as future resources upon which they can draw as they grow and develop.

Nature of Motivation

In terms of its derivation, the word motivates means to move to activate. In general sense, anything, that initiates activity whether external or internal is motivating. Today, the terms means a lot more than this. Motivation is the work a manager performs to inspire, encourage, and initiate people to take required action. Motivation is all about, how behaviour – gets started, is energised, is sustained, is directed, and what kind of subjective reaction is present in the organism while all this is going on. Some of the widely quoted definitions of motivations are given below:

- Predisposition to act in a specific goal by directed way.
- The immediate influences on the directions, vigour, and persistence for action.
- Steering one's actions towards certain goals and committing a curtains part of one's energies to reach them.

Characteristics of Motivation

The important characteristics of motivation are discussed as below:

1. **Motivation is an internal feeling:** Motivation points to energetic forces of individual that drive them to behave in certain ways and to environmental focus that trigger these drives.
2. **Motivation produces goal directed behaviour:** Motivation has got a profound influence on human behavior; it harnesses human energy to organisational requirement. There is the notion of goal orientation on the art of individual; their behaviour is directed towards something.
3. **Motivation contains systems orientation:** It considers those enforce in the individuals and in their surrounding environments that feedback to the individuals either to reinforce the intensity of their drive and the direction of this energy or to dissuade them from their course of action and redirect their efforts.
4. **Motivation can be either positive or negative:** Positive motivation or the correct approach offers something precious to the person in the form of additional pay, incentives, personal benefits, etc., for satisfactory performance. Negative motivation or sick approach emphasises penalties while controlling performance.

5. **Motivation can be monitory or non-monitory:** Monitory may include increase in pay package, promotion, or any other incentive benefit. While non-monitory benefit may include job enlargement, job enrichment, job rotation, recognition, etc.
6. **Motivation means bargaining:** Behaviour is what people do. Motivation is why they don't. Barnard explained motivation in the form of Inducements Contribution Theory. It focuses on workers and organisation endeavouring to find what payouts (inducements) to workers in exchange for what degree of cooperation (contributions) from workers will be satisfactory to both parties. The problem of motivation then becomes one of arriving at compensation to workers that will cost them the output that is required.
7. **Motivation is a complete process:** Five reasons can be provided in support of this statement.
   - **(i)** First, motive is a hypothetical construct. It cannot be seen. Often we observe individuals putting a great deal of overtime. We cannot definitely state whether they are doing it because of additional income they receive or simply because they enjoy their work.
   - **(ii)** Individuals may have a host of needs that are continuously changing, and sometimes, in conflict with each other. As a result, it becomes exceedingly difficult to observe or measure motivation with certainty.
   - **(iii)** People satisfy their needs in many different ways. A salesman may work hard to earn money; a second salesman may be inspired by his achievement motive and so on. By simply observing salespersons in action it is not easy to differentiate between these groups.
   - **(iv)** Promoting an employee to a new and more challenging task may intensify the drive to work harder in anticipation of the next promotion. Thus gratification of a particular need may gradually lead to an increase in its intensity.
   - **(v)** Finally, goal- directed behaviour does not always lead to need satisfaction.
8. **Motivation and satisfaction are related but not synonymous concepts:** Motivation is the drive to satisfy a want or goal. It is concerned with goal directed behaviour. Satisfaction refers to the contentment experiences when a want is satisfied. The term satisfaction is used to analyse out comes already experiences by an employee. Satisfaction is a consequence of rewards and punishments associated with past experience.

Theories of Motivation

All of the theories depend on the individual's perception of what is a valued motivator. What will be perceived as a motivator depends on the individual's needs. The theories of motivation are broadly classified into two as Content, and Process.

1. Content Theories of Motivation: These theories attempt to identify what things motivate people. Some of these theories are:

(i) Maslow's theory of hierarchy of needs,

(ii) McClelland's theory of achievement, power, and affiliation needs,

(iii) Herzberg's two-factor theory of motivation.

(iv) McGregor's X and Y theory of motivation

(i) Maslow's Theory of Hierarchy of Needs

Abraham Maslow was an American behavioural psychologist who worked both in academia and industry. He published a number of human relations books until the early 1970s, but it was his first book, '*Motivation and Personality*' published in 1943, that set out his idea of the hierarchy of human needs.

Maslow assumes that what motivates people is unmet needs. People may be seeking to meet more than one category of needs at a time. Maslow argued that the factors that drive or motivate people to act lie on an ascending scale. Once a group or order of needs is satisfied, the individual will not be motivated by more of the same, but will seek to satisfy higher order needs. What's more, a higher order need will not be a motivator if lower order needs remain unmet. Maslow defined five orders of needs, listed in ascending importance. First three are the lower order needs and last two are the higher order needs.

(a) Physiological needs (the most basic need), are the ones required for survival, i.e., the basic survival requirements of warmth, shelter and food

(b) Security needs, involve keeping oneself free from harm, i.e., protection from danger of threat

(c) Social needs are the desire for love, friendship, and companionship, i.e. relations with others, expressed as friendship, companionship or love

(d) Esteem needs, are the need for self-esteem and the respect of others, sense of personal worth, respect, and autonomy

(e) Self-actualisation needs (the highest-level need) describe the desire to live up to one's full potential. In these needs there is a sense of achieving your full potential

Thus, for example, we won't be concerned about working relationships or professional achievement if we are truly concerned for our own security. By the same token, a manager won't motivate someone by talking about personal ambition and achievement if that person feels she/he is about to lose his/her job.

Of course, Maslow's ideas were applied to the complete range of human experience, whereas for most of us, physiological and security needs are usually met to a large extent. But recent history has shown that when individuals are homeless, hungry and under threat, all social systems and self-respect break down.

Despite this, Maslow's hierarchy still applies to modern commercial life, and managers would do well to think in these terms when trying to motivate staff.

There have been a number of variations on Maslow over the years. Some split physiological needs down into energy (food, warmth) and protection (shelter). Others have added power – the need for influence over the actions of others, either person-to-person, or group-to-group.

(ii) McClelland's Theory of Achievement, Power, and Affiliation Needs

This motivation theory is based on the assumption that through life experiences, people develop various needs. The three needs include:

(a) The need for achievement: The desire to do something better than it has been done before.

(b) The need for power: The desire to control, influence, or be responsible for other people.

(c) The need for affiliation: The desire to maintain close and friendly personal relationships.

People have all of these needs to some extent. The relative strength of the needs influences what will motivate a person.

(iii) Herzberg's Two-factor Theory of Motivation

Frederick Herzberg studied and practised clinical psychology in Pittsburgh, where he researched the work-related motivations of thousands of employees. His findings were published in '*The Motivation to Work*' in 1959. He concluded that there were two types of motivation:

(a) **Hygiene Factors:** that can de – motivate if they are not present – such as supervision, interpersonal relations, physical working conditions, and salary. Hygiene factors affect the level of dissatisfaction, but are rarely quoted as creators of job satisfaction.

(b) **Motivation Factors:** that will motivate if they are present – such as achievement, advancement, recognition, and responsibility. Dissatisfaction isn't normally blamed on motivation factors, but they are cited as the cause of job satisfaction.

So, once you've satisfied the Hygiene factors, providing more of them won't generate much more motivation, but lack of the motivation factors won't of themselves demotivate. There are clear relationships to Maslow here, but Herzberg's ideas really shaped modern thinking about reward and recognition in major companies. Employees' satisfaction and dissatisfaction stem from different sources. Dissatisfaction results from the absence of what Herzberg calls *hygiene factors like* – salary, relationship with others, etc. Satisfaction results from the presence of *motivating factors like* – opportunities, etc. The supervisor has control of many of the motivating factors, including recognition, responsibility, advancement, and personal growth.

(vi) McGregor's X and Y Theory of Motivation

Douglas McGregor published '*The Human Side of Enterprise*' in 1960, in which he suggested that traditional management methods (which he called Theory X) might not be the only way to get people motivated. Instead, we could take a different approach (based on Theory Y) and achieve the same if not more.

Theory X is the traditional view of direction and control, based on these assumptions:

- The average person inherently dislikes work and will avoid it if at all possible.
- As a result, most people have to be coerced, controlled, and threatened if they are to put in enough effort to achieve the organisational goals.
- In fact the average person prefers to be directed, avoids responsibility, isn't ambitious and simply seeks security.

Theory Y is based on the integration of individual and organisational goals, assumes:

- The physical and mental effort of work is as natural as play or rest, so the average person doesn't inherently dislike work.
- We are capable of self-direction and self-control, so those factors don't necessarily have to come from elsewhere.
- Our commitment to an objective is a function of the rewards for its achievement.
- The average person learns not only to accept but to seek responsibility.
- Most people have a capacity for imagination, ingenuity and creativity.
- The intellectual potential of most people is underused in modern industrial life.

Theory Y is not a soft option. Infact, it can take as much management effort as Theory X, but the effects of a Theory Y approach will last longer. The Theory X manager is a dying breed (although it has to be said he's not yet extinct), and Theory Y lies behind most modern approaches to motivation. Nowadays, the terminology is used as a polite way of referring to the old command-and-control approach to management: the trouble is the diehard Theory X manager won't pick up the subtle criticism.

2. Process Theories of Motivation

Process theories look at the process of motivation rather than specific motivators. The way to explain motivation is to look at it as a process. Two major process theories are:

(i) Vroom's expectancy – valence theory of motivation.

(ii) Skinner's reinforcement theory

(i) Vroom's Expectancy – Valence Theory of Motivation:

Victor Vroom assumes that people act as they do to satisfy needs they feel. He sets out to explain what determines the intensity of people's motivation. He explains that motivation depends on two things:

(a) Valence: the value a person places on the outcome of a particular behaviour.

(b) Expectancy: the perceived probability that the behaviour will lead to the outcome.

The strength of motivation equals the perceived value of the outcome times the perceived probability of the behaviour resulting in the outcome. In other words, people are most motivated to seek results they value highly and think they can achieve. This theory is based on employees' perceptions of rewards and whether they are able to achieve those rewards.

- It is important to note that employees may place different values on rewards and their ability to achieve the outcome than does the supervisor.
- Supervisors need to determine from the employees what is rewarding and what is possible to achieve.

(ii) Skinner's Reinforcement Theory of Motivation:

B. F. Skinner says that people behave as they do because of the kind of consequences they experience as a result of their behavior. Broadly speaking, people keep doing things that lead to consequences they like, and avoid doing things that have undesirable consequences. For example, praise feels good, so people tend to do things that get them praised. Supervisors can encourage or discourage a particular kind of behaviour by the way they respond to the behaviour. Consequences can be thought of as:

(a) Reinforcement

- The desired consequence for behaviour.
- This term is used to indicate positive consequences for desired behaviour.
- This is also used to indicate the outcome for ceasing negative behaviour.

(b) Punishment

- An unpleasant consequence of a behaviour a supervisor wants to end.
- This is sometimes described as negative reinforcement

Supervisors must consider individual differences in designing rewards. What motivates one person may not motivate another. Likewise, not all rewards are under the control of the supervisor. Organisational policy, labour contracts, and laws may dictate what an employee may receive. Some supervisors and other managers assume that the main thing employees want out of a job is money.

Based on the content theories of motivation, it makes sense to say that money motivates people when it meets their needs. When a person has high financial demands and relatively low income, money may be a motivator. If an individual is financially comfortable, non-financial rewards, such as a sense of accomplishment, are increasingly important.

Human behaviour in organisation is the study and application of knowledge about how people, individuals, and groups act in organisations. It does this by taking a system approach. That is, it interprets people-organisation relationships in terms of the whole person, whole group, whole organisation, and whole social system. It encompasses a wide range of topics, such as human behaviour, change, leadership, teams, etc. Its purpose is to build better relationships by achieving human objectives, organisational objectives, and social objectives.

Review Discussions

1. Discuss the concept of personality and explain the theories of personality?
2. Critically examine Johari Window?
3. Enumerate the components and characteristics of attitudes. Also discuss the formation of attitudes?
4. Describe the concept of organisational behaviour and its application in the effectiveness of organisational performance?
5. Explain the term motive and its classifications?
6. Discuss the indicators of morale and its relevance to productivity in organisation?
7. What is motivation? Explain the process and content theories of motivation?

♣♣♣♣♣♣

CHAPTER 4
ORGANISATIONAL DEVELOPMENT

After studying this chapter, you should be able to:

- Comprehend the concept and need of Organisational Development.
- Know steps in Organisational Development.
- Be aware of Organisational Development interventions.
- Discern ethics in Organisational Development.
- Be familiar with Organisational Development values.
- Understand Weisbord's model.

Introduction

Organisational Development (OD) is a systematic process for applying behavioural science principles and practices in organisational effectiveness.

Organisational development is an organisational improvement strategy. In the late 1950s and early 1960s, it emerged out of insight from group dynamics and from the theory and practice of planned change. Today, the field offers an integrated framework capable of solving most of the operant problem confronting the human side of organisations.

OD is a field of practice aimed at analysing the functioning of an organisation, facilitating change and, through its process-consulting capabilities, bringing disparate elements of the organisation into alignment, generally around planned change. OD is characterised by facilitation and communication practices. OD frequently employs surveys in its professional work. Its aim is the smooth, coordinated, and aligned functioning of the organisation. OD deals with the overall health of the organisation. It comes into play when the organisation is not functioning properly or will have to alter its way of operating. OD emphasises organisational effectiveness and is called upon when a major change affecting the entire organisation is anticipated or occurring. It relies on consultant intervention, bringing together all the affected players and groups, and facilitating communication and decision making. OD is the field of study and practice that focuses on various aspects of organisational life, including culture, values, systems, and behaviour. The goal is to increase organisational effectiveness and maintain optimal organisational health through planned interventions in process or operations. Generally, OD services are requested when an organisation or one of its major parts requires or experiences significant change. OD consultants provide planned approaches and structured activities to work through change to achieve desired improvements.

OD is characterised by a distinct consulting method that focuses on the people, culture, processes, and structure of the organisation. A primary OD goal is to optimise the entire organisational system by ensuring all elements are harmonious and congruent. Performance suffers when organisational structure, strategy, culture, and processes are misaligned.

Organisational development is now about the people and organisational function and how to get them to function better. The field is based on knowledge from behavioural science disciplines such as psychology, social psychology, sociology, anthropology, system theory, organisational behaviour, organisational theory and management. OD practitioners are consultant trained in the theory and practice of organisational development, with knowledge from the underlying behavioural science.

OD programs are long termed, planned sustained efforts. Such efforts begin when a leader identifies undesirable situation and seek to change it. The leader contacts an OD professional and together they explore whether organisational development suits the task at hand. If the answer is yes, they enlist other in the organisation to help design and implement the change program. The participants develop an overall game plan or strategy that includes a series of activities, each intended to achieve an outcome that moves the organisation towards its goal. The two major goals of OD program are:

1. To improve the functioning of individuals, teams, and the total organisation, and
2. To teach organisational members how to continuously improve their own functioning.

Organisational development deals with the gimlet of 'people problem' and 'work system problems' in organisations like: poor morale, low productivity, poor quality, interpersonal conflicts, and intergroup conflict, in clear or inappropriate goals, inappropriate leadership styles, poor team performance, in appropriate organisational structure, poor relation, inadequate alignment among the organisation's strategy, structure culture, process, and the like. In short, where individuals, teams, and organisation are not realising their potential, OD can improve the situation.

Need for Organisational Development

Organisational development is emerging discipline directed towards using behavioural science knowledge to assist organisation adjust more rapidly to change. Using a system approach, OD has grown rapidly in response to a need for organisation to remain viable and survive in the world of change. Two important factors have caused the use of OD as a technique of planned changes. Firstly, training for change does not work properly only through reward structure on the job unless there is a proper change in the environment of the organisation in which people work. Secondly, there need to be a highly receptive and effective organisation so that changes are implemented and absorbed to make organisation survive and grow. OD helps a lot in this direction. It tries to free up communication tightness by increasing the amount of trust and seek to build problem-solving capability by improving group dynamics and problem confrontation. In short, it reaches into all aspects of organisational culture in order to make it more humanly responsive.

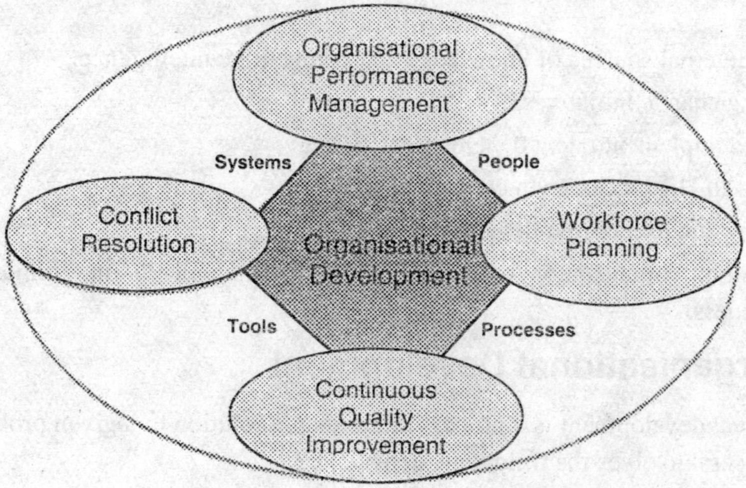

Fig.4.1. Organisational Development Model

When an individual gains new insight into his behaviour he may find it difficult to use new behaviour on the job. One may fear that the other members feel to continue with the old behaviour. There is little evidence that training facilitates organisational change. For an individual to make personal change on the job, an organisation as climate should exist to support these changes otherwise training the individual will have little or no impact on the support of the desired individual change, which is a basic part of the organisational development. Developing the system involves building more effective interpersonal working group. For example, the team may become more efficient, responsive, flexible, and creative from the point of view of the organisation. The concept of team-building lies in the art of organisational development but organisational effectiveness requires more effective teams.

Organisational development is not a program or a project rather it is a continuous process. This process may involve certain project planning and specific programs such seminars, conferences, appraisal, interviews with an object to develop better procedures and supporting climate for dealing with organisational problems. Technological change in industries are well planned and implemented with considerable care but organisational change that is modifying some part of organisational structure or implementing a new process of work is often not deliberately planned but a haphazard activity. Planning, implementation, and evaluating these organisational changes are part for organisational development.

Some of the important aspects of OD are as follows:

1. Contributing to the big picture of vision a reality.
2. Aligning corporate values with individual values.
3. Facilitating towards coaching and mentoring for high levels of performance.
4. Create a culture of improvement through regular forums for best practice.
5. Measuring business impact.
6. Evaluation of system that clearly link best practice initiatives to corporate business goals and priorities.
7. Identify internal sources of knowledge and competitive intelligence.
8. Managing change initiatives.
9. Build and implement talent development strategy.
10. Aligning all HR processes to competencies.
11. Designing and executing relevant forums.
12. Determining organisational designing and implementation initiatives to improve effectiveness.

Steps in Organisational Development

Organisational development is a process rather than a solution to a given problem. Organisational development process involves the following steps:

1. Problem identification and definition.
2. Collection of necessary data.
3. Diagnosis.
4. Planning of change and its implementation.
5. Evaluation of feedback.

1. Problem identification and definition

Understanding and identification of the problem in the organisation is the first step in OD process. The awareness of the problem includes knowledge of the possible problems of organisational growth, human satisfaction, organisational effectiveness, and use of human resources. Having understood exactly what the problem is, the OD practitioner can proceed to collect the necessary data to solve the problem.

2. Collection of necessary data

Data gathering is perhaps the most important activity in the process of OD. Personal interviews, personal observations, and questionnaires are the most common base through which the data is collected. Different data and as such the question of which method to use depends upon the nature of problem the organisation encounters. Having collected the necessary data, organisation proceeds to analyse it.

3. Diagnosis

There is no hook-book formula for accurate diagnosis. It demands considerable skills of analysis and observation as most of the problems are often expressed by organisational members in ambiguous terms. OD program may turn out to be a self-defeating exercise if decisions were to be based on such general vague information. Before decisions are taken, the information collected must be subjected to a microscopic examination, and therefore, experience and judgement are critical to this phase. If organisational leaders were to show in decent haste to arrive at decisions quickly without considering the pitfalls, dangers, it may prove to be very costly at the end. Diagnosis should not be limited to a single problem. Often, important factors like attitudes, assumptions, available resource, etc., must be taken into account in the diagnostic phase. For this purpose attitude surveys can be undertaken through questionnaires wherein the respondents may be asked to evaluate and rate several jobs related factor like working conditions, compensation, benefits, etc. Such surveys will help identify the problem clearly as perceived by the organisational members. Diagnosis assists the planners to locate the source of specific problem and see what changes are required in the system, the structure, or in people.

4. Planning of change and its implementation

After diagnosing the problem, the OD expert turns his attention to the planning of change and implementing it. OD interventions come into picture here. Intervention is considered to be the action phase in OD process. Intervention is a set planned, programmed activities, and techniques by which organisation and their clients collaborate in an OD program. According to French and Bell, 'interventions consist of the long range evolving applications of OD techniques targeted for changing individuals, groups, or the total organisations'.

The range and numbers of available interventions is not small but extensive. The particular interventions to be used depend on the target group in the organisation. One intervention differs from another. In a program it does not consider all interventions, but selects the appropriate one that suits the requirement. But sometimes more than one intervention is used in a program.

5. Evaluation and feedback

Probably one of the important stages in OD process is evaluation. As one stage ends and another stage looms, evaluation is helpful to know as to what has been done, whether it is correctly done or not, and show whether further work is needed before proceeding to the next stage.

Any OD activity is incomplete without proper feedback. Feedback is the process of relaying evaluations to appropriate employees and group by means of special sessions or reports. Feedback must be carefully handled because sometimes emotional factor set in. For instance, when mistakes of some of the members are spelled out then emotional factors accompanying the resentment may creep in. It is important to remember that feedback should be based on the broad array of data and should include the assessment of the change model itself.

Organisational Development Interventions

Some of the OD techniques or interventions for bringing about change might be considered as follows:

1. Sensitivity training

OD is an educational strategy which focuses on the whole culture of organisation in order to bring about a planned change. The change in behaviour pattern of individual within an organisation can be bought about sensitising them. Sensitivity training or T-group training is also known as laboratory training as it is conducted under controlled conditions. It means the development of awareness and sensitivity of behavioural patterns of oneself and others. It is an experience in interpersonal relationships, which results in a change in feelings and attitudes towards oneself and others. T-groups are helpful in unlearning and learning certain things. They help the participants to understand how groups actually work and give them a chance to discover how they are interpreted by others. It also aims at increasing tolerance power of the individual and one's ability to understand others. The sensitivity training programs are generally conducted under controlled laboratory conditions.

Two functions of a T-group or sensitivity development group are as under:

(i) To help its members learn how group actually work.

(ii) To give each member of the group a chance to discover how other people interpret and are affected by his/her own behaviour.

The activity of T-group consists mainly of sitting around a table in a free and open environment in which participants discuss themselves and their interactive process, loosely directed by a professional behaviour scientist who at the group's first meeting simply states that idea of a T-group is to help its members learn about their own behaviour and also learn from other's behaviour. The professional creates the opportunity for participants to express their ideas, beliefs, and attitudes. Specific results sought include increased ability to empathise with others, improved listening skills, greater openness, increased tolerance of individual differences, and improved conflict resolution skills. Members criticise freely the behaviour of each other thereby giving feedback, which may be positive or negative. If individuals lack awareness of how others perceives them, then the successful T-group can effect more realistic self-perceptions, greater group cohesiveness, and a reduction in dysfunctional interpersonal conflicts. Further, it will ideally result in a better integration between the individual and the organisation.

T-group or sensitivity training is an important tool of helping manages to win the cooperation of people working with them.

Despite of popularity of T-group, the value of this training is strongly disputed by some specialists who are willing to concede that a participant may learn a thing which may be helpful at time in his life, but of little use to cope up with his job. It is also said that sensitivity training may cause psychological reactions which a person may not be in a position to bear because of the openness and truth about the situation.

2. Job enrichment

Prior to Herzberg's work many others behavioural scientists were concerned with worker motivation. For several years there was an emphasis on what was termed 'job enlargement' or 'job rotation'. This was proposed to be an answer to the overspecialisation that had characterised many industrial organisations. The assumption was that workers could gain more satisfaction at work if their jobs were enlarged, that is, if the number or varsity of operations in which they engaged was increased.

Herzberg makes some judicious observations about this trend. He claims that doing a snippet of this and a snippet of that does not necessarily result in motivation. Washing dishes, then silverware, and then spots and pans does no more to satisfy and provide an opportunity to grow than washing only dishes. What we really need to do with work, Herzberg suggests, is to enrich the job. Job enrichment is meant to be the deliberate upgrading of responsibility, scope and challenge in work.

An example of job enrichment may be illustrated by the experience an industrial relations superintendent had with a group of janitors. When the superintendent was transferred to new plant, he soon found, much to his amazement, that in addition to his duties, fifteen janitors in plant maintenance reported directly to him. There was no foreman over these men. Browsing through the files one day, the superintendent noticed there was a history of complaints about housekeeping around the plant. After talking to others and observing for himself, it took the superintendent little time to confirm the reports. The janitors seemed to be lazy, unreliable, and generally unmotivated. They were walking examples of theory X assumptions about human nature.

Determined to do something about the behaviours of the janitors, the superintendent called a group meeting of all fifteen men. He opened the meeting by saying that he understood there were a number of housekeeping problems in the plant but confessed that he did not know what to do about them. Since he felt they, as janitors, were experts in the housekeeping area, he asked if together they would help him to solve these problems. 'Does anyone have a suggestion'? he asked. There was a deadly silence. The superintendent sat down and said, 'nothing', the janitors said nothing. This lasted for almost twenty minutes. Finally one janitor spoke up and related a problem he was having in his area and made a suggestion. Soon others joined in, and suddenly the janitors put down their ideas. At the conclusion of the meeting the suggestions were summarised with implied acceptance by all, including the superintendent.

After the meeting, the superintendent referred any housekeeping problem to the janitors, individually or as a group. For example, when any cleaning equipment or material salesmen came to the plant the superintendent did not talk to them but the janitors did. Infact, the janitors were given an office where they could talk to salesmen. In addition, regular meetings continued to be held in which problems and ideas were discussed.

All of this had a tremendous influence on the behaviours of these, men. They developed a cohesive productive team that took pride in its work. Even their appearance changed. Once a grubby lot, now they appeared at work in clean, pressed work clothes. All over the plant, people were amazed how clean and well kept everything had become. The superintendent was continually stopped by supervisors in the plant and asked, what have you done to those lazy, good-for-nothing janitors, given them energy pills? Even the superintendent could not believe his eyes. It was not uncommon to see one or two janitors running floor tests to see which wax or cleaner did the best job. Since they had to make all the decisions including committing funds for their supplies, they wanted to know which time, did not distract from their work. Infact, these men worked harder and more efficiently than ever before in their lives.

This example illustrates that even at low levels in an organisation, people can respond in responsible and productive ways to a work environment in which they are given an opportunity to grow and mature. People begin to satisfy their esteem and self-actualisation needs by participating in the planning, organising, motivating and controlling of their own tasks.

It should be pointed out that the problem of motivation is not always a question of enriching jobs. As Chris Argyrols dramatically showed in his successful use of mentally retarded workers, on the assembly line, some organisations have a tendency to hire people with ability for in excess of the demand of the work.

An example of over hiring happened in the start-up operation of a large plant. As in the case of most new plants, one of the first works was security. The supervisor of plant security set a hiring criterion as a high school education and three years of police or plant protection experience as minimal requirement for applicants. Being the first large industrial plant in a relatively agricultural area, the company was able to hire people not at the minimum level but well over these standards.

When these people began their jobs – which consisted simply of checking badges on the way out-boredom, apathy, and lack of motivation soon characterised their performance. This resulted in a high rate of turnover. When the problem was revaluated, the reverse of the hiring procedures was found to be appropriate. These applicants with a high school education were considered overqualified. Those with police or security experience were also considered overqualified. Rather than experience workers, applicants with fourth-and fifth-grade education, and thus lower job expectations, were hired for these position. Their performance was found to be much superior, and the turnover, absenteeism, and tardiness rates were cut to a minimum. Why? For these workers, a new uniform, badges, and some power were important, but they also found the jobs as one incorporating opportunities for responsibility and challenging work.

3. Survey feedback

One of the tools for assessing attitudes held by organisational members, identifying discrepancies among member perceptions, and solving these differences is the survey feedback approach. Everyone in an organisation can participate in survey feedback, but of key importance is the organisational family – the manager of any given unit and those employees who report directly to him or her. A questionnaire is usually completed by all members in the organisation or unit. Organisational members may be asked to suggest questions or may be interviewed to determine what issues are relevant. The questionnaire typically asks members for their perceptions and attitudes on a broad range of topics including decision making practices, communication effectiveness, coordination between units, and satisfaction with the organisation, job, peers, and their immediate supervisor.

The data from this questionnaire are tabulated and these data then become the springboard for identifying problems and clarifying issues that may be creating difficulties for people. In some cases, the manager may be counselled by an external change agent about the meaning of the responses to the questionnaire and may even be given suggested guidelines for leading the organisational family in group discussion of the results. Particular attention is given to the importance of encouraging discussion and ensuring that discussions focus on issues and ideas and not on attacking individuals.

Finally, group discussion in the survey feedback approach should result in members identifying possible implications of the questionnaire's findings. Are people listening? Are new ideas being generated? Can decision making, interpersonal relations, or job assignments be improved? Answers to questions like these, it is hoped, will result in the group agreeing on commitments to various actions that will remedy the problems that are identified. Thus, the use of questionnaires is to identify discrepancies among member perceptions followed by discussion and remedies are suggested.

4. Process consultation

Consultation gives client insights into what is going on around the client, within the client and between the client and other people. This identifies processes that need improvement. No organisation operates perfectly. Managers often sense their unit's performance can be improved, but they are unable to identify what can be improved and how it can be improved. The purpose of process consultation is for an outside consultant to assist a client, usually a manager, to perceive, understand, and act upon process events with which he or she must deal. These might include work flow, informal relationships among unit members, and formal communication channels.

Process Consultation (PC) is similar to sensitivity training in its assumption that organisational effectiveness can be improved by dealing with interpersonal problems and in its emphasis on involvement.

Consultants in PC are there to give the client insight into what is going on around him, within him, and other people. They do not solve the organisation's problems. Rather the consultant is a guide or coach who advises on the process to help the client solve his or her own problems. The consultant works with the client in jointly diagnosing what processes need improvement. The emphasis is on 'jointly' because the client develops a skill at analysing processes within his or her unit that can be continually called on long after the consultant is gone. Additionally, by having the client actively participate in both the diagnosis and the development of alternatives, there will be greater understanding of the process and the remedy and less resistance to the action plan chosen.

Importantly, the process consultant need not be an expert in solving the particular problem that is identified. The consultant's expertise lies in diagnosis and developing a helping relationship. If the specific problem uncovered requires technical knowledge outside the client and consultant's expertise, the consultant helps the client to locate such an expert and then instructs the client in how to get the most out of this expert resource.

5. Organisational structure

The immediate result of the organising process is the creation of organisational structure which is a framework of the formal relationship that has been established. The purpose of the structure is to assist in regulating and directing the efforts put forth in an organisation so that they are coordinated and consistent with organisation objectives.

There are several types of organisational structure, any one of which may be adopted. If responsibility, authority, and accountability are established in one way, the line and staff structure is created. Another arrangement of relationships is known as the functional type of structure. Each of these structures is briefly described and in addition, the project structure is briefly discussed to indicate how activities can be fitted into structural adaptation.

(i) Line organisational structure: Line structure is created by the functional differentiation downward of primary or basic functions. In manufacturing organisation, these basic functions are production, sales, finance, human resource, quality control, etc. Thus, in the line organisation, all personnel are in the direct chain of command above these functional differentiation outward. One of the decisions common to all types of structure is the selection of bases for grouping divided activities. What has been divided must be combined, if possible, to affect coordinated and unified progress towards organisational goals.

(ii) Line and staff organisation structure: Functional differentiation downward and outward produces a lime and staff organisation. Most business organisations accept to have this type of structure. The people of management have become sufficiently complex so they presumably expect attention will produce more effective result in selected areas. This expertise is introduced into the organisation in an advisory or facilitative manner. In theory, line managers are free to reject the specialised advice or service on the basis of overriding general objectives.

(iii) Functional organisation structure: The adoption of the functional form of organisational structure involves the violation of some principle of organisation previously cited. A functional relationship is established when a staff function is brought directly to bear on the line function with authority to command rather than to advise. Thus, the integrity of line is broken and some personnel are accountable to multiple superiors. If the personnel unit, for example, is set up on a functional bases, it does not recommend that a supervisor accept it as an applicant, but it orders that it be done.

The unit can overrule lower line managers on matters of wages, grievances, training, and the like. Thus, in matter pertaining to personnel the supervisor must look to the personnel unit; in other areas, the supervisor looks to the appropriate line superior.

No firms today are completely fictionalised in all specialised functions. Then significance lies in the provision of a third alternative. Organisers can choose among the following: (a) a function such as hiring can be allocated to the supervisor (line organisation); (b) it can be given to a specialised personnel unit with rights of advice only (line and staff); or (c) it can be assigned to the personnel unit with rights of commands (fictionalised). The third alternative should be used sparingly to prevent distortion of basic general objectives.

(iv) Project structures: A variation of the fictionalised form now coming into wider use, particularly in the aerospace industry, is the project structure. If a management desires to emphasise strongly a specific undertaking or project, a special structure can be created. Such projects are usually unique and unfamiliar to the existing organisation and complex in nature. They require interaction among specialists and have limited work objectives. A project manager is given authority to assemble temporarily the necessary talents and facilities to accomplish on undertaking. In some instance, the usual line and staff departments do the work, but the project manager specifies what efforts are needed and when it will be performed. The operating unit manager may decide who in his or her unit is to help and how the work is to be accomplished. It is apparent that, through the unit manager has line or command authority over personnel, the project manager has functionalised all authority in connection with the work on the particular project.

Business managers have found the project structure supplement to be highly effective in assuring the accomplishment of important goals. The project cannot get lost between departments. It has been found that one person can work for two or more masters and can effectively influence those over whom he or she has no clear authority. The possibility of conflict and frustration is great, but the opportunity for prompt, expeditious, and effective accomplishment is even greater. The coordinative power of the knowledge and expertise of the participating specialists makes up on part for the vagueness and complexity and formal organisational relationships. Both projects managers and supporting unit's managers must maintain an open mind be willing to negotiate.

The typical role of HR managers in project structures is as supporting personnel specialists and to be willing to share in their supervision. For example, a task force may be set up to open a new branch of a outlet chain in a distant city. The personnel unit may be asked to supply an employment interviewer to help in selecting personnel for the new outlet. This interviewer works not only for the project director, but also for his or her more permanent superior, the personnel director. Conflicts can develop when the project director wants more speed in selecting personnel, while the HR manager wants all laws and policies followed. On occasions, the personnel specialist can be a project trader who is authorised to draw temporary help from various parts of the organisation. For example, if the firm wants to put the force of authority behind a program for hiring the culturally disadvantaged, a task force can be formed of line supervisors who temporarily report to the project leader from the personnel unit. One can again visualise possible conflicts between the special projects objectives and the continuing objectives of the line units. The project structure is utilised when one wishes to emphasise two different sets of values. Rather than the ensuring conflicts being settled by the chain of command, the project structure relies upon negotiating skills of project leaders and functional bosses, both of whom possesses overlapping formal authority.

6. Organisational design

Moving from general grouping to the specific, the human resource manager should have an even greater interest in the design and specification of individual's jobs within the organisation. Excessive specification and concentration upon technical efficiency have adverse impact upon the motivation of personal responsible for executing these narrow jobs.

The design of an effective work unit for an individual employee is a highly complete task. It should not be left solely to the line supervisor, the union business agent, or the industrial engineer. The HR Manager has a responsibility to represent the interest of the individuals, which hopefully will be reflected to some degree in the interests of the total organisation. Among the many factors that will affect job designs are as follows:

(i) The proven values of specialisation and respective operations.

(ii) Changing technology.

(iii) Labour union policies.

(iv) Abilities of present personnel.

(v) Available supply of potential employees.

(vi) The interaction requirement among jobs within the system.

(vii) Psychological and social needs of human being that can be met by the jobs.

Specialisation tends to lead to greater productivity as well as ease of hiring. The resulting unit of work undergoes constant modification because of the impact of mechanisation and automation. Some jobs are eliminated, other created and still others altered in content, resulting in different specification of education, experience, personality, and breadth of view point. Labours unions are necessarily involved and seek to retain both present employee's security and union control of these units of work. Thus, calls for alteration of jobs' content despite advances in technology. Economic and organisational values lost in job's design may be recouped in part through enhanced union cooperation.

Management must also be concerned with the practical consideration of quantity and quality of personnel presently available, both within the firms and in the labour market generally. Changes in job content may be made to reflect particular characteristics of specific people available for transfer or hire.

Behavioural scientists have continually stressed the importance of designing jobs and systems work in a manner that will satisfy psychological and sociological needs of people. One of the most commonly cited human relation problems in this area of job design is employed dissatisfaction with jobs that we repetitive, narrow, meaningless, and routine. Engineering efficiency had to lead to the creation of the production and assembly lines. Such lines have proved themselves on the basis of the quantity and quality of production that can be extracted from such a productive arrangement. The major deficiency, however, lies in the human relations area, with such specific problems resulting as:

the boredom of the worker, loss of pride in work, insecurity, and obsessive thinking. These problems are compounded when a moving conveyor links all position together in a 'monster' whose pressure never ceases.

Traditionally, the solutions to excessive specialisations of jobs assignments have involved some means of periodic rotation to provide variety, e.g., change tasks every few hours, or workup the moving assembly line. In recent years, considerable research has been undertaken with respect to more unusual and seemingly risky changes in job content. Among these are jobs enlargement, jobs enrichment, and semi-autonomous groups.

7. Team building

It includes high interaction among team-members to increase trust and openness. Team building utilise high interaction group activities to increase trust and openness among team-members.

Team building can be applied within groups or at the intergroup level where activities are interdependent. Not all groups activity has interdependence of functions. To illustrate, consider a football team and a track team:

Although members on both teams are concerned with the team's total output, they function differently. The football team's output depends synergistically on how well each player does his particular job in concert with his team-mates. On the other hand, a track team's performance is determined largely by the mere addition of the performances of the individual members.

Team-building is applicable to the case of interdependence, such as in football. The objective is to improve coordinative efforts of members that will result in increasing the team's performance.

The activities considered in team building typically include goal setting, development of interpersonal relations among team-members, role analysis to clarify each member's role and responsibilities, and team process analysis. Of course, team-building may emphasise or exclude certain activities depending on the purpose of the development effort and the specific problems with which the team is confronted. Basically, however, team-building attempts to use high interaction among members to increase trust and openness. It may be beneficial to begin by having members attempt to define the goals and priorities of the team. This will bring to the surface different perceptions of what the team's purpose may be. Following this, members can evaluate the team's performance – how effective are they in structuring priorities and achieving their goals. This should identify potential problem areas. This self critique discussion of means and end can be done with members of the total team present or, where large size impinges on a free interchange of views may initially take place in smaller groups followed up by the sharing of their findings with the total team.

Team-building can also address itself to clarifying each member's role on the team. Each role can be identified and clarified. Previous ambiguities can be brought to the surface. For some individuals, it may offer one of the few opportunities they have had to think through thoroughly what their job is all about and what specific tasks they are expected to carry-out if the team is to optimise its effectiveness.

Still another team-building activity can be similar to that performed by the process consultant, i.e., to analyse the key processes that go on within the team to identify the way work is performed and how these processes might be improved to make the team more effective.

8. Intergroup development

OD efforts to change the attitudes, stereotypes, and perceptions that groups have of each other. Major areas of concern in OD are the dysfunctional conflict that exists between groups. As a result, this has been a subject to which change efforts have been directed.

Intergroup development seeks to change the attitudes; stereotypes and perceptions that group have of each other. For example, in one company, the engineers saw the accounting department as composed of shy and conservative types and the human resources department as having a bunch of ultraliberals who are more concerned that some protected group of employees might get their feelings hurt than with the company making a profit. Such stereotypes can have an obvious negative impact on the coordinative efforts between the departments.

Although there are several approaches for improving intergroup relations, a popular method emphasises problem-solving. In this method, each group meets independently to develop lists of its perception of itself, the other group and how it believes the other group perceives it. The groups then share their lists after which similarities and differences are discussed. Differences are clearly articulated, and the groups look for the causes of disparities.

Are the groups' goals at odds? Ware perceptions distorted? On what basis ware stereotypes formulated? Have some differences been caused by misunderstandings of intentions? Have words and concepts been defined differently by each group? Answers to questions like these clarify the exact nature of the conflict. Once the causes of the difficulty have been identified, the groups can move to the integration phase-working to develop solutions that will improve relations between the groups.

Subgroups, with members from each of the conflicting groups can now be created for further diagnosis and to begin to formulate possible alternative actions that will improve relations.

Ethics in Organisational Development

Ethical issues in OD practice, that is, in terms of enhancement versus violation of basic values, Louis White and Kevin Wooten see five categories of ethical dilemmas on organisational development practice stemming from the action of either the consultant or client or both. The types of ethical dilemmas they see are – misrepresentation and collusion; misuse of data; manipulation and coercion; value and goal conflicts; and technical ineptness (These five types largely encompass the several ethical dilemmas reported by Susan Devoget in a survey of OD practitioners).

We shall draw on and modify their categories to suggest what we see as some of the more serious areas for potential ethics violations in OD consulting. Some of these areas apply not only to OD consulting, but to management consulting in general. They are discussed as below:

1. Misrepresentation of the consultant's skills

An obvious area for unethical behaviour would be to distort or misrepresent one's background, training, competencies, or experience in vita sheets, advertising, or conversation. A subtle form of misrepresentation would be to let the client assume one has certain skills when one does not.

2. Professional/technical incompetence

The potential for unethical behaviour stemming lack of expertise is pervasive in OD. To give one example using, Harrison's concepts of depth of intervention, it would seen to be unethical to ask people in a team-building session to provide mutual feedback about leadership style when neither preliminary interviews nor the client group has indicated a readiness or a willingness to do so. Another example would be as follows: A preliminary diagnosis suggests the appropriateness of a feedback intervention, but the consultant has no experience from which to draw in order to design a constructive feedback exercise. The consultant goes ahead anyway. It would be unethical for the consultant to go ahead without some coaching by a more experienced colleague. These situations may call for the 'shadow consultant', the consultant to a single individual in the case another consultant. Thus, we have hypothesised two olations of ethical standards: using interventions that have a low probability of being helpful (and may be harmful in this circumstance), and using an intervention that exceeds one's expertise.

3. Misuse of data

Again, the possibilities for unethical of behaviour in the form of data misuse on the part of either the client or the consultant are abundant. This is why confidentiality is so important in OD efforts. Data can be used to punish or otherwise harm persons or groups. An obvious example would be a consultant's discloser to the boss, the names of those who provided information about the boss's dysfunctional behaviour. Another example would be showing climate survey results from department A to the head of department B without department A's authorisation. Serious distortions of the data would also be unethical. Let's imagine scenario in which the consultant interviews the top twenty members of management and finds several department heads are angry about the behaviour of fellow department head Z and the practices in Z's department. Further, due to Z's hostile and uncooperative behaviour with the consultant in the data gathering interview, the consultant is now angry but is not conscious of the extent of the themes from the interviews to the groups; his or her anger takes the form of overstating and over emphasising the dysfunctional aspects of Z's unit. In an ironic twist, the groups might turn on the consultant and defend Z. As it is said, never attack wrongly the worst member of the group, the group will reject you.

4. Collusion

An example of collusion would be the consultant agreeing with the key client to schedule a team-building workshop when department head Z is scheduled to be on vacation. This tactic is hardly the way to deal with the problem created by Z, and is likely to create reduced trust in the consultant and the key client, Z's boss, and is likely to intensify Z's dysfunctional behaviour. Another example illustrating the power that the consultant colluding with other members of the group to set up feedback situation in which Z's deficiencies will be all too apparent, particularly to Z's boss. Instead of creating a situation in which everyone, including Z, has a chance of improving performance, this pollution is maimed at Z's undoing. If OD interventions are perceived as methods for getting anyone damaged, the OD process is doomed to be a failure.

5. Coercion

It is unethical to force organisational members into setting where they are in effort, required to disclose information about them or their units which they prefer to keep private. The creation of a T-group with unwilling participants would be an example.

6. Promising unrealistic outcome

Obviously, this is an unethical and unproductive practice. The temptation to make promises in order to gain a client contract can be great, but the consequences can be reduced credibility of the key client within his or her organisation.

7. Deception and conflict of values

Deception in any form is unethical and will destroy trust. For example, a telephone company that embarked on a major re-engineering effort after giving assurances of job security, and then proceeded to layoff a huge part of the workforce. The layoffs came after the company had promoted teamwork and empowerment and secured employees' cooperation in streamlining operations. For an OD professional on the scene under such circumstances, the ethical course of action would be to press top management to look at the probable consequences of re-engineering, to look at possible options and to be completely open with employees about the implications of whatever change strategy was selected and the ethical responsibilities of the OD profession and company management extend, of course, to mitigating the impact of any change effort on the lives of individual employees.

Thus, the values underlying ethical OD practice are honesty, openness, voluntarism, integrity, confidentiality, the development of people, and the development of consultant expertise, high standards, and self-awareness.

Organisational Development Values

The OD paradigm values human and organisational growth, collaborative and participative processes, and a spirit of inquiry. The change agent may be directive in OD; however, there is a strong emphasis on collaboration. Concepts such as power, authority, control, conflict, and coercion are held in relatively low esteem among OD change agents. The following briefly identifies the underlying values in most OD efforts:

1. **Respect for people:** Individuals are perceived as being responsible, conscientious, and caring. They should be treated with dignity and respect.
2. **Trust and support:** The effective and healthy organisation is characterised by trust, authenticity, openness, and a supportive climate.
3. **Power equalisation:** Effective organisations deemphasise hierarchical authority and control.

4. **Confrontation:** Problems should not be swept under the rug. They should be openly confronted.
5. **Participation:** The more that people who will be affected by a change are involved in the decisions surrounding that change, the more they will be committed to implementing those decisions.

Organisational development is the field of study and practice that focuses on various aspects of organisational life, including culture, values, systems and behaviour. The goal is to increase organisational effectiveness and maintain optimal organisational health through planned interventions in process or operations. Generally, OD services are requested when an organisation or one of its major parts requires or experiences significant change. OD consultants provide planned approaches and structured activities to work through change to achieve desired improvements.

Marvin Weisbord Six-Box Model (Weisbord's Model)

The six-box model is a framework developed by the American analyst Marvin Weisbord to assess the functioning of organisations. It is a generic framework and is intended for use across a wide variety of organisations. It is based mainly on the techniques and assumptions of the field of organisational development.

The model represents a particular way of looking at organisational structure and design. It gives attention to issues such as planning, incentives and rewards, the role of support functions such as personnel, internal competitions among organisational units, standards for remuneration, partnerships, hierarchies and the delegation of authority, organisational control, accountability, and performance assessment. The model also follows the basic 'systems' approach to organisational functioning including the well known inputs and outputs categories.

The six-box model is comprised of the following components (boxes):

1. **Purposes:** What 'businesses' are we in?
2. **Structure:** How do we divide up the work?
3. **Rewards:** Is there an incentive for doing all that needs doing?
4. **Helpful mechanisms:** Have we adequate coordinating technologies?
5. **Relationships:** How do we manage conflict (coordinate) among people? With our technologies?
6. **Leadership:** Is someone keeping the boxes in balance?

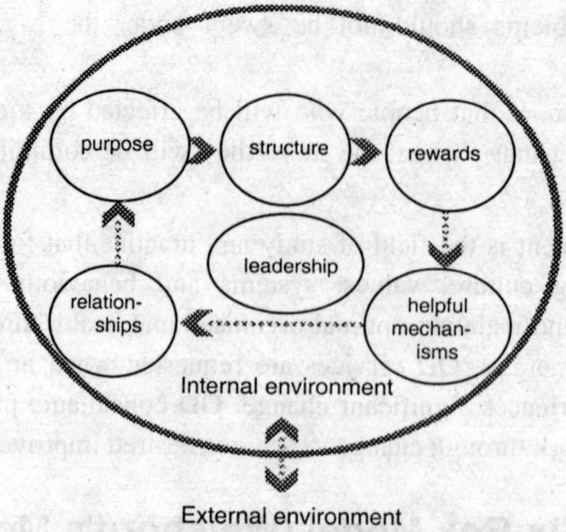

Fig.4.2. Six-Box Model

For several years Marvin Weisbord experimented with 'cognitive maps' of organisations. These are labels that would help us better describe what we saw and heard and understand about the relationships among various bits of data. He started this endeavour when he realised that though he knew a lot of organisational theory, most theories are either too narrow to include everything he wished to understand, or too broadly abstract to give much guidance.

These notes represent a progress report on his efforts to combine bits of data, theories, research, and hunches into a working tool which anybody can use. For want of a more elegant name, he calls this tool the 'Six-Box Model'. This model (Figure 4.2) has helped him to rapidly expand his diagnostic framework from interpersonal and group issues to the more complicated contexts in which organisations are managed.

Figure above provides six labels under which one can sort much of the 'funny stuff' that goes on in organisations, both formal and informal. These labels allow people to apply whatever theories they already know in doing a diagnosis and to discover new connections among apparently unrelated events.

Review Discussions

1. Explain the significance of organisational development in management.
2. What are the intervention strategies in OD?
3. What are the inputs that are required for OD to be of any importance?
4. How does organisational development process provide a planned change and what are the steps involved in it.
5. Explain Marvin Weisbord's Six-Box model.

♣♣♣♣♣♣

CHAPTER 5

CHANGE MANAGEMENT

After studying this chapter, you should be able to:
❍ Understand the nature of organisational change and its management.
❍ Be acquainted with types of organisational change.
❍ Be familiar with levels of organisational change.
❍ Discover reasons of organisational change.
❍ Hit upon resistance to organisational change.
❍ Comprehend why change projects fail?
❍ Identify importance of change management.
❍ Apply change management strategies.
❍ Make out principles of change management.
❍ Distinguish steps involved in change management.

Introduction

Organisation is often viewed as a group of persons contributing their efforts towards achieving its objectives. It is a universal truth that an individual is unable to fulfil his/her needs and desires alone because she/he lacks strength, ability, and resources. So, she/he seeks the cooperation of other people who share goals with him/her. An Organisation is a mechanism with which a management directs, coordinates, and controls the activities of people.

Constant change is everywhere and in everything. Thus, organisational change is also one of the factors in the organisation. Change is most unchangeable. It is said –'change is painful and yet needful'. It is an indispensable function in the organisation.

Like man, organization – whether political, commercial, social or educational has to change to adapt itself to changing situation. Any alteration which occurs in the overall work environment of an organisation implies alterations of structural relationships and role of people in an organisation.

Nature of Organisational Change

Change is a part of life and provides opportunity for growth. It is a conscious decision by the management of organisation. In any organisation, we have people engaged in production, research, development, administration, etc. The organisation in order to change should prepare a stock of the situation and should effect change in their attitude and style of functioning. An organisation is an open system which implies that it is in a constant interaction and interdependent relationship with its environment. Any change can occur in its environment, such as change in consumer tastes and preferences, competition, economic policies of the government, etc. An organisation consists of inter-related and interacting system, to perform complicated tasks such as:

1. Authority and power system.
2. Reorganisation of the tool and techniques used in the system evolving proving of better equipment.
3. Change in the attitudes and behaviours and interpersonal relationship of people working in the organisation through systematic manpower planning.
4. Delayering to flatten structures.
5. Change to multiple reporting relationships.
6. Jobs designed to grow.
7. Increase in job flexibility.
8. Increase in organisational flexibility.
9. Need for clear, measurable, and flexible standards of performance at all level, etc.

Types of Organisational Change

There are different types of change in organisation like:

- Continuous change
- Discontinuous or radical change
- Participative change
- Directive change
- Change by exception
- Paradigm change

Linda Ackerman distinguishes between three types of change as:

- Development change
- Transitional change
- Transformational change

The term 'work change' refers to any alteration that occurs in the overall work environment. Its effect is illustrated in an elementary way by an experiment using an air-filled balloon.When a finger is pressed against the exterior of the balloon the contour of the balloon visibly changes at the point of impact. Here an obvious pressure, representing change, has produced an obvious deviation at the point of pressure. The molecules of air in the balloon represent the organisation's employees. It is apparent that those at the spot of pressure must make drastic adjustment. Though the technical change has in no way made direct contact with the employee, it has affected them indirectly. Though it is fired the employees are displaced and have to adjust to a new location in the balloon. This happens in any work change as well. Organisational change is the observable difference from previous exiting situation to the current situation in the organisation.

Remaining resilient in times like these requires forward thinking. Often when challenges arise, company leaders spend so much of their time and resources preparing for the major change that they don't sufficiently plan for what will happen afterward.

Levels of Organisational Change

'Consistency is the quality of a stagnant mind', says John Sloan. This is rightly said, as it finds great application in the current unpredictable business scenario. Change, resistance to change, and managing change are popular terms and processes in the business world, more so to employees in change-prone organisations.

Well, enthusiasm to change is quite obvious in today's employees. However, whatever it takes to bring out innate change is not ingrained in the change management programs or organisation's conduct. The initiative to hold change management and performance enhancement programs have never fallen apart but the structure and the content of such programs definitely need refurbishing.

Change is possible only if employees are persuaded to think about their jobs in fresh perspectives. A transformation in the attitudes and behaviour of an individual can bring about a fresh outlook to one's job.

There can be three levels of change as mentioned below:

(i) Lifeless-change

Depending on the extent of change desired CEOs could take to any of the three levels of change. The first is related to the outcomes of the business decisions. It has nothing to do with the work patterns or the workplace behaviour of employees. For instance, consider divesting non-core assets to emphasise on core business. In no way does it affect employees change in attitudes or behaviour. This is the least complex, rather the most straightforward level of change that could be brought about in organisations.

(ii) Half-minded-change

The next level involves slightly more complex change process. This level demands of employees' adjustment in the existing practices or adoption of new ones to achieve predetermined targets. A financially unstable company for instance, might solicit change in working patterns or look for innovative ways to reduce or even eliminate waste.

(iii) Abysmal-change

The third and the most complex and deepest of all the levels of change is cultural change. Cultural change involves a complete change in employees' behaviour across the board. If a company could become competitive by changing from being reactive to proactive, hierarchical to collegial, or reflective to externally focused, then cultural makeover is the ideal change that one could look for. Since change is collective and affects the culture of organisations, it must aim at transformation of the minds of all those employees involved in the change.

Essentials of Organizational Change

Senior leaders and their learning partners must keep three key areas in mind as they navigate any major change like: Organisational design, leadership capabilities, and employee engagement.

1. Organisational Design

As an Organisation's strategy shifts to respond to the change, so must its design. The design of an organisation includes a number of important levers that work together to ensure the achievement of the organisation's strategy. These levers include: organisational structure, processes, metrics and reward systems, and people practices. These systems, working in harmony, create focus and harness the collective energy of the organisation.

Realigning these key levers after a major organisational change is often not a top priority, as senior executives are typically focused on the bottom line, shareholder value and employee retention. While a full-scale redesign may not be possible or practical, organisations can begin bringing their systems back into alignment with the new reality by targeting three critical areas:

(i) Values

Having a shared set of values provides a clear sense of purpose to employees and serves as the foundation on which to rebuild the house.

(ii) Goals

Once the foundation has been secured, leaders must ensure that everyone knows what needs to be done to stabilise and start rebuilding. Leaders need to communicate how the goals have changed and how they link to the strategy.

(iii) Roles

Leaders must be clear with employees about how they fit into the newly defined organisation. Do they have new roles and new people they need to interact with to do their jobs? Are their roles the same, but are they part of a different team? Have teams merged? Team leaders should understand the scope of change for each person on their team and be sure to clearly identify the level of change to enable maximum productivity.

2. Leadership Capabilities

Challenging times require a different type of leadership. There are five core leadership competencies critical to driving and enabling change. The logic behind these competencies is simple: a layoff, restructuring, or merger or acquisition causes major disruption, and leaders must focus their capabilities on a narrow list of priorities. The priorities include:

(i) Setting direction

Leaders must define the focus for the organisation and its people by restating the vision and ensuring that the sense of purpose is clear and articulated.

(ii) Aligning employees

Once leaders have set the course, they must make the goals, objectives and mission clear to employees to gain their support.

(iii) Motivating and inspiring people

Enduring a major change can be difficult for the remaining employees and may drain productivity. Leaders can motivate and inspire people by focusing on the organisation's future success.

(iv) Communicating

Change can be unsettling, but people will be more productive if they know what's going on. Leaders must demonstrate strong communication skills and must be honest with employees about the changes in the organisation.

(v) Managing talent

Leaders must scrutinise the redefined organisation's talent needs and secure that talent.

While simple in theory, in practice, the focus and discipline required to successfully execute on these capabilities is not easy. In all likelihood, formal leadership development efforts are no longer practical. However, targeted coaching, action learning and on-the-job tools can help develop these competencies in real time and not only support leaders through the change, but strengthen their capabilities in the process.

3. Employee Engagement

During a workforce reduction, company leaders can be so focused on the employees they're laying off that they overlook the impact of the change on those who stay. To survive and rebuild, it is vital for the organisation to support its people and teams as changes occur.

One way to do this is by directly enlisting employees to play a role in shaping the future of the organisation. Understand what they need to be more individually resilient and provide the training and support to build this capability. While often formed early in life, personal resiliency can be developed, and strengthening personal resilience enables organisational change to be absorbed with minimal impact on productivity and morale.

Leaders also can perform a quick pulse survey, asking employees to answer these key questions:

- Do I know what is expected of me?
- Do I have the right skills, abilities and potential?
- Do I belong here?
- How can I learn, grow or innovate?

Communication is also vital component of employee engagement. Employees should be kept informed through regular communication, such as newsletters and manager roundtables. The communication channels should be two-way, open and honest, and frequent. The more information employees have, the less time they spend guessing about the direction of the company and the more time they have to focus on their work.

While there is no way to predict what changes might affect an organisation in the future, leaders who prepare for the change and its aftermath will ensure their organisations can thrive through the challenges ahead.

Reasons for Organisational Change

Many things cause organisational change. These includes:

- Challenges of growth, especially global markets
- Changes in strategy
- Technological changes
- Competitive pressures
- Customer pressure, particularly shifting markets
- To learn new Organisational behaviour and skills

- Government legislation/initiatives.
- Change in organisational structure
- Change in managerial personnel.

Research indicates that organisations are undergoing major change approximately once in every three years, whilst smaller changes are occurring almost continuously. There are no signs that this pace of change will slow down. Hence, organisations have to modify and change to adapt to the changing internal and external environment.

- Technological innovations have multiplied
- Basic resources have progressively become more expensive.
- Competition has sharply increased.
- Communication and computers have reduced the time needed to make decision
- Environmental and consumer interest groups have become highly influential
- The drive for social equity has gained momentum
- The economic interdependence among countries has become more apparent.

Resistance to Organisational Change

As usual, whenever there is any change, there tends to be resistance. This resistance can fall in two categories – one direct and other indirect. To name a few – finding fault, ridiculing, manipulating, criticism at every point, etc., fall under direct resistance. Indirect resistance will be in the form of not following the change though verbally agreed, showing ignorance, concealing facts or information, etc. Employees resist change because they have to learn something new. In many cases there is no resistance on the benefits of the new process is going to bring, but it is the fear of unknown future and their ability to cope up with it. In many organisations the change management came to a virtual halt due to the resistance it encountered during its implementation.

1. At a staff meeting everyone agrees to utilise a new procedure, but several weeks later you discover that the procedure has not been implemented.
2. When computerisation is introduced, though all staffs insist that they need individual computer, nobody is using them for the purpose for which they were intended.
3. The employee consents to the change by appearing cooperative, but infact doing the things in the same way as he was doing before implementing change.

Why Change Projects Fail?

More often, change projects fails due to the lack of effective change management than any other reason. In many cases, the teams lack the basic understanding of what change management is and how to implement change management tactics. When changes are made, many employees do not have knowledge base of why the change is being made.They also do not share the same accountabilities as managers. The outcome is a hazardous mix of various priorities, different knowledge sets, and different driving forces. If the change is not managed properly, these different values and driving forces clash with each other result in unfortunate outcomes for the organisation.

Change Management

Change is the only constant thing in the lives of individuals, groups, society, nations, and the universe itself. In today's dynamic technological, social, political, economic, and legal environment, change is all-encompassing in organisations. It happens continuously, and often at rapid speed. It is rightly said that 'to be where we are, we have to run fast'! The change we refer here has got a broad list of topics. For an individual, change may mean a new behaviour. Similarly, from the point of view of a businessman, it may mean a new business process or new technology. From the social view, it can be a new act or policy. For the success of change management, active and enthusiastic participation of the employees or people is essential. Change management is concerned with two sets of people, i.e., one those who want to effect change and second is those on whom change is to be effected. Change management is the effective process of a business change such that executive leaders, managers, and frontline employees work in consonance to successfully implement the technology or organisational changes. Every organisation in the recent time is facing the pressure for change may be due to globalisation, government initiatives, or any other reason in order to improve productivity, achieve better results. The pace of change is increasing day-by-day and it is an art to develop the skill of living with the change and also managing the change.

Change management is not a singular concept; rather it includes a set of best practices and experiences, which are used to handle both internal as well as external changes. Change management includes effective management of new methods and systems in an on-going organisation. Change from an existing setup to a new environment has its own set of inherent problems and the problems become multifold when applied in a service institution. It is a continuous, often contradictory process, which brings difficult challenges as well as opportunities. Change is no longer a choice. So, organisations cannot avoid change. Managers, leaders have to be aware of change and take active role in anticipating, planning, facilitating and implementing organisational change through effective change management strategies. Competencies in managing change can help them to be more effective in moving the organisation from the present towards the future.

Change management is not a stand-alone process for designing a business solution. It is the processes, tools and techniques for managing the people-side of change. It is not a process improvement method. Change management is a method for reducing and managing resistance to change when implementing process, technology or organisational change.

Change management is not a stand-alone technique for improving organisational performance. Change management is a necessary component for any organisational performance improvement process to succeed, including programs like Six Sigma, Business Process Re-engineering, Total Quality Management, Organisational Development, Restructuring, and continuous process improvement. Change management is about managing change to realise business results.

Change management can be defined as 'the process of managing changes that occurs because of an event'.

Karen Kaiser Clark states 'Life is change. Growth is optional. Choose wisely.' Management when defined simply is nothing but making wise choices at the correct time.

Change Management includes the changes that lie within and are controlled by the organisation and those that come to terms with the changes occurring in the surrounding environment,i.e.,the events originating outside the organisation and the response to them.

The basic definition of change management has following three important aspects:

- The task of on-going change.
- An area of professional practice.
- A body of knowledge.

Importance of Change Management

'Managing change' refers to making of changes in a planned and managed or systematic fashion where the aim is to implement new methods and systems in an on-going organisation in a more effective manner. The content or subject matter of change management consists chiefly of the models, methods and techniques, tools, skills and other forms of knowledge that go into making up any practice. The subject matter of change management is drawn from psychology, sociology, business administration, economics, industrial engineering, systems engineering, and the study of human and organisational behaviour.

The rate of organisational change has not slowed in recent years, and may even be increasing. The rapid and continual innovation in technology is driving changes to organisational systems and processes. Witness the startling growth of the Internet, which is enabling much faster and easier access to knowledge; add to this the increased expectations of employees as they move more freely between organisations. And, of course, globalisation has seen the tearing down of previous international market barriers. It is no wonder that relentless change has become a fact of organisational life.

While management design and implement strategies that deliver improvement in performance, they often neglect one key area for success –'Managing the change'. Change management is important because understanding this change and its effect on the organisation and its people minimises disruptive aspects and enhances positive opportunities in the change process. These opportunities can include containing costs, realigning resources and respond more quickly to customer demands.

In spite of the importance and permanence of change, most change initiatives fail to deliver the expected organisational benefits. This failure occurs for a number of reasons. One might recognise one or more of these in an organisation which are as follows:

1. Absence of a change champion or one who is too junior in the organisation
2. Poor executive sponsorship or senior management support
3. Poor project management skills

4. Hope rested on a one-dimensional solution
5. Political infighting and tough wars
6. Poorly defined organisational objectives
7. Changing the team through diverting to other projects

Failed change initiatives leave burned out employees, making the next change objective even more difficult to accomplish. It should come as no surprise that the fear of managing change and its impact is a leading cause of anxiety in managers.

Change management helps people to deal with change. Three key benefits are:

- Change management can help people to recognise how powerful the human dynamics are in any change effort, how they dramatically affect the final result and how management can use that knowledge to attain the best possible outcome.
- A change management strategy can act as a map for guiding action.
- Change management ideas and tactics can help the management to develop the relationship needed to maximise the effectiveness of a change.

Change Management Strategies

There are different strategies and procedures that are used to categorise the change environment. The relevance of different change strategies is that they build upon different assumptions about human motivation and hence willingness to engage in change at a particular point of time. These strategies are not intended to be mutually exclusive. Rather they may each be appropriate at a different stage of a particular change process. Once the environment is identified, an effective implementation plan can be composed. Five differing views are presented below:

1. Normative-re-educative strategy

This approach believes that changing the norms, attitudes and values of individuals will lead to changes in their behaviours. It is based upon core beliefs, values and attitudes. So change will occur as individuals change their attitudes and this leads them to want to behave differently. People are social beings and will adhere to cultural norms and values. Change is based on redefining and reinterpreting existing norms and values, and developing commitments to new ones.

2. Rational-empirical strategy

This strategy is based on persuasion, and assumes that individuals are rational and as such they will follow their own self-interest once this is made clear to them. The benefits of a change therefore need to be highlighted and sold to the individuals as being of personal benefit to them. People are rational and will follow their self-interest once it is revealed to them. Change is based on the communication of information and the proffering of incentives.

3. Power-coercive strategy

This strategy is based on the application of power, with the belief that most people are compliant to those who have greater power. A potential issue with this process is that once the power is removed, individuals may revert to previous behaviours. People are basically compliant and will generally do what they are told or can be made to do. Change is based on the exercise of authority and the imposition of sanctions.

4. Action-centred strategy

This focuses on the actions which include problem solving, looking at problems and focusing on remedial actions.

5. Environmental – Adaptive strategy

People oppose loss and disruption but they adapt readily to new circumstances. Change is based on building a new organisation and gradually transferring people from the old one to the new one.

Factors Influencing Selection of Change Strategy

Generally speaking, there is no single change strategy. An organisation can adopt a general strategy for any given situation. It can also adopt mix of strategies in special cases. The following are the factors which influence the strategy chosen to change management:

- **Degree of change:** Radical space in an organisation argues for an environmental- adaptive strategy. It will change the existing on an organisation and build a new one instead of trying to transform the old one.
- **Degree of resistance:** Strong resistance argues for a coupling of power-coercive and environmental – adaptive strategy. Weak resistance or concurrence argues for a combination of empirical – rational and normative reductive strategies.
- **Target population:** Large population argues for the mix of all four strategies. Diverse population also calls for mix of all strategies. This implies that, there should be a careful segmentation.
- **The stakes:** High stakes argue for a mix of all strategy. When stakes are high, nothing can be left to chance. Moderate stakes calls for a power-coercive strategy.
- **The timeframe:** Short-timeframes argue for a power – coercive strategy. Longer time-frames argue for mix of empirical-rational, normative – reeducative and environmental adaptive strategies.
- **Expertise:** Adequate expertise at making change in an organisation argues for some mix of strategies
- **Dependency:** This is a classic double-edged sword. If the organisation is dependent on its people, management's ability to command or demand is limited. Conversely, if people are dependent upon the organisation, their ability to oppose or resist is limited.

Three Phases of Change Strategy

1. Definition phase:

This phase accurately define the change. It involves:

- Problem specification
- Formulation of success criteria
- Identification of performance indicators

2. Evaluation phase:

This phase helps to:

- Generate the options
- Selection of appropriate techniques

3. Implementation phase:

- Development of implementation strategies
- Consolidation

Principles of Change Management

Three important principles are central to the change management approaches which are:

1. Change management is not the goal in itself: it is a means to an end, and the end is an improvement in an organisation's performance. It is about effectively managing a process that will lead to an environment where an improvement in performance can be realised.
2. The 'target' of change must play an active role in realising the change: Successful change projects will identify and communicate the vision, letting the employees know that they are expected and empowered to play an active role in realising the planned benefits.
3. An organisation's employees are their greatest asset: potentially, they are also the greatest challenge. For a vision to become reality, those at the, scoal-faces must believe in the project and have the desire to achieve it.

Steps Involved in Change Management

The important steps of change management are as follows:

Step 1 : Change Management Planning

Before launching a project, the team should conduct the following:

- **Benefit Identification:** The early identification and agreement to the organisational, functional and personal benefits to be produced from any change programme is essential.

- **Executive Sponsorship:** The programmes must show alignment with senior management's business objectives. Gaining executive sponsorship and leadership is the first step to verify that the change to be implemented aligns with the business objectives.
- **Readiness Assessment:** An assessment of the readiness of the organisation to adopt the changes required will enable a realistic implementation plan to be developed.
- **Benefits Planning:** Having identified the benefits of the programme, it is important to structure the plan in a way that demonstrates when and how these benefits will be delivered.
- **Resistance Management:** A major obstacle to successful change management is employee resistance at all levels, typically due to lack of awareness about the change, comfort with the ways things are, fear of losing control or overload of current responsibilities. A strategy will be developed to reduce resistance.

Step 2: Change Management Execution

Once the project has been launched, the project should conduct the following four key execution steps:

- **Communications Plan:** If employees know 'what' the change is and 'why' it's being implemented, then 'how' to implement the change becomes far less challenging. We will develop a carefully structured communications plan to inform the employees about the change management programme and how the change will affect them.
- **Implement the Change Management Plan:** The execution of the actions within the change management plan can be supported by continuously assessing progress and if necessary revising the plan accordingly where the aim is to equip the employees in the organisation with the skills, tools, and techniques required for them.
- **Education and Training Plan:** A key element of the change management plan is the Education and Training plan, to perform an effective role within the organisation once the changes have been implemented.
- **Resistance Management:** By actively listening, feedback on the changes can be constantly monitored during implementation, to identify any areas where resistance is being encountered.

Step 3: Change Management Reinforcement

Once the project is complete, PMIS (Personnel Management Information System) can support clients' through three further steps focused upon sustaining the change. They are:

- **Measuring Benefits:** Measuring the benefits delivered by the programme assessing the progress achieved against the objectives identified at the outset.
- **Identify Gaps and Manage Resistance:** If some of the anticipated benefits have not been realised this may be because of gaps in the actions undertaken or unexpected resistance. The identification of these gaps and resistance will enable the implementation of corrective actions to reinforce the change.

- **Reinforcing Change:** Having achieved the new behaviours, process, practices, etc., it is all too common for organisations to slip back to operating and behaving along the original familiar lines.

On a regular basis, monitor the Organisational performance relative to the goals of the Change Management project, developing where appropriate corrective actions to reinforce the desired changes.

To conclude it can be said that by encouraging employees' involvement and delegating responsibility downward to shape the change becomes continuous. This is because people develop greater awareness and a different mindset with which they actually want to continually improve. To be effective, the project must recognise, respect and leverage the knowledge, insights and opportunities that this change can bring. Effective change is nothing but winning over people in the organization.

Organisational change is increasing yet the high level of failure indicates that effective management of these changes is still lacking. Such a gap indicates that there is much to learn about how to manage change more effectively. Hence, people management and development professionals have significant role to play in any change management process. Change management is a systematic approach to dealing with change, both from the perspective of an organisation and on the individual level. With the widespread commitment of people throughout the organisation, change efforts will succeed. Change does not substantially alter the way a leader leads; change only reinforces that leaders must always use their skills to lead everyday.

Review Discussions

1. Explain organisational change. What are the levels and areas of change?
2. Describe the change management process. What strategies are involved in managing change?
3. Discuss the factors influencing the change management strategies?
4. Explain the phases of strategies in change management?
5. Why some organisations fail to make change and how can it overcome these limitations?

♣♣♣♣♣♣♣

CHAPTER 6

ORGANISATIONAL CULTURE AND CLIMATE

After studying this chapter, you should be able to:

- Be on familiar terms with organisational culture and climate.
- Comprehend uniformity of culture.
- Be acquainted with improving organisational culture.
- Identify components of culture.
- Be acquainted with developing organisational culture.
- Discern how culture affects work.
- Spot characteristics of organisational climate.
- Determine factors affecting organisational climate.
- Originate changing organisational climate.

Introduction

We can compare organisational culture and climate to personality and mood. The former is enduring; the latter is temporary. We acquire our basic personalities early in life, but our moods can shift several times in one day.

Organisational culture is not quite as fixed as personality, however, so the analogy is not perfect. It is hard to change an organisation's culture but not as difficult as changing your personality. Also, organisational climate can last so long it becomes indistinguishable from culture, like being in a bad mood for months on end. Generally, however, climate is easier to change. During an economic downturn, people are worried about their jobs, then suddenly a big order comes in and everyone breathes a sigh of relief, so the climate improves.

Understanding Organisational Culture

Culture is an anthropological term that is applicable to organisations too. It represents a pattern of beliefs and behaviour that have been learned from other members of the society. It is in its broadest sense, the cultivated behaviour, i.e., totality of man's learned experience which is socially transmitted or more briefly behaviours acquired through social learning. It is most frequently described as custom. Just as top executives can influence climate, they can also set the tone for the culture. If the CEO is an entrepreneur, the culture will be one that makes fast decisions, takes risks, and likes to innovate. Apple Computers would be a good example of an entrepreneurial culture. Insurance companies and banks tend to have very different cultures, dominated by avoidance of risk. Such processing cultures need elaborate rules to ensure consistency and efficiency. An engineering culture may be like aircraft manufacturers or phone companies, emphasising on value, technical competence, and high quality. Then there are marketing cultures that are very sales oriented. They tend to be populated by dynamic, lively, and outgoing people. Scientific cultures are common in medical or drug manufacturing companies where there is an insistence on pure research to back up new proposals. It is not this simple, of course. Cultures can vary a great deal within a particular industry. organisations might have a culture of blame, fun, hard work, equality, career development, environmental consciousness, or any other personality trait.

Major culture change initiatives focus on making the company more customer focused, innovative or cost-conscious. It can be a matter of loosening up or tightening up, often accompanied by moving back and forth between centralisation and decentralisation.

Understanding Organisational Climate

Typical climates correspond to human feelings or moods: excitement, depression, anger, fear, optimism, or anxiety. Like human mood, an organisation's climate can be caused by internal and external factors. If the CEO or other prominent leaders are in a certain mood, they can infect the entire organisation. Leaders whose moods are highly variable could lead teams with wildly fluctuating climates. Just as most people won't be in the same mood all the time, we can't expect an organisation's climate to be unchanging. Shifting emotions are a good thing as it makes the organisation seem more human. It would feel like being part of a machine if the climate of our workplace never altered. An emotionally variable climate is, like a similarly expressive person, more open, transparent and understandable. We feel comfortable when we can read another person's feeling. The same applies to our workplace. It is unhealthy to suppress emotion in organisations or people.

Organisational Culture

Culture is the set of important understandings that of a community share in common. It consists of patterns and ways of thinking, feeling, and reactions that are acquired by language and symbols that create distinctiveness among human group. Culture of the organisation plays an important role in the area of motivation and the level of economic rewards. It also influences the level of commitment to work on the part of the members. Organisational culture represents a common perception shared by the member of an organisation and has a tendency to describe the organisational culture in almost similar terms.

The term 'Organisational Culture' refers to the norms and values of an organisation, which together make the personality of the company. Improving organisational culture is the need of the hour, as people want to work for a company that enables them to maintain a balance between their work life and personal life and organisations who give importance to organisational culture increase their productivity and lower are the attrition rates. So, a healthy organisational culture is a win-win situation for all the stakeholders, shareholders, management, customers and employees.

What makes organisational culture enduring is the socialisation process of an organisation. This process familiarises a 'fresher' with the various characteristics of culture and forces him to adjust to it and continues throughout one's entire career in the organisation.

Socialisation process has three stages – pre-arrival, encounter, and metamorphosis. Selection of only 'right type' of person who 'fit' the eligibility requirement (which is laid down in the light of prevailing organisational culture) is an attempt to maintain and perpetuate the existing organisational culture even before the outsider has joined the organisation. If a 'wrong' person (whose individual characteristics do not match with the prevailing organisational culture) gains an entry into the organisation, she/he encounter with the new forces. These forces try to change him/her according to organisation culture. The person may decide either to surrender him/herself to these forces and get completely changed or to leave the organisation.

The various forces which a person has to encounter on him/her entry into the organisation and which subsequently bring about his/her metamorphosis are long-standing unwritten rules, rituals, taboos, jargons, and the prevailing work culture. Every organisation has some long-standing unwritten rules of conduct, which its members meticulously follow. Rituals refer to ceremonies which organisation performs on specific occasions? Taboos refer to the prohibitions imposed on certain forms of speech or acts, e.g., not calling superiors by their first names, not discussing each other's personal lives in public, not coming to the place of work in a drunken state and so on. Jargon refers to the special language, which only the members of the fraternity understand. This is sometimes referred to as 'code language', and may include nicknames for persons, events, and processes, etc.

Characteristics of Organisational Culture

Campbell and others have identified such characteristics as following:

1. **Individual autonomy:** The degree of responsibility and freedom and opportunities of exercising initiative that individuals in the organisation have.
2. **Structure:** The rules and regulations, and the amount of direct supervision that is used to oversee and control employee behaviours.
3. **Support:** The degree of assistance and warmth provided by managers to their subordinate.
4. **Identity:** The degree to which members identify with the organisation as a whole rather than with their particular work-group of professional expertise.
5. **Performance:** Reward the degree to which reward system in the organisation is based on employee performance criteria.

Uniformity of Culture

A common misconception is that an organisation has a uniform culture. All organisations have culture in the sense that they are embedded in specific societal cultures and are part of them. An organisational culture is common perception held by the organisational members. Everyone in the organisation would have to share this perception. There can be dominant culture and subculture as discussed below:

1. **Dominant culture:** A dominant culture is a set of core values shared by a majority of the organisational members. For example, most employees at South-West Airlines seem to subscribe to such values as handwork, company loyalty, and the need for customer service. At Hewlett-Packard, most of the employees seem to share a concern for product innovativeness, product quality, and responsiveness to customer needs.

2. **Subculture:** Culture is a unique concept. Within any organisation we can find variations in culture known as subculture. It is unique but natural that within a society, substantial variations do exist in culture. A subculture is set of values shared by a minority, usually a small minority of the organisation's member. Subculture typically is a result of problems that are shared by members of department or unit. It is however possible to classify these subcultures into institutional (vertical subculture) and professional (horizontal) subculture as discussed below:

(i) **Institutional subculture:** An institutional subculture comprises of the behaviour patterns of a particular group of a department within the company of a company as a whole. For instance, a company may place tremendous emphasis on the safety and accident prevention. Similarly, in some organisations, high priority may be on quality of work. Thus, safety in the former and quality in the later will become the part of subculture of that organisation.

(ii) **Professional subculture:** These encamps the customs associated with a particular professional of occupational group within an organisation. Therefore, they are also called as horizontal culture. Some professionals also develop certain code of conduct or ethics applicable to their profession. For example, accountants have some code of conduct and they perform their duties and functions irrespective of the consequences to the particular organisation for which they work.

Improving Organisational Culture

Some of the important ways of improving organisational culture are discussed as follows:

1. Training and development of employees in the right way is an important step towards improving the organisation's work culture.
2. Analysing the existing culture and comparing it with the expectations and perceptions of employees brings changes accordingly.
3. Create a diverse team of enthusiastic people, who are interested in working as a team and improving the work atmosphere as a whole.
4. Healthy communication, good leadership with strategies adopted to build an attractive culture.
5. Handling conflicts by way of creating an unbiased, transparent and impartial conflict resolution mechanism.
6. Team-building along with synergy is a must to attain the organisation's objectives to build effective culture. Synergetic and cooperative teamwork is manifestation of a healthy organisational climate.

Components of Culture

Culture factors manifest themselves in a number of ways in formal organisations. Conveniently, culture can be classified into two parts – material and non-material as discussed below:

1. Material culture: It comprises of all the things that man artifacts. The manmade objects are created by technology and often referred to as material culture. Food, clothing, housing, tools, and transportation devices, are all visible items, whereas advancement in science like X-rays, and Gamma,-rays, all belong to the category of invisible items. These material aspects of culture have a great relevance to the way in which organisations are created and made operative.

2. Non-material culture: This type of culture refers to the intangible beliefs, philosophies, habits, culture among the members of organisation or society. Non-material culture has the following befitting examples:

(i) **Rituals:** One feature of non-material culture is the use of ritual in union according to prescribed formulae. They are usually associated with the ceremonies and tribal observations requiring a number of people to act. These rituals are not limited to religion and religious ceremonies alone; they are followed in our society and very much in business organisations.

(ii) Taboos: Another feature of non-material culture is taboos. Every society has a system of taboos. These represent generally the nature of acceptable human conduct affecting morality. In any organisation for example, it may be wrong to accept gift from costumers or suppliers. Infact, in almost all organisation, groups exists to punish the members for non-compliance of the existing taboos.

(iii) Jargons: The most important of all factors is jargons or the language used by people when they are in a group. For instance, teenagers develop a type of slang that is virtually incomprehensible and unpalatable to many adult members. Further railroaders have a special language which they use when they join as a group. Similarly, musicians have special words for ordinary things and deeds of day-to-day life.

Developing Organisational Culture

Many companies lack an accurate understanding of their own culture and therefore don't provide the right information to attract candidates who are the best cultural fit. It's crucial for employers to determine and define the company's culture so they can assess potential employees' capacity to fit within that culture.

Company culture is very important because it can influence large-scale managerial decisions, company ethics and more. However, culture is also something that evolves as things like company staff or location change, or as the organisation grows or shrinks in size.

Many companies confuse their brand with their culture. Just because a company sells the hippest mobile device on the market doesn't guarantee that the culture of their office will mirror their brand personality and commercial success. Conversely, just because a company offers a product or service that may seem staid or boring, it doesn't mean they have an office environment to match.

Here are a few steps employers can take to help evaluate their corporate culture:

1. Conduct a company self-evaluation

Is the company culture really what employers think it is? Ask employees to anonymously describe the company culture to determine if there is consistency in their answers and if their answers mirror the beliefs held by the executive team.

2. Use objective evaluation

Bring in a few objective observers for a day or two to provide feedback on the culture. These could be friends of staffers, temporary staff or professional consultants.

(i) Institute a new dress code (slightly more casual or slightly more formal).

(ii) Arrange to buy the staff lunch once a quarter or bring in bagels every other Friday.

(iii) Organise an afternoon for teams (or the company, based on its size) to volunteer.

(iv) Invite staffers to bring in something indicative of them personally or professionally to use to decorate the office.

3. Don't settle for the bandages

Many companies are tempted to solve cultural problems by throwing a company party or engaging in other quick-fix tactics. Not only is that unsustainable, but it usually also further degrades company culture because employees see that it is not a genuine attempt at creating lasting cultural change.

4. Nurture your culture

Just as employers have strategic goals for the business, they should develop strategic goals to grow and sustain the company culture.

5. Broadcast it

If employers find they have consensus on the corporate culture, they must then articulate that message on the corporate.

No matter how great a candidate looks on paper, the relationship will not last if he or she is not a fit with the corporate culture. In economic times like these, many job seekers are reticent to do anything that may jeopardise a job offer, irrespective of whether they think they will thrive in the cultural environment.

It is therefore incumbent on employers to remember that hiring employees is about more than just the duties they perform; it is also about how they will fit in with the 'personality' of the company.

Guidelines for Developing Culture

Based on researches, Collins and Poras have provided following guidelines for developing suitable organisational culture:

1. Preserve core ideologies while allowing for change.
2. Stimulate progress through challenging objective, purposeful evolution, and continuous self-improvement.
3. Encourage experimentation and accept mistakes.
4. Accept paradox while rejecting either or thinking.
5. Create alignment by translating core values into goals, strategies, and practices.
6. Grow new managers internally by promotion from within.

How Culture Affects Work?

Even before the employment, people have a tendency to develop some basic values by integrating with the environment. These basic values by integrating with the environment will be so ingrained that they become difficult to change. Keith Davis points out certain values like freedom, equality, security, and opportunity as discussed below:

1. Freedom: Autonomy or freedom represents a basic cultural value that affects work in good many organisations. Freedom here refers to freedom from authority and freedom to do as one feel like doing anything she/he wants. This is to say, this freedom is within some prescribed bonds. It may mean different things for different people.

2. Equality: This value states that all people are equal, having equal rights when compared with their neighbours. However, this value gives due recognition to different mental, emotional, and social differences and reward. Another associated idea is equity, which states that there should be justice in rewarding performance.

3. Security: People in a dynamic environment seek security. People want/prefer full employment rather than handout. Some sorts of mental tension prevail in the mind of employees as long as she/he is economically insecure and she/he may not contribute effectively to organisational goals. Security is, thus a highly regarded value in culture.

4. Opportunity: Another value that affects people in work organisation is the opportunity. People expect good many opportunities to climb the ladder in organisation. Modern education, policies of promotion from within and similar factors affect the opportunity of employees.

Organisational Climate

A concept that management cannot afford to ignore is, 'Organisational Climate'. All organisational theoreticians and researchers unanimously agree that a sound climate is extremely important for the ultimate achievement of organisational climate though abstract in nature, is normally associated with job performance, and job satisfaction and morale of the employees. It is therefore a commonly experienced phenomenon and often referred to by many expressions as atmosphere, surroundings, milieu, environment and culture, etc. Organisations like fingerprints and snowflakes are always unique.

Organisational climate is a very important factor to be considered in studying and analysing organisations as it has a profound influence on the outlook, well-being, and attitudes of organisational members and thus on their total performance. It affects the behaviour of people in three ways:

1. Defining the stimulus that confronts the individual.
2. Placing constraints upon the individual's freedom of choice.
3. Providing source of reward or punishment.

It further provides a platform for understanding such characteristics of organisations such as stability, creativity, innovation, etc.

Meaning of Organisational Climate

Organisational climate is the human environment within which an organisation's employees do their work. It may refer to the environment within a department, a major company unit such as a branch plant, or an entire organisation. Climate for the organisation is somewhat like personality for a person. 'Just every individual has a personality that makes each person unique; each organisation has an organisational climate that clearly distinguishes its personality from other organisation.'

Climate can influence motivation, performance, and job satisfaction. It does this by creating employee expectation about what consequences will follow from different actions. Employees expect certain rewards, satisfaction, and frustrations on the basis of their perception of the organisation's climate. Although intangible, organisational climate is a real phenomenon. In the literature of organisational behaviour several definitions have been advanced and almost all have a greater degree of commonality.

Organisational climate is a relatively enduring quality of internal environment that is experienced by its members, influence their behaviour, and can be described in terms of the values of a particular set of characteristics of the organisation.

According to Joe Kelly, 'climate may be thought of as the perception of the characteristics of an organisation'.

Forehand and Gilmer, have defined organisational climate as a set of characteristics that describe an organisation and that:

- Distinguish one organisation from another,
- Are relatively enduring over a period of time,
- Influence the behaviour of people in organisation.

It is thus a summary perception which people have about an organisation. It is a global expression or the manifestation of attitude of organisational members towards the organisation itself. An organisation tends to attract and keep people who fit in its climate so that its patterns are perpetuated at least to some extent.

Perhaps one of the most important and significant characteristics of a great workplace is its climate. Organisational climate, while defined differently by many researchers and scholars, generally refers to the degree to which an organisation focuses on and emphasises:

- Innovation
- Flexibility
- Appreciation and recognition
- Concern for employee well-being
- Learning and development
- Citizenship and ethics
- Quality performance
- Involvement and empowerment
- Leadership

Organisational climate, manifested in a variety of human resource practices, is an important predictor of organisational success. Numerous studies have found positive relationships between positive organisational climates and various measures of organisational success, most notably for metrics such as sales, staff retention, productivity, customer satisfaction, and profitability:

- Denison (1990) found that an organisational climate that encourages employee involvement and empowerment in decision-making predicts the financial success of the organisation.
- Schneider (1996) found that service and performance climates predict customer satisfaction.
- Patterson, Warr, and West (2004) found that manufacturing organisations that emphasised a positive organisational climate, specifically concern for employee well-being, flexibility, learning, and performance, showed more productivity than those that emphasised these to a lesser degree.
- Potosky and Ramakrishna (2001) found that an emphasis on learning and skill development was significantly related to organisational performance.
- Ekvall (1996) found a positive relationship between climates emphasising creativity and innovation and their profits.
- Hansen and Wernerfelt (1989) found that organisational climate factors explain about twice as much variance in profit rates as economic factors.
- Thompson (1996) found that companies utilising progressive human resource practices impacting climate such as customer commitment, communication, empowerment, innovation, rewards and recognition, community involvement/environmental responsibility, and teamwork outperformed organisations with less progressive practices.

Organisational climate clearly influences the success of an organisation. Many organisations, however, struggle to cultivate the climate they need to succeed and retain their most highly effective employees. Hellriegel and Slocum (2006) explain that organisations can take steps to build a more positive and employee-centred climate through:

- **Communication:** How often and the types of means by which information is communicated in the organisation
- **Values:** The guiding principles of the organisation and whether or not they are modeled by all employees, including leaders
- **Expectations:** Types of expectations regarding how managers behave and make decisions
- **Norms:** The normal, routine ways of behaving and treating one another in the organisation
- **Policies and rules:** These convey the degree of flexibility and restriction in the organisation
- **Programs:** Programming and formal initiatives help support and emphasise a workplace climate
- **Leadership:** Leaders that consistently support the climate desired

Making a climate change in your organisation is one of the core fundamental steps to beginning to create a great place to work.

Organisational climate should be viewed from total system point of view. There may exit different climates within different organisation, and there subclimates will be integrated in the similar fashion of integrating attitudes of employees, so as to form the organisational climate. In organisations, there may be differences in climates in different work units as we commonly observe. It is because, one type of climate may be suitable for one particular unit and the same may not be suitable for another unit. It should be noted that the climates of different organisational subsystems are radically different. Therefore, instead of taking a fragmented view of climate in particular subsystem, the total system is more useful to study and analyse.

Characteristics of Organisational Climate

The nature of organisational climate will be clear from its following characteristics:

1. **General Perception:** Organisational climate is general expression of what the organisation is all about. It represents the summary perception which people have about an organisation.
2. **Qualitative Concept:** It is an abstract and intangible concept. It is difficult to explain the components of organisational climate in quantifiable units.
3. **Distinct Identity:** It reflects how an organisation is different from other organisations. It gives a distinct identity to the organisation.
4. **Enduring Quality:** It is built-up over a period of time. It represents a relatively enduring quality of the internal environment that is experienced by the organisational members.

Factors Affecting Organisational Climate

In every organisation there exist certain elements that exert profound influence on the existing climate. In some organisations certain factors like structure or process play a major role while in other organisation, some other factors may play a major role. Lawrence James and Allan Jones have tried to identify five factors as discussed below:

1. Organisational context: The first factor that affects the climate is management philosophy. If the company is wedded to such a policy that it effectively utilises its resources both human as well as non-human, then it can be concluded that the climate is good. The manpower policy is generally expressed by rules, regulations, and policies and so on. The climate is said to be highly favourable when the existing management techniques are such that employees goals are perfectly matched to the ideals of the organisation.

2. Organisational structure: Structure represents another variable that affects climate. Any structure is a framework that establishes formal relationships and delineates authority and functional responsibility. Further, the actual arrangement of hierarchy is also to be considered, for it affects climate. Highly decentralised structure results in sound climate when the management feels the necessity of high degree of employee input, whereas if the management feels the necessity of maintaining grated degree of consistency in operation regarding decision making, it will be wedded to centralised climate.

3. Organisational process: In every organisation, certain processes are vital so that it runs it well. Communications, decision-making, motivations, leadership, etc., are some of the very important process through which the management carries out its objectives. In all these process, the relationship between the superior and the sub-ordinate is visible and therefore the superior cannot afford to ignore this visible interface. For instance, let us consider the leader-follower relation. It is the leader's choice whether to delegate decision making, give assignments, performance management, etc. A leader thus should be aware of the possible influence, of his actions on the climate when deciding about the most appropriate supervisory technique for a given situation. It should be noted that a failure to this subject results in a disturbed climate of the organisation.

5. Physical environment: The external conditions of environment the size, and location of the building in which an employee works, the size of the city, whether or in which an employee works; all affect the organisational climate. An employee's performance in a job in a relatively clean, quiet, and safe environment will undoubtedly have a favourable perception of the organisational climate. Office décor, size, and space a person has in doing his work are important factors to be borne in mind. For Example, high level of noise brings bad feelings and leads to disturbance, frustration, and aggression and thus has a negative effect on the climate.

6. System values and norms: Every organisation has certain values and norms where certain kinds of behaviours are rewarded and encouraged, and certain kind of behaviour faces an individual to formal sanctions. This is then communicated to employees through rules, regulations and so on. Although in every organisations, informal systems also exist but knowing the values and norms of these is very difficult. But from the point of view of both the organisation and its climate, informal and formal; exert influence on this climate.

Changing Organisational Climate

While is changes in an organisation are easily made or immediately made, research evidence demonstrates the facts that change in climate is possible and has occurred. In one study by McClelland and Bumhanc, it has been found that by making the managers aware of the climate they had created significant changes in climate that can successfully be accomplished at group level.

The pertinent question is when to change the climate? If in the view of top management the effectiveness of the organisation can be improved by an alteration in the climate, steps will be taken to bring about the desired change, sometimes when there is something wrong with the existing climate, a change in climate is called for. For instance, in one study by Robert Rock, it has been found that to overcome serious problems at International Harvester, a change in the climate was suggested in terms of change in structure design, planning, management development, and reward systems. The changes were implemented and the follow-ups study indicated definite improvements in some areas with problems remaining in some other areas.

Thus, changes in climate are possible, but are gradual rather than overnight occurrences. Since climate is the manifestation of the attitudes of organisational members, it certainly takes sometime:

- To change the managerial philosophy.
- To change the rules, regulations and procedures.
- To observe the reaction of human resources to change.

Organisational culture and organisational climate overlap to a certain extent, with perceptions of culture's patterns of behaviour being a large part of what climate research addresses. However, organisational members may describe organisational features (climate) in the same way but interpret them differently due to cultural and subcultural influences (Rosen, Greenlagh, and Anderson 1981). For example, structured leadership and limited participation in decision making may be viewed as negative and controlling from one perspective or as positive and legitimate from another. Social influence reflecting the organisation's culture shapes the interpretation members make of organisational features and activities. Thus, it would seem appropriate to assess both climate and culture simultaneously in investigating the impact of the organisation on the well-being of members.

Review Discussions

1. Explain organisational culture and organisational climate. What is their significance in organisational management?
2. How will you promote organisational culture?
3. How does organisational culture affect the working of people?
4. What are the factors responsible for changing organisational climate?
5. Making a climate change in the organisation is one of the basic steps to create, 'a great place to work'. Comment on this statement.

♣♣♣♣♣♣

CHAPTER 7
CONFLICT MANAGEMENT

After studying this chapter, you should be able to:

- Know the meaning of conflict.
- Identify the types of organisational conflict.
- Make out the sources of conflict.
- Comprehend the levels of conflict.
- Discern functional and dysfunctional features of conflict.
- Be acquainted with to manage conflict.
- Be familiar with avoidance of conflict.
- Recognise the competency in resolving tough conflicts.
- Be aware of Pondy's conflict episode process.
- Be familiar with Thomas-Kilmann conflict model.
- Be on familiar terms with role conflict, role ambiguity, and role analysis.

Introduction

Organisations are responsible for creating a work environment that enables people to thrive. If disagreement and differences of opinion escalate into conflict then the organisation must intervene immediately. Conflict in the organisation can be constructive or destructive for an organisation. In fact, the Chinese character for 'conflict' represents two meanings, opportunity and danger. As a manager we need to find and focus on how to make it beneficial and how to minimise the negative aspects. We need to create an organisational culture that encourage and even rewards good conflict management, our goal has to be to increase the benefits achieved from managing and encouraging beneficial conflict, like task and process conflict, while managing, resolving and reducing the negative effects of relationship conflict. Different writers have defined organisational conflict in different way The common key words, which are used in these definitions, are frustration, incongruence incompatibility and mismatch.

Meaning of Conflict

Conflict is a psychological state of mind when people are in a state of dilemma whether to do or not to do a thing. In organisational conflict, it may imply difference of opinion with persons or groups and sometimes they manage to show down and slow down other and plan strategies for that.

Conflict may be defined as breakdown in the standard of decision making and it occurs when an individual or group experience difficulty in selecting an alternative.

The concept of conflict may be understood as collision or disagreement. The conflict may be with an individual when there is an incompatibility between his or her own goal and event; may be between two individual or between two groups of organisation. According to Chaung and Megginson, conflict is 'the struggle between incompatible or opposing needs, wishes, ideas, and interest of people'. Conflict arises when individual or group encounter goal that both parties cannot obtain satisfactorily. The term conflict, evasion fights, riots, or wars have become pervasive and, infact, virtually every day of every year one can find dozens of armed combat situation somewhere in the world. These are more violent expression of conflict but a manager encounters more stubble and non-violent type of opposition such as arguments, criticism and disagreement. Conflict can be positive and negative-constructive or destructive. It may be cognitive or affective. Cognitive conflict refers to differences in perspectives or judgements about issues. Affective conflict is emotional and directed at other people. Affective conflict is likely to be destructive because it can lead to anger, bitterness, goal displacement and poor decisions. Cognitive conflict, on the other hand can air legitimate difference of opinion and develop better idea and solution to problem, when conflict occurs within the company team and between the team and outsider it can reduce morale, lower productivity, increase absenteeism, and cause smaller large-scale to serious and violent behaviour.

Types of Organisational Conflict

Task, roles, process, organisational direction, external pressure, and relationship issues, all create conflict. While each area may call for different strategies to identify and address the root cause of these conflicts, six best practices talent leaders can use to guide effective resolution in the workplace are discussed as below:

1. **Task conflict:** Task conflict relates to the content and goal of the work. According to Graves, task conflict arises among members of team and affects the goals and tasks they are striving to achieve. It can be based on differences in vision, intention, and quality expectation. It is essential to focus and channel any task conflict so that these differences become collaborative and lead to improvements in the way and go about accomplishing current and future task. Converting conflict to friendly competition might be one way of taking the best from both sides.

2. **Role conflict:** Conflict surrounding roles and responsibilities are especially common during or immediately following organisational change, particularly restructurings. People may be unclear on who is responsible for which decisions and outputs.

For example, after an international strategic business consulting firm restructured its managerial staff, an individual who formerly managed two key customer segments was unwilling to relinquish all the responsibility to the new manager. He continued to question staff and issue orders while his replacement was trying to set a new direction. With two managers giving input, employees were stuck in the middle, which created conflict among them as well as between the managers.

To identify the root cause of a role conflict, each party needs to examine his or her responsibilities as well as the other persons. One or both may need to change their perception, and then they will need to collaborate to clarify who will handle what.

3. **Process conflict:** This is related to how the work gets done. This form of conflict centres around, the process, procedures, steps or methods used to reach goal. One person might like to plan many steps ahead while others might like to dive in headfirst. These differences in approaches or processes can lead to communication break downs and ultimately conflict. Healthy differences in approaches to process will often lead to improved way of doing job.

Process conflict commonly arises when two departments, teams, or groups interact on a process. They may view the process differently and disagree on how it should be accomplished or point fingers rather than communicating effectively when problems arise.

For example, at a global manufacturer of heavy lifting equipment, three shifts were involved in the production of a machine, which often suffered from poor quality or low production rates. No standard process existed to build the machine, and each shift believed its approach was best. If one shift ended before the product was completed, the next group would either send the machine through without completing it – which resulted in poor quality – or take it apart and rebuild it – which slowed production.

To identify the root cause of process conflict, examine the process controls in place and how employees interact with them. Get teams or individuals to collaborate to define the process more effectively and establish communication channels to address problems.

4. Directional conflict: Directional conflict arises when organisations are forced to rethink their strategies and focus on shorter-term activities, as many did during the economic downturn. Employees may not know how to prioritise long-term versus short-term needs, or one department may work tactically while another remains strategic.

For example, a regional insurance brokerage, representing several prominent insurance providers, was developing a succession plan and selected several managers to be groomed as next- generation leaders. This action resulted in directional conflict because the managers were unclear whether to focus on meeting their short- term goals or on the longer-term succession efforts.

To identify the root cause of directional conflict, individual employees should ask themselves: What do I believe our direction is or should be? Is that aligned with what others are saying? What are senior managers saying? Answering these questions will enable individuals to change their own direction if necessary and help others change theirs.

5. External conflict: External conflict arises when pressures from customers or other stakeholders impact internal decisions. Recent economic challenges compelled organisations to adjust and adapt, for example, by lowering prices while providing enhanced customer service. Sales or customer service personnel advocating for customers' needs may have come into conflict with operations trying to meet internal goals.

For example, a health care software company was pushing to bring a new product to market. Sales and customer service employees continued to bring customer input to the programming group, which did its best to incorporate the ideas into the product. As the requests continued to come in, it extended the development process beyond the planned release date. When management finally decided to release the product without further enhancements, additional conflict arose because customers now complained that their inputs are not incorporated.

To identify the root cause of external conflict, ask if anyone internally has the control to resolve the problem. It may be possible to create a can- do list, which may answer questions such as: What can we do to address the external demand? The solution might involve collaboration among several departments to adjust to the external pressures more effectively.

6. Relationship conflict: It focuses on interpersonal relationship. They are directly between people and may be over roles style, resources or even personalities. This conflict can penetrate and damage all aspect of an organisation. Relationship conflict can quickly demand all the attention and energy.

Although poor chemistry between individuals can exist, most interpersonal conflict tends to grow from the other five sources of conflict. For instance, when two managers attempt to direct the same department or when employees see external circumstances differently, interpersonal conflict builds.

However, at times, genuine interpersonal conflict may exist. For instance, a national business services firm hired a new vice-president whom the divisional personnel disliked because they felt he was not as open and direct as his predecessor. This created conflict between the leader and the team, which affected performance.

To find the root cause of interpersonal conflict, look for a particular bias or prejudice. Can negative emotions be overcome? An open, direct conversation is always the best way to bring issues out in the open and begin working on a resolution.

Sources of Conflict

There can be following common causes of conflict:

1. **Conflicting needs:** Whenever people compete for scarce resources, recognition, and power conflict can occur.
2. **Conflicting styles:** Because individual bear unique, they all have different styles, everyone should understand their own style and learn how to work with others who have different style.
3. **Conflicting perceptions:** When person have alternate images of the same stimulus and each will attend and interpret the information in somewhat different manner. In this people may view the same incident in dramatically different ways memos, performance reviews, rumours and hallway comments can be sources for conflicting perception.
4. **Conflicting goals:** Problem can occur when people are responsible for different duties in achieving the same goal.
5. **Conflicting roles:** This conflict occurs when one task is assigned to more than one person and may put certain constraints to role.
6. **Different personal values:** Differing personal values politics, religion, can cause conflict, colour ethnicity differences can lead to conflict.
7. **Unpredictable policies:** Whenever policies are changed inconsistently applied or non-existent misunderstanding are likely to occur. The absence of clear policies or policies that are constantly changing can create an environment of conflict.
8. **Informational factors:** When various points of views have been developed.

Levels of Conflict

Conflict continuously occurs in our social life, they occur at various levels within individuals, groups, or organisations. Conflict arises from disagreement over the goals to attain or the methods used to accomplish them. In organisations, conflict among different interests is inevitable and sometime the amount of conflict is substantial.

It occurs when they have one or more alternatives and they have to choose few or one out of these. There are different levels of conflicts and they are as follows:

1. **Conflict at Personnel/Individual Level**

   Conflicts at individual or personnel level in an organisation may be viewed in two ways:

   - **Intra-individual or personal conflicts:** It is a situation in which an individual is in a problem of decision making within him/her, e.g., role ambiguity.
   - **Inter-individual or inter-personal conflicts:** When two individuals; are in confrontation with each other, it may be called as inter-personal conflict. This may be between two individuals of the same group; in that case it may be called intra-group conflict. If the conflict is between two members of different groups then it may simply be regarded as inter-personal conflict but if it is blown up, it may develop as inter-group conflict.

2. **Conflicts at Group level**
   - **Intra-group conflicts:** e.g., conflict between subgroups
   - **Inter-group conflicts:** e.g., conflict between different groups

3. **Conflict at Organisational Level**

   These conflicts may also be intra-organisational conflict or inter-organisational conflict.

   - **Intra-organisational conflicts:** All inter-individual, intra-individual, inter-group or intra-group conflicts are intra-organisational conflicts.
   - **Inter-organisational conflicts:** Inter-organisational conflicts are between two organisations or between a business organisation and the government (Government Policies).

Functional Features of Conflict

More often conflicts lead to positive or functional outcome such as:

1. Provide chance for self-determination through analysing the situation.
2. Helps to seek clarification.
3. Generates challenging spirit among individuals/managers.
4. Develops spirit of unity even among heterogeneous group when sources of conflicts are common.
5. Indicates the situation calls for improvement.
6. Long-standing problems can be dealt through creativity of people in resolving situation.
7. Sometimes conflicting situations are created to divert the attention from many other problems in the organisation.
8. Leads to personal growth and change.
9. Acts as major stimulant for change.

Dysfunctional Features of Conflict

Conflicts are sometimes very disastrous and needs certainly elimination due to following reasons:

1. Wastage of time and efforts, affects productivity of individuals.
2. People work for their own defects/interests rather than organisational objective.
3. Creates suspicion in the mind against individual, organisation or management.
4. Increase employees turnover.
5. Creates disloyalty and rebellious attitude and loses creativity.
6. Unresolved anger among people.
7. Increased personality clashes.
8. Less self-esteem among people.
9. Psychological well-being is threatened.
10. Creates negative climate.
11. Group cohesion is disrupted.
12. Create stress in people.
13. Leads to frustration.

Managing Organisational Conflicts

Conflict management is the process of planning to avoid conflict where possible and organising to resolve conflict where it does happen, as rapidly and smoothly as possible. For any organisation to be effective and efficient in achieving its goals, the people in the organisation need to have a shared vision of what they are striving to achieve, as well as clear objectives for each team/department and individual. This could happen for all the government organisations and NGOs. The process of managing conflict may be as follows:

1. Preliminary step: This step involves knowing of full details of the conflict and the first thing to note is the stage of the conflict. The more advance the stage of conflict, the more efforts are required to manage it. Moreover, strategy used is also dependent upon the stage of conflict. Keep on top of what's happening in the unit and throughout the organisation, including any changes in unit's environment or changes in colleagues' moods. The informal way of communication is also one of the ways to discover grievances, although it is not a reliable source of information. Intervene at an early stage.

Never think, if I ignore the problem, it will go away. It probably won't. You may not want to address your coworker's complaint, perhaps damaging unit morale and further isolating you among the staff. So, once you recognised the abnormal situation, you should react immediately. It is the duty as well as the responsibility of the manager to resolve the problems.

A small campaign or test designed to gauge internal happenings. i.e., trial balloon approach can be implemented. Without telling the information to a new person, she/he has to allow working in that line and his/her view about the work environment has to be recorded for further proceedings.

Always do not expect others to automatically tell you when they are animosities at something. If your coworkers were not properly communicating with you as well as with their colleagues, or if they avoid making eye-contact, you should understand that they were unhappy with something. Obviously they feel embarrassed to express, you should take initiative to open conversation about the issue.

2. Diagnosing the issue: Under this stage, the issues involved should be analysed and understood what the conflict is about, it may arise due to facts, goals methods and values. Next thing in diagnosing is to know why these differences have arisen; the difference may be informational, perceptual, role factors and the like.

When someone addresses criticism to you listen to what she/he is saying whether or not you feel his/her complaint is valid. She/he may need to vent her feelings. Don't interrupt and don't make quick judgements. When he/she's finished, you'll have a chance to address her complaint.

Get to the root of the problem. Ask questions by yourselves. What is that is happening? Is it really a problem for all the workers or it is for one in particular? Always be supportive to the employees, hear the complaint and try to resolve it immediately by putting your actions in any of the form. Don't hesitate to do *ad hoc* enquiry.

3. Conflict handling modes: Plan yourself, how you are going to deal with the internal conflict, from where you are going to start and how it should be, how you are going to finalise. Do it after planning properly.

There may be numerous modes of conflict handling and these may be as under:

- To avoid appearance of conflicts and for this purpose like-minded people should be appointed.
- Mediating involves sweeping out differences by mediation through persuasion, highlighting the merits and demerits of their case.
- Letting the parties to settle their scores. It is better when both the parties adopt a rigid stand to their views.
- Mutual problem-solving approach is suitable when both parties are interested in resolving the conflicts and are not rigid in their stand.

Avoidance of Conflict

There are four key steps to reduce and manage conflict according to Kevin J. Sensenig as mentioned below:

1. Align on shared values and direction: Without a sense of commonality of vision and direction, underlying frustration, fear and conflict will fester despite attempts at resolution. Ask questions such as: Are we on the same page? Are we pursuing the same direction?

2. Take personal ownership: No one wants to be wrong. Once people stop assigning blame and responsibility to others, resolution becomes easier.

3. Deal with facts first, emotions second: Identify the problem and root cause of the conflict, and find a way to resolve the issue. With a resolution in place, handle the emotional component. If emotional issues are left unresolved, people won't buy into the solution.

4. Build collaboration: Without this step, people will resume work without interacting. This will renew the conflict. Align groups and departments to prevent future problems.

Building trust is at the core of conflict resolution. Lack of trust is also a common reason why conflicts arise in the first place. With mutual trust, problems tend to be resolved quickly without escalating into conflict. To rebuild lost trust, follow these steps:

(i) **Set the ego aside:** Learn to say: It is not about me; it is about getting the best result. How can I interact with this individual at a human level to resolve the conflict?

(ii) **Review the situation honestly:** Ask, what assumptions do I bring to the table, and are those the real facts or just temporary feelings? Is there really an issue, or am I reading too much into the situation? When people are feeling low, tired or emotionally drained, conflicts arise more quickly.

(iii) **Meet with the other party:** Candidly explain the situation and how it creates a challenge or conflict. Ask for the other person's perspective. What was he or she trying to accomplish and why? Listen intently to gather information without refuting each statement directly.

(iv) **Reach a decision:** Determine whether trust has been broken and needs to be rebuilt or whether there was a simple misunderstanding that can be quickly clarified and resolved.

(v) **If trust has been broken, begin rebuilding it immediately:** Clearly articulate and share information on why the actions that broke trust were taken. Listen to the other person's perspective and articulate your own based on facts, not personalities. Don't tell the other person what to think, what the problem is and how to fix it. Listen and arrive at a resolution together.

(vi) **Reach an agreement:** Once both parties have articulated their perspectives, agree on how to move forward to build trust.

(vii) **Honour agreements:** Both parties have to hold up their end of the bargain. Do exactly what was promised or trust will fall to an even lower level. Continue to demonstrate trustworthiness day-by-day, activity-by-activity.

People tend to rely on status and position to handle conflicts. Both create mindsets that discourage people from taking personal responsibility for conflicts. However, while people may be unaccustomed to taking ownership of conflict and are uncomfortable about seeking out an opposing party directly, these steps are essential to resolve conflict and build trust.

Competency in Resolving Tough Conflicts

According to Jennifer S. Goldman, the ability to resolve conflict is a core competency for leaders in all types of organisations. It's no wonder there's lots of advice out there on the topic.

The good news is that much of it is excellent. The bad news is that most of it pertains to 'routine' conflict – conflict that arises every-day and is best addressed by using interest-based, or principled, negotiation that produces win-win solutions.

But what about conflicts that reappear despite our best efforts to resolve them? For example, what about the family business in which a father has threatened to sell the company rather than pass it on to his children? Or a newly merged company suffering from a long - standing conflict between two of its highest - profile members?

For all its successes, principled negotiation has its limitations. A new framework called CIVIC aims to enable organisations to effectively deal with persistent conflicts. CIVIC is an acronym for the five core competencies individuals need to do this: complexity, interconnectedness, values, imagination, and courage.

1. Complexity – According to researcher Peter T. Coleman, many long-standing conflicts involve multiple parties, issues and relationships. The first step in solving long-term conflicts is to recognise this complexity. The second step is learning how to anticipate the potentially complex consequences of our own and others' actions.

For example, in the case of the family business in which a father wants to sell the business rather than pass it down to his children, it is important for all parties to ask themselves a set of questions about the potential consequences of their actions before taking a next step. Some important questions include: What are the possible unintended consequences of my behaviour down the road for others? For myself? For the company? For future generations of my family and the company's leadership? When we take this long range view, we may gain a new perspective that can help us prevent conflict from escalating.

2. Interconnectedness – Conflicts often are made up of interwoven interests and needs between the parties. For example, consider a company in which the sales leaders and the R&D individuals can't see eye-to-eye. If they didn't need one another, they could simply walk away. But sales would have nothing to sell if R&D didn't create the products, and R&D would have no way of putting new products into customers hands without a sales force.

In the heat of a conflict, it can be easy to lose sight of the ways in which we depend on one another. A first step out of the conflict is for the parties to simply appreciate the fact that they are interconnected. It helps to map out our relationships and put on the map at least one new person, place or event that we haven't previously considered to be part of the situation. We should also put on the map at least one positive contribution that each person, place or event brings to the situation. Doing so can help us shift our perspective.

3. Values – If conflicts persist over a long period of time, the parties are invariably getting something out of it. If they weren't, they would have ended the conflict long ago.

An important question to ask ourselves is: What benefits do I personally receive from staying in this conflict? The answer may uncover important – but hidden or taboo – values that each party holds. For example, we may benefit from staying in a conflict if we get to feel that we are right and the others are wrong or if we get sympathy or attention from others. Sometimes, staying stuck in a conflict simply allows us to avoid having to deal with it or make a difficult decision. These are all legitimate values or needs that we have, but bringing them to light allows us to find ways to attain them through other means.

4. Imagination – This core competency has two parts. The first is the ability to envision a better future. This requires that we take a step back and ask ourselves: What would this situation look like in its ideal state? Keeping in mind complexity and interconnectedness, what is the ideal state not just with regard to one other party, but for all involved? Map this out.

The second part of this competency refers to the ability to communicate this vision. If you are a leader in the conflict, you may need to communicate your vision both to your own team and to the other parties. Ask others to contribute to your vision of a compelling future.

5. Courage – At the end of the day, we may have the greatest ideas on how to get things back on track to produce superior results. But if we don't do things differently than before, we'll stay stuck in the same patterns. We must consciously choose to act differently, one small step at a time. This takes courage. It may take being unconventional or pushing past our comfort zones. We can study the actions of our favourite courageous leaders – real and imaginary – and choose to live by their example.

Pondy's Conflict Episode Process

Pondy developed a conflict process model, which is useful to understand how a conflict starts. He has delineated five steps that he calls as 'conflict episode' as discussed below:

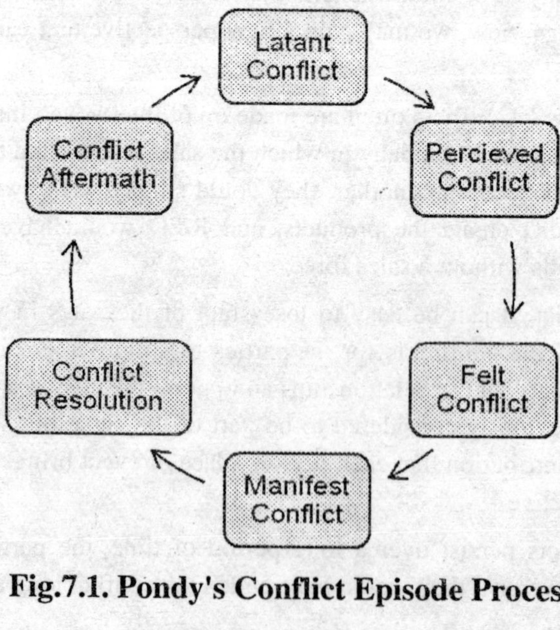

Fig.7.1. Pondy's Conflict Episode Process

1. Latent Conflict: It is the first stage of conflict-promoting situations appears on the scene between individuals and groups. In this stage potential conflict inducing forces exit. For example, demand for various resources by departments when some may get and be satisfied and others may not get and be dissatisfied. Hence there may exist, a situation between two groups. At this stage the seeds of dissatisfaction have been sown.

2. Felt Conflict: When one party frustrates the desire of other party, people perceive that a conflicting situation exists. For example, sales department may need additional budget for promotional activities which finance department may not release. The sales department may attribute lack of finance as potential cause for fall in scales. Thus, a conflict between the two may brew. At this stage the conflict does not surface.

3. Manifest Conflict: At this stage, there is not only recognition or acknowledgement of conflict but also manifestation of conflict by covert or overt behaviour. It is a stage of open dispute. Both parties devise their strategies to face each other. In the above example, sales department may make the point for additional funds for promotional activities especially during festival season. Finance department may openly turndown the request since they might have allots additional funds for procurement of better raw materials for production department. Sales department may argue that better raw materials have no meaning unless the facts are brought to the notice of costumers, which can only be done through promotional campaign. The debate may be unending and frustrating.

4. Conflict Resolution: There can be resolution of conflict and once the conflict is resolved between two parties, there is always a party, which is looser because the resolution is the outcome of win-lose or the compromise strategy, a stage is set for subsequent conflict episode.

5. Conflict Aftermath: A party, which feels defeated, may start preparations and be on the lookout for the assault to take the revenge. Conflict aftermath is a direct function of the results of the conflict resolution style adopted and exercised in any given situation.

Thomas – Kilmann Conflict Handling Model

Whenever we face a problem related with organisational conflict the solution are there in the form of conflict management strategies. Kenneth Thomas and Ralph Kilmann developed their model of how we deal with conflict whilst working together at the University of Pittsburgh.

Their ideas are based on research observations and on well-respected psychological theory (Jung, Blake, and Mouton, etc.). The model describes how individuals behave when faced with conflict: a situation in which the concerns of two people appear to be incompatible. Like many such models, there is no one right style: to handle conflict effectively requires both parties to be versatile. But we will each have our preferred style(s), and it helps to be aware which ones these are, and how to extend into the other boxes on the grid.

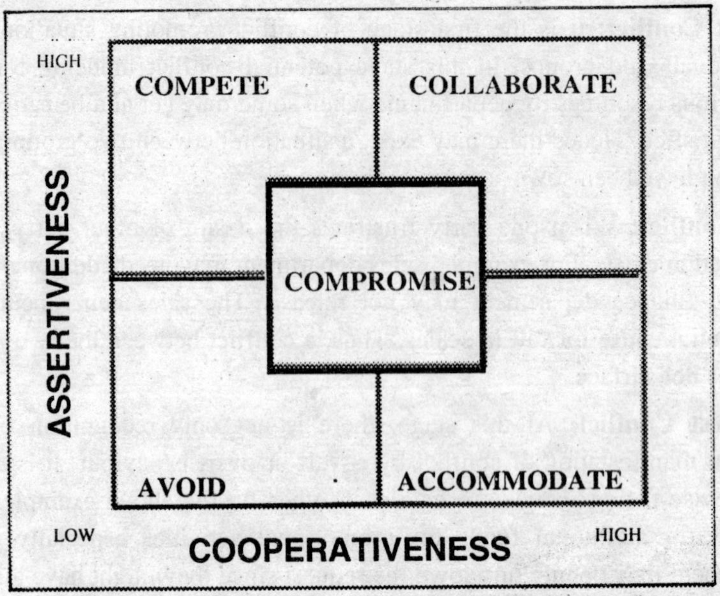

Fig.7.2. Thomas-Kilmann Conflict Handling Model

The strategies commonly adopted by the organisation are as follows:

1. Avoidance: In this the conflicting parties may either withdraw or conceal the incompatibility. Organisation uses avoiding strategies. Where there is clear advantage of waiting to resolve the conflict. Avoiding is appropriate if companies are too busy with more important concern.

We don't pursue our position, or that of the other person, and so don't address the conflict. We might simply not talk about it, postpone the issue, or withdraw from the situation. Avoidance is effective when the situation is charged with emotion that will prevent rational discussion, when you have no prospect of satisfying your concerns, (e.g., company policy) or when other people might be better placed to resolve the problem.

2. Competition: It is a kind of win-lose approach in which a person seeks to satisfy his or her own interest, regardless of the impact on the other parties to the conflict. Organisational strategies is used when they deal with strong personalities. In this senior person use their power to diffuse the conflict. We aim to assert or 'win' our position with no concern for the needs of the other person. We use whatever power (rank, intellect, etc.), we can to achieve this goal. Competing behaviour can be effective in emergency situations, or where tough actions are required that are not in the interests of the other person, e.g., cost reductions, redundancies, rules, and discipline.

3. Collaboration: In collaborating, the intention of the parties is to solve the problem by clarifying differences rather than by accommodating various points of view. It is a kind of win-win solution that allows both parties to achieve their goals. The use of collaborations is inappropriate when time is of the essence, issues are unimportant, and goals of other party are wrong or illegal. Collaborating is considered to the one of the best strategies, especially when the organisation interest are at the stake, this strategies is generally used when organisation feel that the concern is important.

This strategies is used mostly in all the organisations, where we have to solve interpersonal conflict. It promotes creative problem-solving. It takes more time than other strategies.We actively work with the other person to satisfy fully the concerns of both parties. We analyse and gather data, seek out underlying causes, and try to see the issue from both sides, so that neither side has to give ground. Collaboration helps to merge very different insights on a problem, (e.g., the solution is one that neither person would have produced alone), to gain commitment from others who will have to implement the solution, and to build long-term partnerships.

4. Accommodation: It is a kind of lose-win situation in it one party seeks to appease an opponent, that party may be willing to place opponents interest above his or her own, i.e., in short, one party willing to be self sacrificing. When conflict is upon fairly unimportant issue, organisation in order to resolve the conflict uses accommodating strategies. We neglect our own concerns for the interests of the other person. We tend towards selfless generosity – even charity – and are entirely non-competitive. Accommodation is useful for the longer-term, e.g., giving in on this point will build better relations in the future, or when harmony is more important than this particular issue.

5. Compromising: It is a well-accepted strategy for resolving conflict. In it there is no clear winner or loser. It is a kind of situation in which each party is willing to give up something. Its use is appropriate when cooperation is important but time/resources are limited or finding an outcome, even less than best is better than being without any solution. It is not suitable when creative solution is essential. Compromising strategies come under the second choice by the organisation. Organisation use compromising strategy when they are dealing the moderately important issues. It can often lead to quick solution. We aim for a solution that both parties can accept, which partially satisfies their concerns. It requires willingness to give and take, and assumes both sides are able to give ground. Compromise is useful for achieving a temporary settlement to a complex issue, or an expedient solution under time pressure, and when satisfying your concerns, whilst important, is not worth the effort or disruption of more assertive styles.

It is the role of the manager to have a view about his unit activities. The employees must be keenly viewed frequently. Unfortunately, when coworkers are unhappy with each other or their work situation, they are not always upfront about what is bothering them. Instead, they may be filled with angry but never try to show it. The classic 'Win-Win' outcome that we often seek when resolving a disagreement by negotiation should really be achieved through Collaboration, but is often the result of compromise. A compromise Win-Win will resolve the immediate conflict, but may not address underlying disagreements or differing attitudes.

Role Conflict, Role Ambiguity, and Role Analysis

Famous writer Shakespeare said that world is a stage and all men and women are merely players in it. Therefore, we all are actors, each playing a role by enacting certain behaviour. So, a role can be defined as a pattern of behaviour that is expected of a person. Each individual within the organisation and outside plays numerous roles. A worker plays the occupational role of a worker, a subordinate, a supervisor, a union representative or he may play family role of a parent, spouse, a child or a member of a social group. They way an individual assumes the role in the organisation depends upon two most important variables which may be expectation of the individual and expectation of the organisation.

The behaviour pattern expected out of person in each role differs from person-to-person. Similarly perception regarding an individual role also differs from person to person. This difference in expectations and perceptions gives rise to role conflict.

Role Conflict: There are some occasions when there are forces in the work environment which cause an individual to feel that there are opposing elements being placed upon him or her. Being caught between such opposing forces puts a person in role conflict because it is difficult to meet one set of expectations without rejecting the other. A mismatch in the expectations of an organisation and the individual can cause such a role conflict. A situation may arise when an individual has to abide by the rules and policies, calling for strictly following the job description; on the other hand she/he may have to give away to the pressure of demand from his/her colleagues or subordinates. Secondly, the conflict can also be caused between the role and the personality. Now every individual differs in his/her temperament, attitudes, outlook, views, and ideologies. Suppose an employee had been an ecology student and therefore is ecological conscious. Also, she/he is working in a firm which is major source of pollution. Therefore, demands from his/her roles are clashing with that of views and values. Role conflict also arises when a person has to play two or more roles at the same time. For example, a company needs an employee to work for longer hours, whereas his/her family also needs him/her to spend minimum time with them. Therefore, there is conflict between the occupational role and the family role. Role conflict is fairly common in most work environments and can be caused in number of ways. Usually the existence of role conflict is due to particular incident and is of relatively short duration. If a role conflict is major and is of enduring nature, most of individuals would find the pressure intolerable and can quit the job.

Role Ambiguity: This can be defined as the lack of clarity concerning the type of behaviour which is expected of a person in an organisation by others. When role ambiguity exists people are not sure how they should act in a given situation. They are not sure of what is being expected of them. Unlike role conflict where a choice can be made between two or more differing expectations, role ambiguity has a state of uncertainty. The existence of ambiguity in work can mostly be blamed upon poor communication. Incomplete vague instructions and explanations can leave the individual in a position of not knowing exactly what is expected of him. So an employee, who is left to his or her interpretation of the situation, may take some action that is considered inappropriate by the organisation. Without any proper guideline to channelise the action and person's action becomes inconsistent and meeting the expectations of the supervision and the others becomes a trial and error experience. The role ambiguity can effect to a large extent the job performance and job satisfaction. So, only when the role is clearly understood and accepted then the individual can properly fulfill the role given to him. Otherwise a role ambiguity can often cause confusions, misunderstandings, and also role conflict.

Role Analysis: As far as the role is concerned role analysis helps the employees and employer in the organisation to clear confusions relating to expectations, obligations, and tasks and duties. Especially for the new entrants, role analysis programs are conducted to make them clear about their role. Many formal organisations may involve role analysis technique having various methods. Firstly, studying and examining various major roles, their position and significance in the organisation and then various activities can be classified under it. After doing this role can be properly defined and described. Secondly, the expectations of others from an individual's role and the expectations of his/her from others' role can be studied, discovered, revived, and modified from time-to-time and if something new can be added to the expectations that can be done and then can be commonly agreed upon. Role negotiations also help in solving largely the role conflicts. It is a kind of agreement or a settlement between two parties, to modify and change each other's behaviour for each other's benefits and effective work performance. Role analysis is automatically done when a person sees to it that she/he is not over lapping or interfering in other's role and also he/she shares some of his activities under the role. One should continuously revive his/her role and with the changing situations and needs it should be modified from time-to-time. She/he must try to adjust his/her role in such a way, that she/he can cope up with presence of day-to-day demands. She/he should analysis various aspects of the role and understands his/her role clearly so that others can easily anticipate his/her behaviour in a given situation to interact with others accordingly. Therefore, there is proper interaction, communication, a feeling of understanding, and cooperation which leads to coordination of work. Role analysis gives a person a deep insight into his/her own role as well as the other's role.

The very success of the arrangement lies in the order, structure, and consistency of approach and action. This can be possible by reducing role conflict and role ambiguity, for the better progress and goal attainment of the organisation.

Conflict can serve as a constructive mechanism for change. It allows an opportunity to work with someone who you ordinarily would not, understand that conflict will happen but don't let it damage your organisation. Try to resolve them as quickly as possible.

Some situations offer neither fight nor flight – one just has to live with the situation. This problem ultimately affects the individual and it totally disturbs his quality of work life. So it is the primary duty of the departmental head to review the employees' performance, if they found anything serious, they have to adopt strategies which ruled out the entire problem of the employees.

Review Discussions

1. Explain the term conflict. What are its functional and dysfunctional features?
2. What are various types of conflict? Explain its sources.
3. What are the various levels of conflict?
4. Explain conflict resolution model.
5. Describe Pondy's conflict episode process.
6. Explain Thomas-Kilmann conflict handling model.

♣♣♣♣♣♣

CHAPTER 8

TEAM BUILDING

After studying this chapter, you should be able to:

- Comprehend team and essentials of successful team.
- Be familiar with the types of team.
- Be acquainted with the stages of team development.
- Know Belbin team roles.
- Be aware of team building procedure.
- Make out the purpose of team building.
- Identify the selection of key subordinates in team building.
- Be familiar with team building interventions.
- Recognise management of team building activities.

Introduction

A team is a group of individuals who are working together towards a common goal. It is a collection of people relying on group collaboration to attain success and goal achievement. Importance of team is a joint, concerted, and coordinated effort which generates positive energy to achieve goals. Team-building is a group level activity, although the effectiveness of a team is not exclusively a group phenomenon but depends very much on the activities and behaviours of individual team-members. In general, it can be said that team-building is an Organisational Development (OD) technique aimed at improving overall performance. Team-building is an important component for the growth of an organisation. It is difficult because people with individual differences join organisation with different personalities, value system, attitude, and needs. To integrate and polymerise the effort of the people it is important that leader must understand their need hierarchy, problems, attitude, and value system.

Team-building is an attempt to assist the work group in learning how to identify, diagnose, and solve its own problems. It directly focuses on the identification of problem relating to task performance and lays down concrete plans for their elimination. A team building program deals with new problems on an on-going basis. It is an effective technique by which members of an organisational group diagnose; how they can work together and plan changes that will improve their effectiveness.

The work group problems may be related to task or personality conflicts. The task related issues can be streamlined by changing the ways in which things are done, by redirecting the resources to be utilised and re-examining the work processes. The interpersonal relationships within the team can be improved by creating an environment where people freely communicate their feelings and thoughts, where leadership evolves on the basis of respect and functional excellence and where conflicts are resolved on the basis of mutual understanding.

Why Teams?

Teams are formed when a combination of skills, knowledge, and expertise are required to undertake a particular task. A single individual may not have such a combination and there may be challenges such as falling profits, improvements in quality standards, putting together a new project, tackle major change initiatives and cross functional coordination in large and complex organisations. Teams may be formed for many purposes. The list is only a broad indicator for the kinds of teams that may be formed.

Essentials of Successful Team

Some of the prerequisites of a successful team are discussed as follows:

1. There has to be an understanding between the members of the team and the leader. There is a need for participation and involvement by all the members and their understanding that they are engaged in a group task and not individual activities.

2. Inter-personal relationship in an organisation is very important for effective teamwork. Unless there is an atmosphere of understandings in the organisation, the people working in the group will be uncomfortable to get along with one other.
3. Another important element in team-building is use of power by leader in a proactive way to the advantage of the team.
4. The team leader must be able to encourage discussion with openness and flexibilities, making its members equally responsible for decision taken.

Successful teams have components of qualities summarised in acronym 'TEAMWORK'.

Fig.8.1. Teamwork

Types of Teams

The major types of teams are as follows:

1. **Problem-solving Team:** This is the team created for solving specific problems or performs specific tasks.
2. **Cross Functional Team:** This team is created from same hierarchical level of different function to work on common goals.
3. **Self-managed Team:** This is a group of people working together in their own ways towards a common goal which is defined outside the team.
4. **Virtual Team:** This is the team which cannot interact physically but on the internet or by digital resources.

Stages of Team Development

Bruce W. Tuckman is a respected educational psychologist who first described the (then) four stages of group development in 1965, soon after leaving Princeton. Looking at the behaviour of small groups in a variety of environments, he recognised the distinct phases they go through, and suggested they need to experience all four stages before they achieve maximum effectiveness. He refined and developed the model in 1977 (in conjunction with Mary Ann Jensen) with the addition of a fifth stage. Since then, others have attempted to adapt and extend the model – although sometimes with more of an eye on rhyme than reason.

Tuckman and Jensen have described the sequence of the team evolution in their work which is the best model to understand and manage teams. Teams have to go through certain process before it can settle down and work effectively. Understanding the stages of development of the team is a key to successful team management.

Tuckman described the four distinct stages that a group can as it comes together and starts to operate. This proce can be subconscious, although an understanding of the stages can help group reach effectiveness more quickly and less painfully. The stages are as discussed below:

Stage 1: Forming

This is the stage when the team-members assemble and get together. People are very polite, get acquainted with each other and try to assess their own roles in the team. Uppermost in the minds of the new team-members at the formation stage is where and how they fit in with the team. This stage is marked by easy acceptance of each other, avoiding controversies, and direction and support from team leader in settling down.

Stage 2: Storming

This stage introduces conflicts and competition as each individual begins to start work on the plan. Work stress with individual differences on issues crop up. Sometimes, the issues could be cultural, ethnic or simply an issue of asserting one's own strength in the overall team equation. Interpersonal and communication issues dominate this stage leading to a flare up of conflict and confrontation.

The leader needs utmost restraint and maturity at this stage of team development. She/he has to bring forth all his/her networking skills, emotional intelligence, and people management abilities in creating the right atmosphere, create winning relationships between team-members and bring their focus back on team vision and goals.

Stage 3: Norming

As conflicts begin to get resolved, the work flow picks up speed. People settle down to more harmonious working relationships. The focus now shifts to common team objectives and performance related issues. A cohesive team which knows its strengths and weaknesses now moves to peak performance leveraging the complementary skills of its members. This is also the stage where the team leader begins to delegate more effectively. Giving the team-members a certain level of functional autonomy leads to unleashing the creativity of its members making for a high performing team.

Stage 4: Performing

This is the final stage where a perfect group identity is created. There is independence and interdependence, learning as well as sharing knowledge, speed and efficiency. All glitches have been smoothened out by the team leader. There are very high levels of autonomy giving rise to emergence of new leaders. The performance is in its peak due to high motivation.

A successful team leader understands the different stages of the group formation and development. She/he manages the team effectively by moderating his/her team managerial styles according to the stage of development in which the team is passing through.

As the proverb goes, 'if you are wise, your wisdom will reward you: if you are a mocker, you alone will suffer'. Proverbs 9:12-Bible.

Ten years after first describing the four stages, Bruce Tuckman revisited his original work and described another, final stage.

Stage 5: Adjourning

This is about completion and disengagement, both from the tasks and the group members. Individuals will be proud of having achieved much and glad to have been part of such an enjoyable group. They need to recognise what they have done, and consciously move on. Some authors describe stage 5 as 'Deforming and Mourning', recognising the sense of loss felt by group members.

Tuckman's original work simply described the way he had observed groups evolve, whether they were conscious of it or not. But for us the real value is in recognising where a group is in the process, and helping it to move to the perform stage. In the real world, groups are often forming and changing, and each time that happens, they can move to a different Tuckman stage. A group might be happily norming or performing, but a new member might force them back into storming. Seasoned leaders will be ready for this, and will help the group get back to performing as quickly as possible.

Many work groups live in the comfort of norming, and are fearful of moving back into storming, or forward into performing. This will govern their behaviour towards each other, and especially their reaction to change.

Belbin Team Roles

R. Meredith Belbin published 'Management Teams – why they succeed or fail' in 1981. Driven by the increasing importance of team-working in organisations at the time, Belbin set out to identify what made a good team, based on research in the UK and Australia. Although the book offered a number of important factors, it is the team roles that became famous. Belbin found that in successful teams all eight roles could be seen in operation, and concluded that when selecting people for a team, filling the eight roles was as important as choosing technical skills or experiences.

Belbin's ideas continue to be used by thousands of organisations because they make sense and they work. We can buy all sorts of tools to identify individuals' preferred roles, and help teams to make the best use of each role. Although our preferred roles are relatively unchanging over time, most of us can happily perform two or three of the roles, thus filling any gaps in the team's profile. That also means that one person can cover more than one role – clearly important if we have a team of less than eight people.

The concept works best when used openly within a team or across an organisation. Individual preferences are only useful if they are known to others, so teams can assess who can best fulfil each role. We can use role identification as a form of team-building: it reinforces the fact that everyone is bringing something to the team, so we all need each other if we are to be successful.

The eight roles are follows: The brief descriptions are of the 'pure' roles that we are unlikely to find in practice. What we will see depends on the mix of preferred roles in each individual. The abbreviations after each title are the common shorthand used when describing and charting the roles.

Extrovert Roles – Outward looking people whose main orientation is to the world outside the group, and beyond the task(s) in hand.

Plant **PL**	The innovator, unorthodox, knowledgeable and imaginative, turning out loads of radical ideas. The creative engineroom that needs careful handling to be effective. Individualistic, disregarding practical details or protocol can become an unguided missile.
Resource Investigator **RI**	The extrovert, enthusiastic communicator, with good connections outside the team. Enjoys exploring new ideas, responds well to challenges, and creates this attitude amongst others. Noisy and energetic, quickly loses interest, and can be lazy unless under pressure.
Chairman **CH**	Calm, self-confident and decisive when necessary. The social leader of the group, ensuring individuals contribute fully, and guiding the team to success. Unlikely to bring great intellect or creativity.
Shaper **SH**	Energetic, highly-strung, with a drive to get things done. They challenge inertia, ineffectiveness and complacency in the team, but can be abrasive, impatient and easily provoked. Good leaders of start-up or rapid-response teams.

Introvert Roles – Inward-looking people principally concerned with relations and tasks within the group.

Monitor Evaluator **ME**	Unemotional, hardheaded and prudent. Good at assessing proposals, monitoring progress and preventing mistakes. Dispassionate, clever and discrete. Unlikely to motivate others, takes time to consider, may appear cold and uncommitted. Rarely wrong.
Team Worker **TW**	Socially-oriented and sensitive to others. Provides an informal network of communication and support that spreads beyond the formal activities of the team. Often the unofficial or deputy leader, preventing feuding and fragmentation. Concern for team spirit may divert from getting the job done.
Company Worker **CW**	The organiser who turns plans into tasks. Conservative, hard working, full of common sense, conscientious and methodical. Orthodox thinks who keeps the team focussed on the tasks in hand. Lacks flexibility, and unresponsive to new ideas.
Completer Finisher **CF**	Makes sure the team delivers. An orderly, anxious perfectionist who worries about everything. Maintains a permanent sense of urgency that can sometimes help and sometimes hinder the team. Good at follow-up and meeting deadlines.

Different roles are important at different times, and the effective team will be aware of who should be 'centre stage' at a given time. We can of course link Belbin roles to personality types, where we will find common words like 'Extrovert' and 'Analytical', but remember that Belbin roles are less definitive. A sales team might apparently be full of extrovert, expressive and energetic people, but someone will still be able to act as the company worker or completer finisher.

Principles of Effective Team

Individual department or functional managers need to embrace ownership and responsibility for success and accomplishing defined strategic initiatives. However, to maximise the effectiveness of the organisation, managers must be able to work with one another to achieve common goals.

According to Dr. Rick Johnson, for an effective team the following six principles apply:

1. Accountability must be at the forefront of every initiative. Employees do want to be held accountable and they willing accept responsibility given the necessary training, information and the organisation encourages empowerment.

2. Minimise oversight through confidence and empowerment. Do not micro manage. Workers will accept more responsibility if management is not constantly looking over their shoulder. This encourages innovation and creativity but it requires effective communication.
3. Managers need to function more as facilitators and leaders. Coaching is a skill set that should be required training for all managers to improve team management. Regular performance discussions should be scheduled and strictly held to.
4. Performance management and performance measurement are key contributors to improved team management. Goals should be measurable and specific. Creating score cards is an effective tool to improve team performance.
5. Information sharing and effective communication are critical. Teams must have unrestricted access to all relevant information. If you can't trust someone on the team then they shouldn't be on the team.
6. Manager skill sets must be continuously reviewed and upgraded to allow them the opportunity to adopt new skills specifically related to coaching and mentoring. The manager's role must be redefined for the team environment and an emphasis on the servant style of leadership.

Organisations that maximise success embrace the concept of 'Team Leadership' and their managers are skilled at leading group problem-solving sessions maximising collaboration across all functional units. A forum exists to educate and train managers on the problems and concerns of other functional departments. Communication is kept at the 'Adult' level and an explicit understanding of respect exists throughout the culture of the organisation. This feeling of mutual respect, trust, and maturity becomes the foundation for teamwork and problem solving.

Team-building Procedure

Team-building procedure as formulated by Kurt Lewin includes – Unfreezing, Moving, and Refreezing.

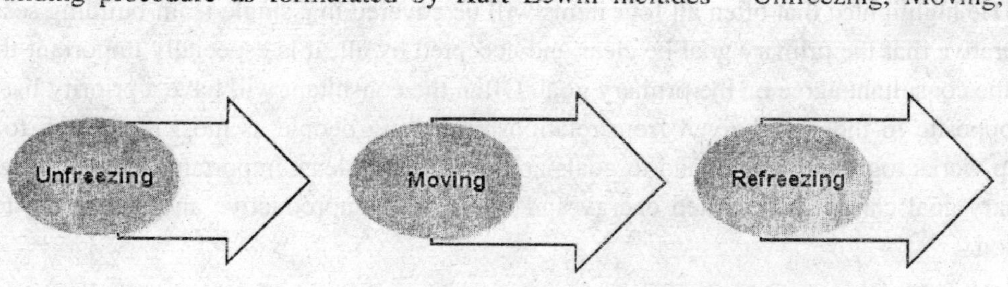

Fig.8.2. Team-building Procedure

1. Unfreezing: The first task is to make the team aware of the need for change. A climate of openness and trust is developed so that the group is ready for change. It consists mainly of a series of experience-based exercises to unfreeze the various teams and get them ready to accept change.

2. Moving: Using a survey/feedback technique, the team makes a diagnosis of where it is and develops action plans to get to where it wants to go. The data are collected on organisational climate, supervisory behaviour, and job content from all supervisors. The data so gathered are openly discussed especially the problem areas and recommendations are made by developing specific plans for the changes to be accurately carried out on the job.

3. **Refreezing:** Once the plans have been made, the team starts to stabilise into more effective performance. Each team meets as a whole to identify barriers to effectiveness, develop ways of eliminating the barriers and agreed upon plans to accomplish the desired changes. The purpose is to establish collaboration on shared goals and problems and generalise the OD effort to the total organisation.

Purpose of Team-building

Team-building session may be directed towards problem-solving for task accomplishment, examining and improving interpersonal relationship, or managing the group's culture and processes. In fact, one of these issues may be principle reason for holding the team-building meeting. For example, suppose that the meeting is designed as a team problem-solving session to examine the impact of the team of new function or task being added to the group's work requirements. Even in this case the position of the session will probably be reverse on how the team becomes more effective at both the task level and the process level.

Richard Beckhard lists, in order of importance, the four major reason or purpose involved in having teams meet other than for the sharing of information:

- To set goals and/or priorities.
- To analyse or the way work is performed.
- To examine the way a group is working – its processes/such as norms, decision making, communications, etc.
- To examine working relationships.

He highlighted that often all four items will be covered in a single team-building session, but it is imperative that the primary goal be clear and accepted by all. It is especially important that the leader and the consultant agree on the primary goal. Often the consultant will have a priority list of items that are opposite to those just given from relationship among people as most important, to the way the group works together as next, and to goals and priorities as least important. Lack of agreement of the primary goal can lead to wasted energy and a generally unproductive and frustrating team-building session.

We agree with Beckhard when he states that the consultant should help to implement the group leader's goals for the session, not the consultant's goals.

Bell and Rosenzweig relied heavily upon team-building workshop in an OD program in a Municipal Government Organisation and commented on the overall nature of team-building sessions as follows:

'We have come to believe strongly that initial improvement efforts should be task oriented rather than focused on interpersonal relations. It is usually safer, less resisted, and more appropriate in terms of the problems and opportunities identified by the client. We have tended not to focus on team-building *per se;* rather, we find that it occurs as a natural byproduct of learning to solve problems in a group setting. However, we don't avoid interpersonal or team ineffectiveness issues if they are getting in the way of effective and efficient problem-solving.'

When a team engages in problem-solving activities directed towards task accomplishment, team-member's build something together a sense of camaraderie, cohesion, and spirit of oneness.

A large block of uninterrupted time to work on high priority problems or opportunities that are identified are worked in ways that are structured to enhance the likelihood of realistic solutions and action plan that are implemented enthusiastically and followed up to assess actual versus expected results.

Many consulting firms have increasingly come to designate these sessions as, 'team-building problem-solving workshops' which are clear signal to them and the client that for a more effective team-building, problem-solving interventions are to be a cornerstone of OD technology.

Selection of Key Subordinates in Team-building

If managers have a narrow range of behaviour; one may think they can expand their flexibility (without changing their own behaviour) by carefully choosing the people they gather around them. If leaders are careful to bring into the organisation key subordinate who complement their leadership rather than replicate it, the organisation may develop a wider range of potential style that can be brought to bear on the contingencies they face. To avoid personality conflicts and to increase the likelihood of building on the strength of others, it is important to select subordinate who understand each other's roles and have the same goals and objectives, even through their styles might be somewhat different.

It is important to print but that it is not always necessary for superiors and subordinates within an organisation to have similar styles. People do not have same personalities to be compatible. What is necessary is that they share perceptions of each other's roles and have common goal and objectives. It is often more appropriate for a manager to recruit key subordinates who can compensate for areas in which they have shortcomings than to surround themselves with aides who are alike. Yet there are large companies today that have created problems for themselves by a sting and selection process that eliminates personalities not congruent with the norm. The usual process is to measure the values and styles of the top management and then selects new people who are compatible with those patterns. The assumption is that if those people got to the top, their values and style must be what is needed to be successful in the organisation in saying that this is a best style, at least for this organisation.

One of the reasons that hiring 'likes' became popular is that they led to a more harmonious organisation. For example, if we have the same set of values and like to behave in a similar ways, are we going to tend to get along? Yes, because we will tend to be compatible. There will probably not be much conflict or confrontation. On the surface, this kind of creeping appears to be very positive. Yet we have found that this approach can lead to organisation and management inbreeding which stand to stifle creativity and innovation. To be effective in the long run, we feel that organisational need an open dialogue in which there is a certain amount of conflict, confrontation, and differing points of views to encourage new ideas and patterns of behaviour so that the organisation will not lose its ability to adjust to external competition. organisations that have had these problems almost have been forced to break their prior policy of promoting only from within and have had to hire some key people from outside who can encourage open dialogue.

What is often needed in organisation is more emphasis on team-building in which people are hired who complement rather than replicate a manager's style. For example, Henry Ford, who was considered a paternalistic leader, placed in key positions in the organisation men who supplemented him rather than duplicated his style. Henry Bennett, for one, acted as a hatchet man, clearing deadwood from the organisation (high task). Another subordinate acted as a confidant to Henry (high relationship). While these styles differed considerably. Ford's success during that time was based on compatibility of expectations, each understood the other's role and was committed to common goals and objectives.

Other examples could be cited. This kind of team-building is common in sports like football, Assistant coaches may have differential task roles, i.e., line coach, backfield coach, and so forth, but may have different behavioural roles with the players. The same may be with principles and vice-principles and so on.

Team-Building Interventions

Probably the most important single group of invention in OD is team-building activities, the goals of which are the improvement and increased effectiveness of various teams within the organisation. Some interventions focus on the intact work team composed of a boss and subordinates, which we call the formal group. Other interventions focus on special team due to mergers, organisational structure changes, or plant startup, task forces, cross-functional projects teams, parallel learning structures, and committees.

Team-building interventions involve team-building activities of formal and special groups involving:

1. **Diagnostic meetings to:**

- Unfreeze the members to be ready.
- Gather joint data collection
- Get feedback data and discuss problem areas of group.

2. **Team-building focused on areas like:**

- Task accomplishments: including problem-solving, decision making, role clarification, goal setting, resource utilisation, etc.
- Team relationships: including building and maintaining effective interpersonal relationships between boss, subordinate and peers; and also the resolution of inter unit conflict, underutilisation of each other as resources.

- Team processes: including understanding and managing group processes and culture, identify barriers and seek collaboration.
- Role analysis: for role clarification and definition.

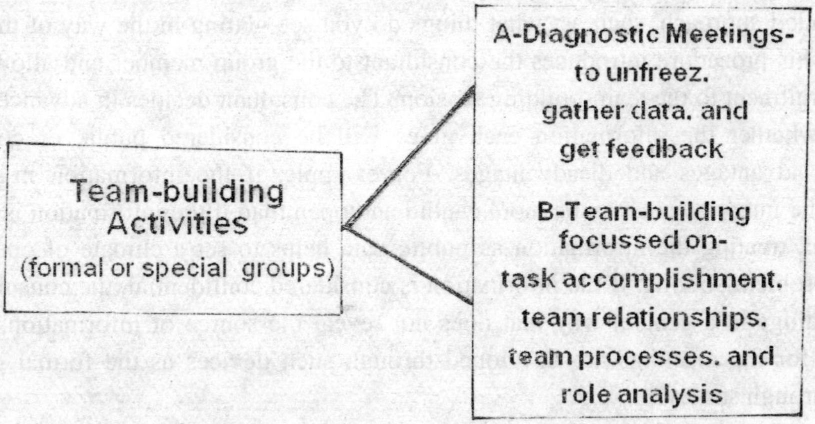

Fig.8.3. Team-building Activities

It is necessary to understand how teams/work groups are configured and operate so as to understand the implications of the OD interventions applicable to them. While work group is a number of persons usually reporting to a common superior and have face-to-face interaction and have some degree of interdependence in carrying out tasks for the purpose of achieving organisational goals. Team is a small number of people with complementary skills and is committed to a common purpose.

Cross-functional teams comprise of individuals who have a functional team as a base but regularly form part of a group, meeting to solve problems needing input from various functions.

The formal group team-building meeting has the goal of improving the team's effectiveness through better management of task demands, relationship demands, and group processes. It is an inward look by the team at its own performance, analyses its way of doing things, and attempts to develop strategies to improve its operation. Sometimes, the purpose of the meeting is a special agenda item, such as developing the group's performance goal for the coming year.

The usual practice for these sessions is to have the consultant interview each of the group members and the leader prior to the meeting, asking them what the strengths of the group are, what their problems are, how they think the group functions, and what obstacles are in the way of the group performing better. These interview data are categorised into themes by the consultant, who presents the themes to the group at the beginning of the meeting. The group examines and discusses the issues, ranks them in order of their importance, examine the underlying dynamics of the problem, and begin about the change deemed desirable. It is impressive to have follow-up meetings to determine whether the section steps that were outlined were taken and to determine whether those steps had the desired effects. This flow of events constitutes the team-building meeting.

The meeting may be called for a special purpose, such as a new member coming into the group, an organisational structure change, or planning for the next year; or it may primarily be devoted to maintaining and managing the group's culture and processes if it is a special purpose meeting. Time should still be allocated to an examination and critique of the group's dynamics.

As mentioned previously, it is often desirable for the consultant to interview the entire group, using open-ended approach, such as 'what things do you see getting in the way of this group being a better one'? This procedure introduces the consultant to the group member and allows the consultant to assess commitment to the team-building session. The consultant decides in advance and informs the interviewers whether the information each gives will be considered public or confidential. Each approach has advantages and disadvantages. For example, if the information in the interview is confidential, the interviewers may be more candid and open than if the information is to be public. On the other hand, treating the information as public data helps to set a climate of openness, trust and constructive problem-solving. If the information is considered confidential, the consultant is careful to report the findings in a general way that does not reveal the source of information. Other ways the agenda items for the meetings are developed through such devices as the formal group diagnostic meetings or through survey.

The consultant presents the interview results in terms of themes. When everyone understands the themes, these themes are ranked by the group in terms of their important the most important ones form the agenda for the meeting. In the course of the meeting much interpersonal and the group process information will be generated, which may also be examined. The group thuds works on the items that emerge from the interactions of the participants. As important problems are discussed, alternatives for action are developed generally the team-building meeting involves deciding on action steps for remedying problems and setting forget dates for, 'who will do what and when'.

Significant variations of the team-building session entail devoting time to problem-solving methods, planning and goals setting methods, conflict resolution techniques, and the like. These special activities are usually initiated in response to the needs demonstrated or stated by the group. The consultant often makes conceptual inputs or structures the situation so that a particular problem or process becomes the focus. A wide variety of exercises may be interspersed into the meeting, depending upon the problems indentified and the group phenomena that emerge.

Factors affecting the outcomes of team-building activities may be:

- Length of time allocated to the activities.
- Teams's willingness to undrestand the process.
- Lengthe of the time the team has been working to gather.
- Team's performance.

Activities relevent to one or more individuals may be:

Diagnostic

- Helps members to better undrestand their motivation style or emotions in group context.
- Results in the members gaining a better understanding of the way these affect the problem-solving and other group process.

Developmental

- Include coaching, 360 degree feedback, assistance with conflict, etc.
- Attempt to alter group's on-going processes by focussing on the behaviours and attitudes of individual members.

Activities oriented to group's operation and behaviour may be:

Diagnostic

- Data gathered includes information on:
    - Leadership styles and behaviour.
    - Goals, objectives, and decision making process.
    - Organisational culture, communication pattern, interpersonal relationships and process.
    - Barriers to effective group functioning.
    - Task and related technical problems.
- They establish a framework within which further work can be done through development activities.

Developmental

- An inward look by the team at its own performance, behaviour, and culture for the purpose of dropping out dysfunctional behaviours and strengthening functional ones.
- They include role clarification, improving goal clarity and member commitment, modifying the decision making and problem-solving process, changing norms, increasing risk taking and trust, and improving communications.

Activities affecting group's relationship with rest of the organisation may be:

Diagnostic

- Focus on understanding the group's organisational role – how its goals support the larger organisation, and how the group interact with other groups.

Developmental

- Actions that improve all the above.

Managing Team-building Activities

A team culture is necessary for success. Working together effectively is not automatic. It takes a specific effort and the development of a culture that is supported by executive management. Shared experiences create unity and value. Knowledge transfer is essential for an organisation to grow. Without knowledge transfer and the sharing of success it is difficult for the group to share any vision and work towards common goals. The effective management of team building activities invloves following strategies:

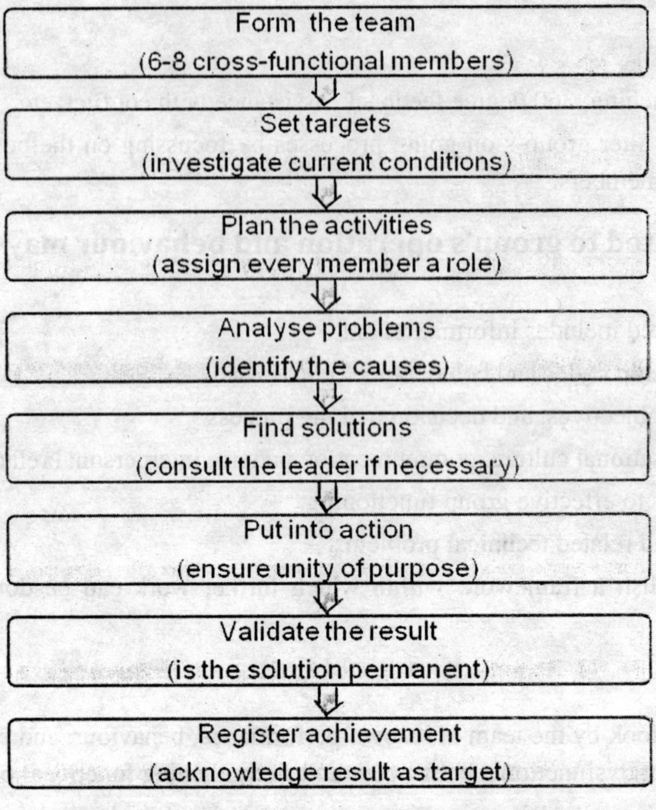

Fig.8.4. Managing Team-building Activities

1. **Form the team:** A team may be formed taking 6-8 cross-functional members and create an intentional communication strategy. Management team must understand and support a common vision. This requires clarity. Clarity begins with effective communication. Make sure communication from management team reaches all employees.

2. **Set Targets**: Investigate current conditions and do not set up intentional competition in the workplace. Try to insure that individual skill sets complement one another rather than compete with one another. Spread the responsibility and authority around by alternating leaders for various tasks. Look for star potential and introduce coaching and mentoring as a skill set.

3. **Plan the activities:** Assign every member a role. Create team ownership in the decision making process but it's not management by committee. Avoid group think by making sure that individuals express opinions openly without intimidation. Responsibility must be accompanied by authority and accountability. Build trust and respect by giving trust and respect. Act as a coach or mentor and not a boss.

4. **Analyse the problems:** Identify the causes of problems. Take complex plans and strategies and assign accountability and ownership. This creates more efficiency and leverages creativity. Assign responsibility according to individual passions.

5. Find solutions: Consult the leader if necessary. Ask for solutions assigning both responsibility and empowerment. Ownership of ideas and initiatives builds commitment. Involving the team in creating direction and solutions through empowerment generates commitment to the tasks necessary to meet objectives.

6. Put into action: Ensure unity of purpose. Brainstorming must be encouraged to release team innovation. Bouncing ideas of one another stimulates creative thinking which leads to creative solutions. This in itself bonds individuals into a common purpose.

7. Validate the result: Facilitate permanent solution. Don't just talk about empowerment and delegation, believe in it and demonstrate that belief by allowing the team-members to make decisions and take independent action.

8. Register achievement: Acknowledge result as target. Reliance on team effectiveness minimises risk by being more flexible and adaptive than relying on a single individual. No one individual alone can jeopardise success. The loss of one team-member can be overcome without losing sight of the objectives.

'Teamwork is the ability to work together towards a common vision. It is the ability to direct individual accomplishments towards organisational objectives. It is the fuel that allows common people to attain uncommon results'.

– Andrew Carnegie

Team-building and teamwork is the key driver in organisational productivity. Organisations are now looking to build teams with people of complementary skills to work towards achieving the corporate objectives and goals.

It is for this reason that companies organise training programs in areas such as team-building. The trainer or facilitator of the program not only gives theoretical explanations or conducts discussions on team functioning, but also carries out various activities on effective team-building. These are fun, and yet with important underlying factors that encourage the participants to look deeper into the topic of the day.

Review Discussions

1. Define team. Discuss its significance and what are the principles of effective team?
2. What are the different types of teams? Explain the prerequisites of successful team?
3. Describe the stages of team development.
4. What is the purpose of team-building in an organisation? Also discuss team-building interventions.
5. How is team-building activities managed?

♣♣♣♣♣♣

CHAPTER 9
ORGANISATIONAL EFFECTIVENESS

After studying this chapter, you should be able to:

- Understand organisational effectiveness.
- Identify interpersonal relationship.
- Be aware of transactional analysis.
- Be familiar with group dynamics.
- Differentiate formal and informal organisation
- Be acquainted with human resource development system.
- Comprehend organisational efficiency and effectiveness.
- Make out organisational effectiveness model.
- Be acquainted with Likert's model of organisational effectiveness.
- Identify role of human resource professional in enhancing organisational effectiveness.

Introduction

Organisational effectiveness is the concept of how effective an organisation is in achieving the outcomes the organisation intends to produce. The idea of organisational effectiveness is especially important for non-profit organisations as most people who donate money to non-profit organisations and charities are interested in knowing whether the organisation is effective in accomplishing its goals.

An organisation's effectiveness is also dependent on its communicative competence and ethics. Ethics is a foundation found within organisational effectiveness. An organisation must exemplify respect, honesty, integrity, and equity to allow communicative competence with the participating members. Along with ethics and communicative competence, members in that particular group can finally achieve their intended goals.

Foundations and other sources of grants and other types of funds are interested in organisational effectiveness of those people who seek funds from the foundations. Foundations always have more requests for funds or funding proposals and treat funding as an investment using the same care as a venture capitalist would in picking a company in which to invest.

Organisational effectiveness is an abstract concept and is basically impossible to measure. Instead of measuring organisational effectiveness, the organisation determines proxy measures which will be used to represent effectiveness. Proxy measures used may include such things as number of people served, types and sizes of population segments served, and the demand within those segments for the services the organisation supplies.

For instance, a non-profit organisation which supplies meals to house bound people may collect statistics such as the number of meals cooked and served, the number of volunteers delivering meals, the turnover and retention rates of volunteers, the demographics of the people served, the turnover and retention of consumers, the number of requests for meals turned down due to lack of capacity (amount of food, capacity of meal preparation facilities, and number of delivery volunteers), and amount of wastage. Since the organisation has as its goal the preparation of meals and the delivery of those meals to house bound people, it measures its organisational effectiveness by trying to determine what actual activities the people in the organisation do in order to generate the outcomes the organisation wants to create.

Activities such as fund raising or volunteer training are important because they provide the support needed for the organisation to deliver its services but they are not the outcomes *per se*. These other activities are overhead activities which assist the organisation in achieving its desired outcomes.

The term organisational effectiveness is often used interchangeably with organisational development, especially when used as the name of a department or a part of the human resources function within an organisation.

Interpersonal Relationship

Interpersonal relationship is the process of one individual reaching out to other individual and establishing a relationship with him or her. This has several significant aspects. Communication is important aspect. How people communicate with one another is not only important in itself, but also because it has implications for the relationship building between two or more individuals. Similarly, collaborative and competitive processes, which result in conflicts or cooperation, represent another important dimension. Individual need for recognition and affiliation plays an important role in building interpersonal relationship within the organisation. Attention may be paid to such processes in order to increase the effectiveness of interpersonal relationship and this lays the foundations for the effectiveness of individuals, the working of groups, and even for the total organisation. People need people and human experience involves interaction and relationship with other person. Each person represents the behaviour of people in an organisation and is concerned with improving organisational behaviour. The environment is developed in such a way as to motivate the people to work hard to accomplish the organisational goal. The organisational behaviour seeks to fulfil both employees' needs and organisational objectives. Organisational behaviour has some fundamental concepts around which nature of people and nature of organisations revolve. The three basic foundations of interpersonal relationships are:

- Need for affection-showing concern for one another.
- Need for recognition-acknowledging one another.
- Need for affiliation-inclusiveness of one another.

Transactional Analysis

Transactional Analysis (TA) is a personality and psychotherapy for personal growth. It has wide applications in clinical psychology, organisations and education also.

Transactional Analysis was developed by Eric Berne as an approach to psychoanalysis and therapy in the early 1950s, but was adopted by commercial organisations in the 1960s as they tried to improve the ways that people in general interacted. It defines some basic ego states and life positions that individuals can adopt, and uses those to describe how transactions then occur between two people. The idea is that if we know your own state, and can determine the other person's state, we can use our behaviour to influence the interactions between the two of us.

Ego States

Berne defined three basic personalities or ego states, each with characteristic attitudes, feelings, behaviours and language. Two of the states subdivide into two further facets:

PARENT	Critical Parent	makes rules and sets limits disciplines, judges and criticises
	Nurturing Parent	advises and guides protects and nurtures
ADULT		concerned with data and facts considers options and estimates probabilities makes unemotional decisions plans and makes things happen
CHILD	Free (Natural) Child	fun-loving and energetic creative and spontaneous
	Adapted Child	compliant and polite rebellious and manipulative

Fig. 9.1.Ego States

Life Positions

The other building block of TA is the view we have of ourselves in relation to other people around us. There are four life positions, shown as a grid that became known as the 'OK Corral'. The quotation in each box typifies the attitude of each life position:

I'M NOT OK **YOU'RE OK** 'I wish I could do that as well as you do'	**I'M OK** **YOU'RE OK** 'Hey, we're making good progress now'
I'M NOT OK **YOU'RE NOT OK** 'Oh this is terrible – we'll never make it'	**I'M OK** **YOU'RE NOT OK** 'You're not doing that right – let me show you'

Fig.9.2. Life Positions

People will move around the grid depending on the situation, but have a preferred position that they tend to revert to. This is strongly influenced by experiences and decisions in early life.

'I'm OK, you're OK' people are in the 'get on with' position. They're confident and happy about life and work, and interact by collaboration and mutual respect, even when they disagree.

'I'm OK, you're not OK' people are in the 'get rid of' position. They tend to get angry and hostile, and are smug and superior. They belittle others, who they view as incompetent and untrustworthy, and are often competitive and power-hungry.

'I'm not OK, you're OK' is the 'get away from' position. These people feel sad, inadequate or even stupid in comparison to others. They undervalue their skills and contribution and withdraw from problems.

'I'm not OK, you're not OK' is the 'get nowhere' position. These people feel confused or aimless. They don't see the point of doing anything, and so usually don't bother.

Transactions

The central concept of TA is that transactions between people can be characterised by the ego state of the two participants. What's more, the ego state adopted by the person who starts the transaction will affect the way the other person responds.

For example, Mr. A says 'what time will they arrive'?, and Mr. B replies 'at 2pm'. This is a simple adult-to-adult transaction.

However, if Mr. A adopts a child state – 'I'm worried that they might not arrive on time', that will tend to produce a nurturing parent response from Mr. B: 'Don't worry, we'll still have plenty of time to talk to them'.

This model shows how the transaction 'balances' between the two people: if one drifts into parent that will encourage the other to move to child, and *vice versa*. The preferred state for most business transactions is adult-adult, but it's OK to move to another state as long as you're aware of it and are ready for the changed response from the other person.

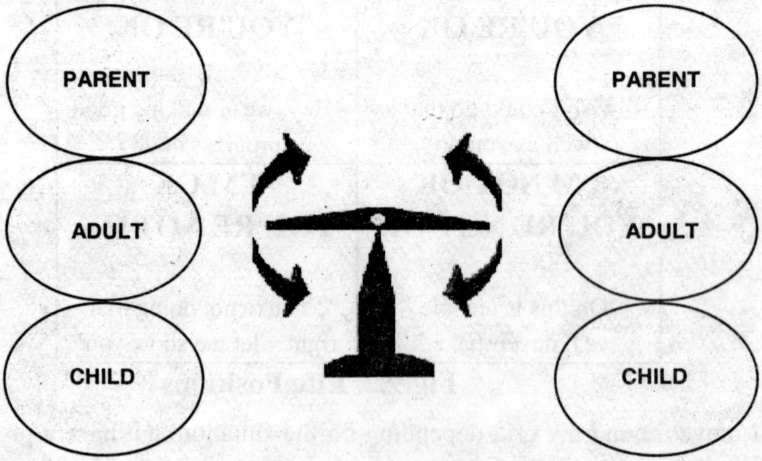

Fig.9.3. Transactions

Of course it doesn't always work that way, and an adult state can sometimes be met with, say, a parent response: 'What time will they arrive'? 'How should I know, I didn't arrange it'!

Strokes

We all need and seek care, attention, love, and recognition from others, and in TA, a stroke is defined as a unit of recognition. With children, strokes are obviously sought and given: they show off their new toy, or misbehave to get attention, and know that adults will respond right on cue. The grownups do the same: working hard, deliberately making mistakes, arriving late or simply arriving home and sighing 'what a day'!

Strokes can be positive or negative, and it's generally better to give a negative stroke than none at all (because that may be taken as negative anyway). But in many business organisations, strokes are subject to a set of unwritten rules:

- Don't give positive strokes freely;
- If you give positive strokes, make them conditional;
- Don't ask for positive strokes – certainly not directly;
- Most positive strokes are insincere ('plastic');
- Never give a physical stroke – by touching someone;
- Don't miss a chance to give a negative stroke.

The result is a cold, unfeeling environment where normal human emotions are generally suppressed. Even in 'warm' organisations where it's OK to express feelings, strokes are still subject to certain norms – such as not giving them to people above you in the hierarchy.

In the absence of a free exchange of strokes, people manipulate others in order to get the strokes they crave, and start playing games.

Games

The complexity of the TA model leaves it open to manipulation, or 'Games'. We adopt a child state because we want someone's help, or a parent state to make them do something for us. But often the games end up damaging the relationship, and the type of game someone plays is influenced by his or her life state.

Examples of games players are:

The Persecutor: 'if it weren't for you', 'see what you made me do', 'yes, but'.

The Rescuer: 'I'm only trying to help', 'what would you do without me'?

The Victim: 'this always happens to me', 'poor old me', 'go on, kick me'.

Group Dynamics

A group is a collection of two or more people who have a common goal or interest and interact with each other to accomplish their objective, and perceive themselves to be a part of the group. Group behaviour is a pattern of behaviour that is expected of an individual when she/he interacts with others. Individuals play multiple roles adjusting their rules to the group in which they are part. The expected role is more or less a formal rule. It is what other people expect from an individual. The expected role is the behaviour that a person actually carries out. Generally speaking, people join group because they expect it to satisfy their needs. Cohesion develops when these hopes are realised. Group cohesiveness is an important indicator of how much influence the group as a whole has over the individual members. It can be thought of as the strength of the 'glue' which holds the group together. It is defined as the degree to which members are attached to one another and share the group's goals. Cohesiveness cause more harmonious behaviour in group members. A cohesive group is able to act as one body to achieve its goal.

Group dynamics means the study of forces operating within a group for the social interaction. Group dynamic deals with interactions and forces among the members of the group in a social situations when this idea is applied to the study of organisational behaviour, the focus is on the dynamic of the members of formal or informal work group.

The main question is that why individuals form into groups? Before discussing some very practical reasons, it would be beneficial to example some of the classic theories of group formation or why do people affiliate with one another.

The most basic theory explains affiliation is propinquity. This interesting word simply means that individual affiliate with one another because of spatial or geographical proximity. The theory would predict that students sitting next to one another in a class for example, are more likely to form into a group than to those who are sitting at the opposite ends of the room. In an organisation employees who work in the same area of the plant or office, or managers with offices close to one another would more probably form into groups than to those who are not physically located together. A more comprehensive theory of group formation and more propinquity come from the theory based on activities, interactions, and sentiments. These three elements are directly related to one another.

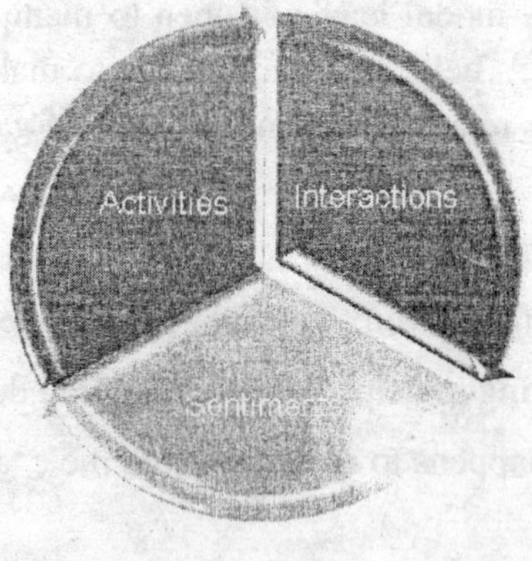

Fig.9.4. Elements of Group Formation

The more activities persons shares, the more numerous is their interactions and the stronger will be their sentiments which determine how much other persons are liked or disliked. The more interactions among persons, the more will be their sheered activities and sentiments and the more sentiments persons have for one another, the more will be their sheered activities and interactions. This theory lends a great deal to the understanding of group formation process. Persons in group interact with one another is not first in physical propinquity sense but also to accomplish many group goals, such as cooperation and problem-solving.

Characteristics of Effective Group

Some of the important characteristics of group in the effective functioning of organisation are as follows:

1. Members are skilled in various leadership and membership rules, and functions are required for interaction between leaders and members; and between members and other members.
2. The group has well-established and relaxed working relationships among all its members.
3. Members of the group are attracted to it and are loyal to its members, including the leaders.
4. The values and goals of the group are a satisfactory integration and expression of the relevant values and needs of its members.
5. Each member is motivated to all that she/he can reasonably do to help the group achieve its control objectives.
6. All the interaction, problem-solving, and decision making activities of the group occur in a supportive atmosphere while members accept that there are real and important differences of opinion. The focus is on arriving at sound solutions and not on aggravating conflict.
7. The group is eager to help each members develop his or her full potential.
8. Each member accepts willingly and without resentment the goals and expectations that the group has established.
9. Members provide mutual help, when necessary or advisable, so that each can successfully accomplish his or her goals.
10. The supportive atmosphere stimulates creativity.
11. The group knows when to use its effort and for what purposes.
12. There is high motivation on the part of each member to initiate and receive communications openly.
13. Members are flexible and adaptable in regard to their goals and attitudes.
14. Individual members feel secure in making decisions that seem appropriate to them because his or her goals and philosophy of operation are clearly understood by each member.

Types of Group

There are various types of group, but within organisations the most important distinction usually prescribed is formal and informal groups and people are assigned positions in these groups to fulfil specific tasks which are clearly related to the organisational purposes. Formal groups are usually of two types and are based on their duration. They can be permanent, like departments in an enterprise, or temporary, like committees or task forces. Informal groups on the other hand, are formal on the basis of common interests, friendship, or social needs. There are usually three types of internal groups.

1. The horizontal clique (a group of people who work in the same area and are of the same rank and status).
2. The vertical clique (a group of people of different rank and status within the same department), and
3. The mixed clique (a group of people of different ranks and status from different departments in different locations).

The creation of informal groups depends very much on the physical locations of people, the nature of their work, their time schedules and so on. These groups therefore, arise out of a particular combination of 'formal' factors and human needs.

The Hawthorne studies were the first to point out their importance for organisational effectiveness while numerous studies have focused on work groups; one of the most enlightening things for the manager is that of Leonard Sayles. Although many approaches to group behaviour do not differentiate among types of groups, he recognised the fact that some groups consistently react quite differently from others; and one aspect in which non-management work groups vary considerably in their level of protest activities or their tendencies to petition for improved working conditions.

Between 1951 and 1955, Sayles studied three hundred work groups from a hundred plants in a variety of industries to determine the factors which influence the nature and frequency of protest actors taken by work groups. In reviewing the data from his sample of groups, he determined that there were basic styles in which work groups reacted to authority in apathetic, erratic, strategic and conservative manner.

1. Apathetic groups: These consisted of relatively low paid and low skilled assembly line workers who were dependent on each other. It was hard to identify the leaders of these informal groups, if they had any. These groups were least likely to develop grievances or engage in concerted action to pressurise the management or the trade union activities.

2. Erratic groups: These consisted semi-skilled workers who worked together in groups doing jobs that were homogeneous and required interaction. They tended to choose, as their leaders, strong big men who were autocratic and tended to concentrate power in themselves. These groups showed more frequent protest activity than the apathetic groups. Their overall behaviour was termed erratic because the seriousness of the issue on which they objected frequently had little relation to the intensity of their reactions.

3. Strategic groups: They were composed of skilled employees who were capable of judgement. Their jobs were not interdependent but were better or key jobs in the plant. They chose as leaders several people who did their jobs well and represented the groups quietly. In contrast to the erratic groups they were not characterised by sudden flashes of activity but were sensibly calculating pressure groups which demanded constant attention to their problems and could reinforce their demands by group actions.

4. Conservative groups: These consisted of the most highly skilled workers in the plant who worked on their own. The leaders chosen by them were the most technically competent workers, who do their work quietly and stayed in the background. This was the most stable of all the groups because there was little evidence of turmoil, trouble, or concerted action on their part.

Thus, while the erratic groups are most troublesome because they are unpredictable; the apathetic workers tend to remain continually quiet and focused; the strategic groups have a very rational approach and the conservatives usually go about their business without any trouble. The management usually spends most of its time dealing with the strategic groups and trying to keep the erratic groups in line.

Formal and Informal Organisation

In a general sense organisations are collections of individuals with collective tasks to perform. The collective tasks are dissected into subtasks, and members are assigned to perform them, creating organisational positions. Their positions prescribe the duties, activities, and authority relationship of each organisational member. The classical organisational structure is built around positions and not around people. In reality, such a formal structure shows only one set of relationships, the officially planned relationship between groups and individuals working together. Other important relationship exist is often called the informal organisation where exists powerful influence upon a workable system for getting the work done in a smooth way. Both formal and informal relationship is necessary for group activity. As pointed out by Keith Davis, they serve to preserve the organisation from the self-destruction that would result from literal disobedience to rules and regulations.

The informal organisation can be viewed as a shadow organisation. It arises naturally, spontaneously for the interaction of people. It refers to unofficial and unauthorised relationship that inevitably occurs between individuals and groups within the formal organisation. It exists within the confines of the formal authority structure. However, the interactions that occur informally are not prescribed by the formal structure nor can they be completely controlled by the formal structure. It use by-product of human nature and is affected by the formal structure.

Comparisons and Contrast of Formal and Informal Organisation

The formal and informal organisations can be compared and contrasted under following heads:

Origin:

Formal organisation is goal-oriented they are tightly built around the general principles of organisation and are the result of conscious thought processes. Informal organisation develops naturally. Informal structure reflects individual and group goals rather than organisational goals. Changes in informal organisational structure occur through collective agreements between members. In contrast changes in informal organisations occur through administrative policies.

Basic structural components:

Formal organisations have a definite structure reflected in the organisational charts providing a pictorial representation of authority relationships. These organisational charts are built around positions and exhibit officially based relationships. The organisation tends to be mechanical and impersonal. Informal organisations are built around people. They are without structure. Moreover, they are initiated but the workers themselves tend to serve the needs of workers. The basic purpose is to improve human relationships.

Goals:

The informal organisation has its own goals, objectives and authority patterns and these factors may or may not coincide with those of the formal structures. Formal organisations are wedded to well defined goals created by management. These goals may be the social satisfaction of its members. It is the primary duty of every manager to provide meaningful goals to organisational participants so that there is no conflict between individual (informal) and organisational (formal) goals.

Influence processes:

In formal organisations, positions conferred on individuals are the centres of power and influence. Authority is equalised with influence. People enjoying authority are supposed to be powerful. In contrast; influence in the informal organisation is attached to the person. The individual with the most influence is the person who is most able to satisfy the needs of the groups.

Control process:

Formal organisations are tied to a rigid system or rules and regulations. Control points are established to constrain behaviour and restrain the members from going off the track. Informal organisation are not glued to any rigid system of rules but are governed by group norms. Norms are standards of behaviour designed to regulate social behaviour along with acceptable lines. Formal rules may be so much of a waste once they are not approved by the informal groups.

Communication:

Formal organisations depend on formal, official channels of communication to seal the ideas of management to the organisational members. These officially based instruments are employed meticulously to convey the feelings of management to workers. Communication thus largely is a one way traffic. The informal organisation designs its own channel of communication, popularly known as 'grapevine', for both organisational and social communication purposes. The grapevine can spread rumours and false information as rapidly as it can spread facts. It tends to outstrip formal channels on speed.

Size:

Formal organisations can balloon to gigantic unmanageable proportions depending on the degree of success enjoyed by them in the market. In contrast, informal organisations tend to be small and manageable.

Human Resource Development System

In organisational context Human Resource Development (HRD) can be defined as a process in which the employees of an organisation are continuously helped in a planned way to:

- Acquired or sharpen capabilities required to perform various tasks and functions associated with their or future expected roles.
- Develop their general capabilities as individuals so that they are able to discover and exploit their own inner potentials for their own and for organisational purposes.
- Develop an organisational culture where superior-subordinate relationships, teamwork, and collaboration among different subunits are strong and contribute to the organisational health.

A sound HRD system is perhaps the most important element in the organisation which not only ensures smooth performance but also long-term survival and growth of the organisation. While other resources like technology, capital assets can be bought, only resources which can't be bought is motivated human resources which help in the growth of the organisation. Hence, HRD has become very important. The HRD can play effective role in:

1. Optimising the use of employees for the growth of organisation by providing them opportunities for self-development and recognise that they constitute the most important asset of the company.
2. Enabling employees to growth with organisation by ensuring maximum personal contribution to the effective working of the organisation.
3. Helping in the congruence of individual aspiration and organisational expectations.
4. Promoting collaboration and team spirit by establishing a climate of trust, openness, and interdependence.
5. Maximising the effectiveness of the employees and the organisation.
6. Maximising managerial effectiveness by having involved committed and highly motivated team of managers to ensure satisfaction of various needs of individuals for achieving their maximum contribution towards organisational goals.
7. Building or acquiring the skills necessary to maximum individual development of human resources, and meet existing and long-term organisational needs.
8. Providing a favourable work environment and dependable management style based on trust, cooperation, and respect for human personality and well-being of the individuals.
9. Achieving good employer-employees' relations through due regard to basic human values and treat employees as self-respecting individuals.

Organisational effectiveness results from trained and developed employees working in a healthy organisational climate which results from both individual development interventions and organisational development plans or interventions.

The HRD system which is so much concerned with overall organisation cannot succeed without the total commitment of the top management in implementation of HRD plans for developing committed human resources and the work environment congenial to human resources.

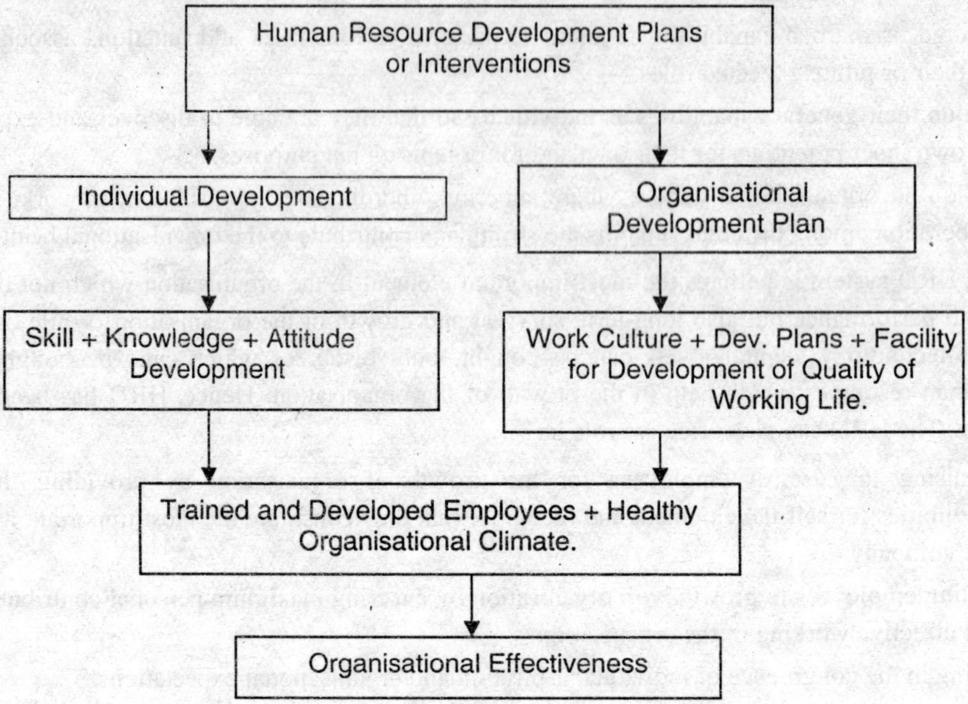

Fig.9.5.HRD Model

Organisational Efficiency and Effectiveness

The effectiveness of an organisation is doing right things and the efficiency of an organisation is doing the things right. Organisational effectiveness is result-oriented and organisational efficiency is process-oriented. It can also be said that organisational effectiveness is people-oriented, whereas organisational efficiency is system oriented. The distinction between effectiveness and efficiency is very important to explain why some-organisations are effective but highly inefficient, or highly efficient but ineffective. Effectiveness is a multidimensional concept which can't be measured by a single criterion. But efficiency can be measured by the ratio of input to output. In other words, efficiency considers the issue of how much input is necessary to attain a given level of output.

The concept of efficiency is closely related to effectiveness though the exact nature of the relationship is open to question. For instance, a decline in cost per unit of output is an indicator of improving efficiency. But this does not guarantee increased effectiveness. It is possible that an organisation's efficiency in production is improving, but it is incurring losses because it is faced with a declining market. On the other hand, an organisation may be inefficient, but it is able to make high profits because of a rising market. Efficiency is primarily a criterion on the internal life of the organisation and it is concerned with the economic and technical aspects of the organisation. But effectiveness is a very broad concept as it considers the survival prospects of the organisation which are not determined solely by the efficiency of the internal system. Effectiveness considers organisation-environment interface and also takes care of the human side of the organisation. But efficiency, on the other hand, concentrates on the technological aspects of the organisation.

An efficient organisation is not necessarily effective and an effective organisation is not necessarily efficient. It is however desirable that an effective organisation is also an efficient one. Efficiency may help an organisation in becoming effective. It increases the possibilities for energy storage and is conducive to long run growth and survival, but it is still only an aspect of organisational effectiveness. Chester Barnard has explained the relationship between the concepts of 'effectiveness' and 'efficiency' in the following words – 'When unsought consequences are trivial, or insignificant, effective action is efficient; when unsought consequences are not trivial, effective action is inefficient'.

The vitality of the organisation lies in the willingness of the individual to cooperate in the achievement of its goal. Willingness of the member cease if the purpose of the organisation that exists cannot be attained. The effectiveness of an organisation is determined by the degree to which it attains its goals. The efficiency of the organisation is measured by the output. Generally, the output is closely related to goals. But organisational effectiveness is not synonymous with organisational goals. The maintenance of human resource must be considered as vital element in encouraging organisational effectiveness. Scientific management pointed out technique of high productivity but overlooked the resentments, hostilities, adverse motivation and attitudinal aspects of human system. The negative attitudes are not in the long run interest of any organisation but results in high employee turnover, frustration, low morale, aggression, etc. Thus, for organisational system to be effectiveness and efficient it must have the capacity to survive, adopt, maintain, and grow regardless of a particular function it fulfills.

Bennis pointed out the following three criteria for efficiency and effectiveness:

1. The adaptability to solve problems and to react with flexibility to changing environment. There is a need of sense of identity, knowledge, and insight on the part of the organisation of what goals are and what it is to do.
2. The ability to search out and to perceive correctly the real properties of the environment.
3. The integration among the subparts of the total organisational system in such a manner that the efforts are not being neutralised. The system level of criteria of organisational effectiveness must be a multiple criteria involving adaptability, a sense of identity, capacity to test reality, and internal integration.

Thus, efficiency and effectiveness of an organisation do not depend on one factor but on multiple factors. Organisational effectiveness is one of the most important concepts in the study of a social organisation. Organisation can only exist under following conditions:

- It must be effective (it must accomplish objectives of the system).
- It must be efficient (it must satisfy individual motives by and for their cooperation).

The effective organisation must fulfill the following conditions:

- It should have high output (qualitatively and quantitatively).
- Organisational flexibility (it is the ability to assimilate external and internal changes).
- The absence of internal organisation strain due to conflict or tension between organisational subgroups.

Organisational goals do help us in maintaining organisational effectiveness. Organisational effectiveness is based primarily on the judgement as to which all the multiple goal in an organisation is made. The efficiency and effectiveness of the organisation are centred in its continuous existence and growth.

Organisational Effectiveness Model

Organisational effectiveness can be defined by the way of a model. The model must be characteristics of organisation and describe in operating terms, the element of dimension that contribute to effective organisational behaviour.

Following are the important components which should be there in the model of organisational effectiveness:

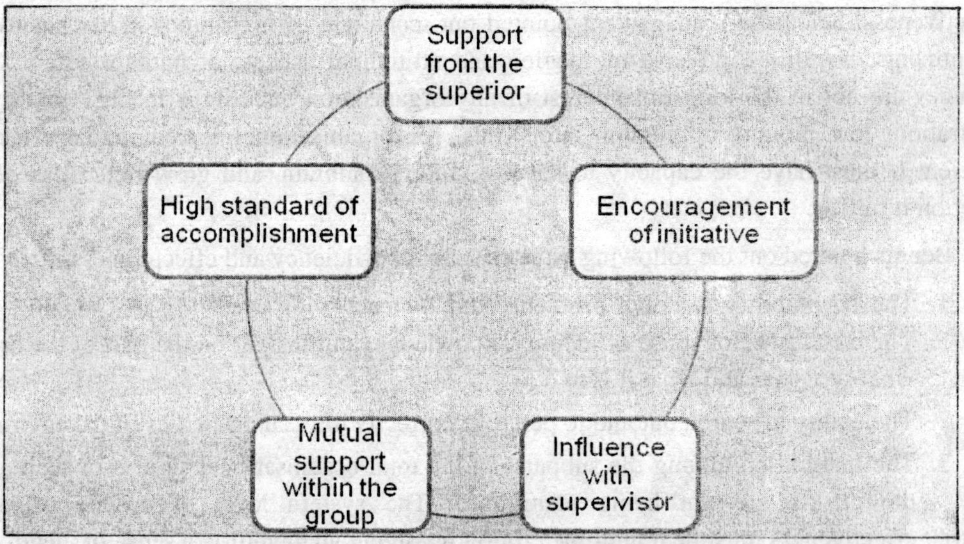

Fig.9.6. Components of Organisational Effectiveness Model

1. **Support from the superior:** It stems from the superior seeing he/she move in the role of a coach rather than that of a boss. It places the supportive supervisor in the role of a communicator with higher management, distinct from the role of an agent of higher authority.
2. **Encouragement of initiative:** It shows that the superior assumes his/her people as responsible, trustworthy, and able to handle authority. She/he believes they will act accordingly, accept challenge, show initiative, and respond to the need of the situation.

3. **Influence with supervisor:** It reflects openness and trust, achievement of upward communication, and acceptance from those responsible for decision making.
4. **Mutual support within the group:** It indicates the willingness of the members of the group to provide required support to meet the challenges, overcome problems, and accomplish the shared goals.
5. **High standard of accomplishment:** It recognises the leader for improving communications for gaining commitment, goal setting, and decision making as important element of group action. These elements must be coupled with which the group in turn accepts and work for.

Likert's Model of Organisational Effectiveness

In discussing effectiveness we concentrate on evaluating the results of individual leaders or managers. These results are significant, but perhaps the most important aspect of effectiveness is its relationship to entire organisation. Here we are concerned not only with the outcome of a given leadership attempts but with effectiveness of the organisational unit over a period of time. Rensis Likert identifies three variables which are, causal; intervening; and output or end-result; which are useful in discussing effectiveness over a period of time. These variables are described as under:

1. **Causal Variables**

   Causal variables are those factors that influence the course of development within an organisation and its results or accomplishments. These independent variables can be altered by the organisation and its management; they are not beyond the control of the organisation, like general business conditions. Leadership strategies, skills, styles, management decisions, philosophy, objectives, policies and structure of the organisation, technology, etc., are examples of causal variables.

2. **Intervening Variables**

   According to Likert, intervening variables represent the current condition of the internal state of the organisation. They are reflected in the commitment to objectives, motivation and morale of members and their skills in leadership, communications, conflict resolution, decisionmaking and problem-solving, etc.

3. **Output or End-result variables**

   Output or end-result variables are the dependent variables that reflect the achievements of the organisation. In evaluating effectiveness, perhaps more than 90 per cent of managers in organisation look at measure of output alone. Thus, the effectiveness of business managers is often determined by net profit; the effectiveness of college professors may be determined by the number of articles and books they have published and the effectiveness of basketball coaches may be determined by their won-lost record. Many researchers talk about effectiveness by emphasising similar output variables. Fred E. Fiedler, for example, in his studies evaluated leader effectiveness in terms of group performance on the group's primary assigned tasks. William J. Reddin, in discussing management styles, thinks in similar terms about effectiveness. He argues that the effectiveness of a manager should be measures objectively by his profit centre performance – maximum output, market share, or other similar criteria.

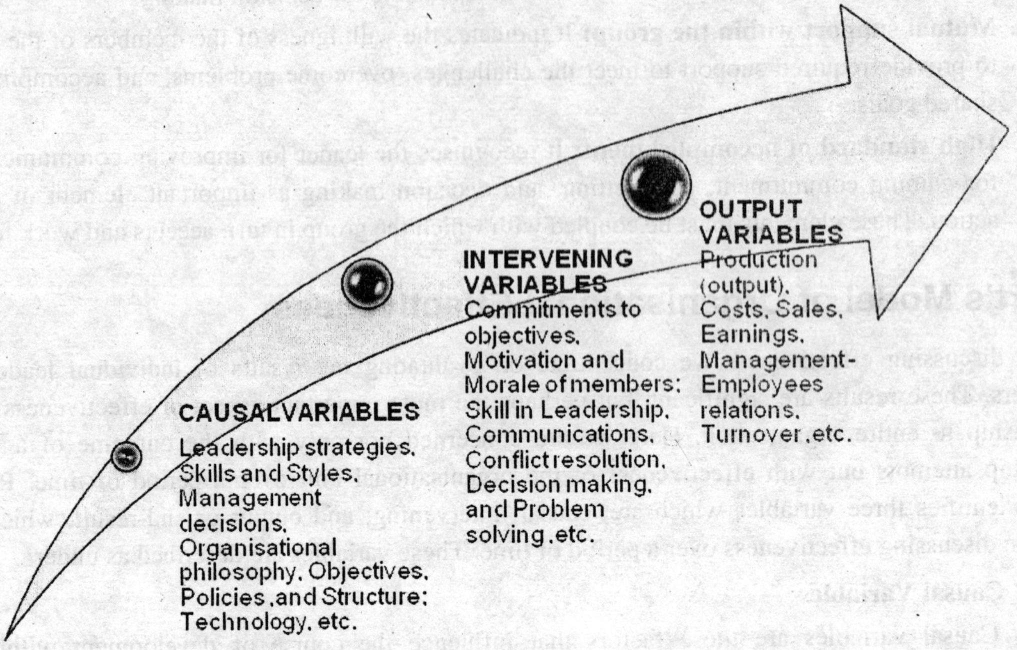

Fig. 9.7. Relationship between Casual, Intervening, and Output variables

We might visualise the relationship between the three classes of variables as stimuli (causal variables) acting upon the organism (intervening variables) and creating certain repossess (output variables), as illustrated in Figure. 9.7

The level or condition of the intervening variables is produced largely by the causal variables which in turn has influence upon the end-result variables. Attempts by top members of the organisation to improve the intervening variables by endeavouring to alter this variable directly will be much less successful unless the effort is directed towards modifying them through altering the causal variables. Similarly, efforts to improve the end-results variable by attempting to modify the intervening variables usually will be less effective without changing the casual variables.

Factors Affecting Organisational Effectiveness

Effectiveness is typically measured in terms of performance, productivity, profit, and so forth. Thorndike identified several criteria as productivity, net profit, mission accomplishment, and organisational growth. Campbell employed the following measures to determine organisational success or effectiveness:

1. Overall performance
2. Productivity
3. Employee withdrawal

4. Rate of return on investment
5. Employee job satisfaction and motivation
6. Stability and growth of organisation
7. Flexibility or Adaptation
8. Evaluations by external entities.

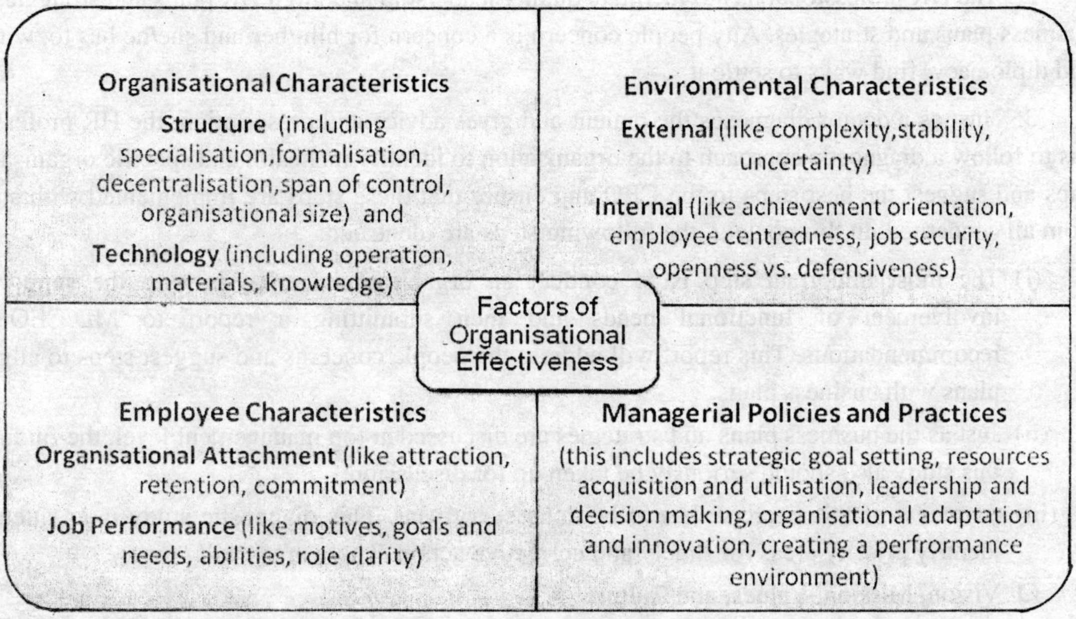

Fig.9.8. Major Sets of Variables that Potentially have their Influence on Effectiveness

Role of Human Resource Professional in Enhancing Organisational Effectiveness

An organisation can achieve its goals only if all employees are fully committed and competent to perform and contribute. With their innovative spirit and effective teamwork, they can make a difference even in the most difficult period only if every individual accepts accountability for performance, but true accountability is the act of an individual driven by personal integrity and commitment. A nurturing and motivating environment has to be developed and maintained that will inspire employees to perform, contribute, develop and hold themselves accountable for results.

Accountability and performance depends on the quality of leadership supported by a conducive culture. Unlike production, marketing and finance departments, human resource department is concerned with all people issues cutting across all departments. HR department has the responsibility to initiate steps that will integrate and align the efforts of all employees in all departments towards building up an effective organisation. In this regard, some of the important roles that HR professional has to play are discussed below:

1. The role of HR department is to initiate steps to develop and maintain committed and competent individuals and work teams who will work with an urge to excel in whatever they do. The HR professional should have the knowledge and skills to rise to the level of an adviser to the CEO in all matters relating to various organisational issues and people cutting across all departments.

2. The HR professional has to facilitate quality leadership and align HR plans and strategies with business plans and strategies. Any people concern is a concern for him/her and she/he has to, with tact and diplomacy, find ways to settle it.

3. Just as a doctor diagnoses the patient and gives advice and prescription, the HR professional has to follow a diagnostic approach to the organisation to identify its health and specific organisational gaps and suggest the best steps to the CEO and ensure that these steps are implemented with support from all concerned. In this context, the following steps are identified:

(i) The most important step is to conduct an organisational analysis with the support and involvement of functional heads and then submitting a report to MD/CEO with recommendations. This report will address the people concerns and suggest steps to align HR plans with business plans.

(ii) Just as the business plans and strategies are discussed at top management level, the findings of this study also should seriously be taken up for discussion.

(iii) A review of this exercise has to be done every year. This diagnostic study is an attempt to identify priority areas for timely and corrective action. These areas will cover:

- Vision, Mission, Values, and Culture
- Organisational structure
- Goal setting process
- Systems and procedures relating to manpower planning and recruitment, communication, performance management, rewards and benefits, learning and development, and managing change for organisational renewal.

4. A gap in any of these subsystems will be a restraining force on the organisation. Therefore, identification of specific areas for improvement is a very important step towards organisation's renewal, survival, growth and effectiveness.

5. It is necessary to provide, continuous learning opportunities so that all members in the organisation will be able to discover their own potential, manage and develop themselves. And in turn they will develop others. This process if supported by a conducive culture, individual development will gradually contribute to organisational development.

6. Organisational development is possible only when proper emphasis is given on the right values, attitudes, and habits apart from knowledge and skills. Each individual has to move in a maturity continuum from dependence to independence and then from independence to interdependence. In other words each and every employee irrespective of the level has to effectively

relate with others to form an effective organisation based on trust and understanding. This is an important aspect of learning and development strategy.

7. Efforts should be made to identify and address the specific concerns/issues relating to each department. There will be both learning and non-learning interventions for performance improvement and better results. Management's concern should be to develop and maintain highly effective self-managed teams.

8. Next step is to determine the specific learning and development needs of employees in various departments to resolve the specific concerns/issues referred to above and to allocate a budget for learning and development activities. Later, appropriate learning and development programs have to be designed and conducted.

9. Once the training programs are over the HR department has to conduct a post-training study and then compare the findings/observations with the situation prevailing during the pre-training phase. The purpose is to ensure that transfer of learning really takes place and better results are accomplished at individual, departmental and organisational levels.

10. To repeat, the role of HR department is to take initiative in this regard and make things happen in the right direction. In this exercise HR professional is a facilitator and an internal consultant supporting and helping department heads and the CEO. She/he has to play the role of business partner and help in aligning HR plans with business plans. She/he can thus reduce their concern and get better visibility, acceptability and recognition.

Human resource professional has the role of an adviser to CEO. She/he has to continuously update himself/herself and enhance his/her competency so as to get acceptance from CEO and other functional heads. The HR professional may not have all the skills for this ambitious role, but can get the help from the colleagues and also take help from external consultants on need base. One point needs to be emphasised here is the readiness of the organisation for these various initiatives has to be ascertained before venturing to do anything, otherwise the results may not be effective and no doubt will be frustrating for all concerned.

The concept of effectiveness appears to be simple, but it is very difficult to simplify the concept. The reason for this lies in the fact that the organisations and the people that run them often have multiple goals which may be in conflict with each other. Even the interpretation of organisational goals may be subject to different viewpoints.

Organisational effectiveness is the extent to which an organisation achieves its goals with the given resources and means. An organisation is said to be effective if it is able to achieve its goals. The goals must be achieved within the constraints of limited resources as none of the resources provided by an organisation's environment are really unlimited. The level of output an organisation achieves with its limited resources determines its efficiency, and the extent to which it is successful in doing what it is set out to do determine its effectiveness.

Review Discussions

1. Explain the concept of organisational effectiveness in context to HRD framework.
2. Describe the concept of transactional analysis in brief.
3. Explain group dynamics? Discuss the process of group formation.
4. What is formal and informal organisation and how do they operate?
5. Explain the interrelationships between organisational effectiveness and organisational efficiency.
6. Explain the important components of an organisational effectiveness model.
7. Describe Likert's model of organisational effectiveness.
8. What are the factors of organisational effectiveness? Discuss the role of HR professional in organisational effectiveness.

♣♣♣♣♣♣

CHAPTER 10

ORGANISATIONAL STRESS MANAGEMENT

After Studying this chapter, you should be able to:

- Comprehend stress and it effect on job performance.
- Discern stress factors.
- Be familiar with consequences of stress.
- Relate organisational development and stress management.
- Be acquainted with organisational stress management strategies.
- Be acquainted with organisational development intervention stress management (ODISM) - model.
- Identify work life balance.

Introduction

Stress is what individuals experience when they feel they have difficulty coping with the pressures and demands placed upon them. Pressures can arise from an individual's personal life as well as from work and people vary in their capacity and ability to cope with different types of pressure. Stress is a complex and sensitive issue. It is also a confusing one, as people use the word in different ways. For some it represents the pressures and demands they have to deal with both within and outside of work ('I am under stress...'); for others it refers to their typical experience when faced with pressures and demands ('I feel very stressed...'). What is clear is that while the pressures and demands of some situations prove disturbing to most people, quite idiosyncratic things can also upset each of us. Further, a situation that proves enjoyable and stimulating one day might also prove upsetting on other occasions. In other words, it is the ways we react to pressures and demands, not just the pressures themselves, which affect our experience.

Stress and Job Performance

Stress has become a part of one's life and has assumed enormous proportions. Stress is a condition of strain that has a direct bearing on emotions, thought process and physical conditions of a person. Stress is anything that places a demand on us physically, mentally, or emotionally. It makes us change the normal way we like. Most of us think of stress as a crisis, but not all stress is bad. Without stress (astress), life would be boring. There would be no growth and no change.

Stress has both negative and positive consequences. Eustress is positive stress, laying emphasis on meeting challenges accompanied by achievement. It is beneficial as it encourages going ahead against hindrances. Excessive amount of stress leads to distress and is harmful in nature and cause loss of feelings, helplessness, desperation, and disappointment. Conditions that cause stress are termed as stressors.

Stress and job performance go together. It can be helpful or harmful depending upon the level of it. Increase in stress enhances job performance as it encourages the workers to meet the job requirements and face challenges. When stress reaches saturation point it exhibits day-to-day performance capability of an individual. At the point additional stress does not bring about any improvement, on the other hand it starts creating hindrances. If stress continues for a longer period, the employee's behaviour undergoes a change. She/he is unable to take decisions, develops erratic behaviour and is unable to cope with the situation. This leads to burnout condition and the job performance is hampered.

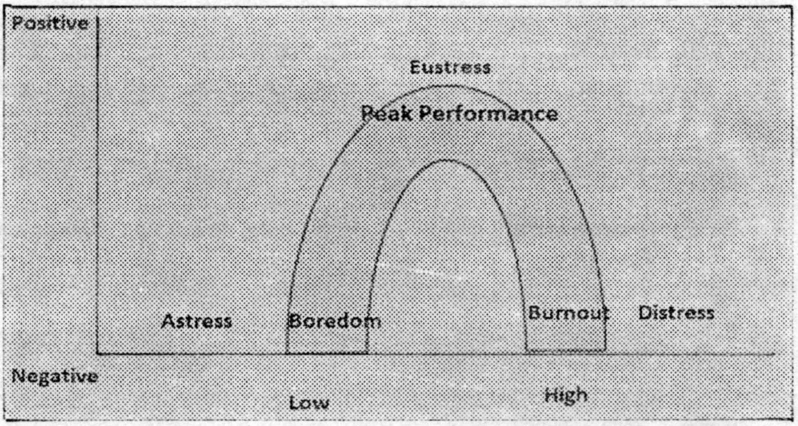

Fig.10.1. Stress and Job Performance

Occupational stress is not only damaging to individuals but to organisations as well, through poor work performance, damaged personal relations, absence due to ill health, increased staff turnover, and so on. Some people thrive on stressful situations while others are overwhelmed.

Stress Factors

The workplace had become a high stress environment cutting across many organisations. Employees do experience high level of stress due to various factors such as high workload, tight deadlines, high targets, type of work, lack of job satisfaction, long working hours, pressure to perform, etc. Interpersonal conflicts at the workplace, such as superior-subordinate relationships and relationships with peers, are also a source of stress.

Thus, stress occurs when people become mentally, emotionally and/or physically distressed, or disturbed, as a result of the ways a person perceives and reacts to pressures and demands. Stress can be experienced because of work, (e.g., a feeling of carrying an excessive load, or of not having the requisite skills to undertake a task or their role in general); relationships, (e.g., bullying, harassment); when people perceive situations to be violating important values, (e.g., 'fairness') or impeding the achievement of important goals through conflicting pressures from within and outside of work, (e.g., work/home interface) or because of a life crisis such as bereavement, divorce,etc.

The severity of a person's stress is influenced by many things including the mismatch people see between the demands they feel are being made of them at a particular time, their view of their ability to respond to them satisfactorily and the possible consequences of a failure to do so. The cumulative impact of different pressures and demands over the longer-term can be particularly damaging to psychological and physical health.

Stress is a complex and sensitive issue. Dr. Sanjay Bhattacharya (2010) has broadly classified stress factors as environmental and personal. Life is tough and getting tougher by the day. The stress of daily living, especially as the pressure to excel mounts, impacts everyone, not just on the work front but in every single area of an individual's life. In today's world of doing more with less, employees find themselves with more work, fewer resources, and less time. With a tight deadlines and a competitive work environment only the best performers are guaranteed continued employment.

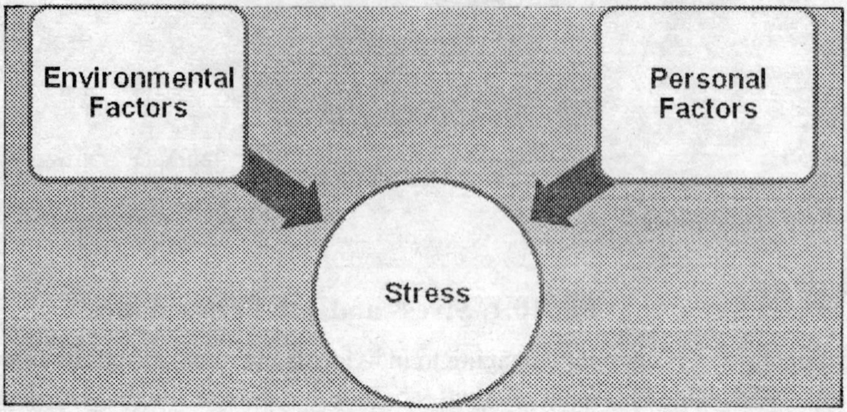

Fig.10.2. Stress Factors

All of these factors add up to a very stressful work environment. Ultimately employees take work home and worry about missing deadlines or performing inadequately and end up working longer hours.

Stress can be caused by many things in life, pressures from work, the family, social commitments and other everyday events. The word stress is derived from the Latin term 'Stringers' which means 'to draw tight'. Some define stress as the non-specific response of the body to any demands made on it. Stress is our physical, mental, and emotional response to the various demands, changes, and events in our life. It is an internal phenomenon and a mental attitude.

1. Environmental Factors – are the widespread provision which surrounds individuals and has bearing towards their stress. These factors may be economic worries, political reservations, organisational structure, organisational policies, and leadership style.

- **(i) Economic Worries:** The job insecurity may tend to create economic worries. Losing a job can be an occasion for stress. Because individuals are individual humans, they also share common physical risks. Someone who loses a job may be concerned, but their confidence in their ability to obtain another quickly and easily can result in only minor stress.
- **(ii) Political Reservations:** The political uncertainties creates adverse situations in the setting causing environmental pressures and demands which they have to deal with both within and outside of work.
- **(iii) Organisational Structure:** More over the organisational structure at times comes as a barrier in terms of expression and communication, causing role conflict and role ambiguity leading to stressful environment for the person.
- **(iv) Organisational Policies:** At times unfavourable organisational policies or inability to cope up with the organisational policies may also cause stress for individuals.

(v) **Leadership Style:** Some may find difficulty to acknowledge the manner of leadership of the superior due to their ineffectual leadership style causing mental, emotional and/or physically distress, or disturbance to the subordinates, as a result of the way they perceive and react to environmental pressures and demands in work.

2. **Personal factors** – Are lack of individual's capacity to overcome their problems for meeting the expectations for the future. These factors may be family problems, interpersonal relationship, role demands, and coping capacity.

(i) **Family Problems:** Family problems like ending a close relationship – whether with a friend, a partner, or a valued family member, discovering a health problem, life crisis such as bereavement, divorce, etc., can be stressful. Reactions vary because individuals are unique. They interpret their experiences differently. Also, some people react to these facts very differently than others. While some will be anxious, others will be stoic.

(ii) **Interpersonal Relationship:** Lack of good interpersonal relationships among the people creates unhealthy climate within the organisation. Unjust treatment like bullying, harassment, etc., at work by an unreasonable supervisor, disrespect by others or just simple indifference to justice will cause stress for nearly anyone when they perceive situations to be violating important values like fairness or impeding the achievement of important goals.

(iii) **Role Demands:** Stress can also be experienced because of work pressure like a feeling of carrying an excessive load, or of not having the requisite skills to undertake a task or their role in general where a person is not able meet the role demands.

(iv) **Coping Capacity:** One of the major factors is the attitude of the person in the given situation that determines the coping capacity of a person. If you feel you can overcome serious hurdles quickly or without major loss, you will evaluate fewer external events as a cause for stress. When you do experience it, the degree of stress will be less. The severity of a person's stress is influenced by many things including the mismatch people see between the demands they feel are being made of them at a particular time, their view of their ability to respond to them satisfactorily and the possible consequences of a failure to do so.

Consequences of Stress

In some cases, stress motivates and encourages us to complete a task we find difficult so that we can take pride in ourselves and what we achieve.

Hans Selye was one of the founding fathers of stress research. His view in 1956, which holds true today also, was that stress is not necessarily something bad it all depends on how one takes it. In an ideal world, there should be just enough stress to keep employees working to their full potential, but not enough to cause overwhelm or excessive anxiety. Too much or too little stress is where we run into problems. Stress symptoms begin to manifest themselves when an individual perceive or feel that life demands are exceeding their ability to deal with them. When stress begins to take its toll, they may experience both physical and psychological effects.

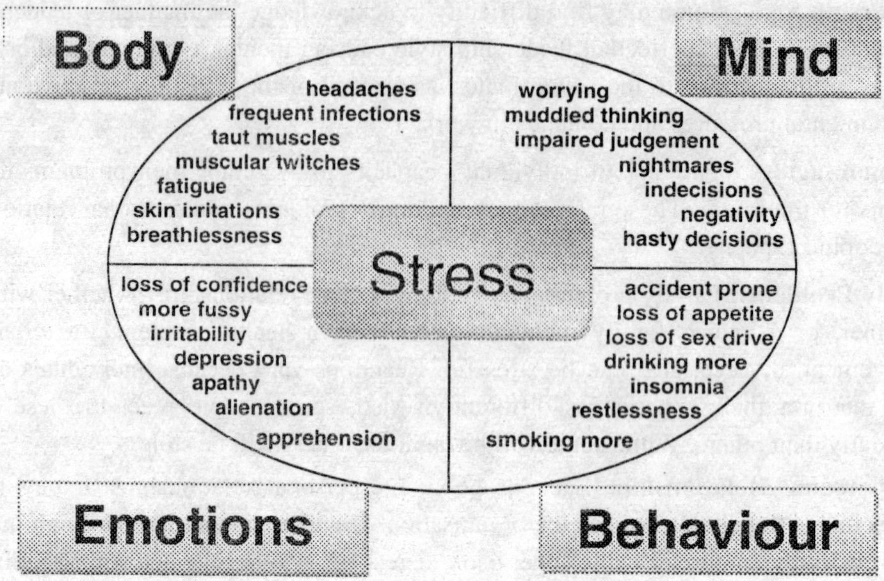

Fig.10.3. Stress Symptoms

Experts believed that the dysfunctional aspects of stress could directly impact an organisation's performance and also affect the well-being of its employees. Stress at the workplace is linked to absenteeism, higher attrition, and decreased productivity. Stress led to fatigue, irritability, poor communication, and quality problems/errors. High stress levels also affected the morale and motivation of the employees. Prolonged exposure to stress without effective coping mechanisms could lead to a host of physical and mental problems. For instance, stress could lead to stress-induced gastrointestinal problems, irritable bowel syndrome, acidity, acid reflux, insomnia, depression, heart-disease, etc. Organisations are gearing up to provide employees with a stress-free healthy environment and have started implementing various unconventional methods to decrease stress at the workplace.

Some individuals will recognise that their health is affected and will seek help others will not recognise or acknowledge that they are stressed although it may be apparent to their manager and work colleagues. Although in itself, stress is not an illness, there is evidence that stress can lead to mental and physical ill health. The cumulative impact of different pressures and demands over the longer-term can be particularly damaging to psychological and physical health.

The negative effect of stress may be physiological as well as psychological symptoms like chronic headache, hypertension, anxiety, depression, etc. Therefore, the stressed individuals have to be helped to relate themselves to others and experience growth opportunities in accordance with their needs and opportunities to cope up with these personal and environmental factors for organisational development.

Organisational Development and Stress Management

Organisational Development (OD) is the process through which an organisation develops the internal capacity to most efficiently and effectively provide its mission work and to sustain itself over the long-term. This definition highlights the explicit connection between organisational development work and the achievement of organisational mission. This connection is the rationale for doing OD work. If organisational development is to achieve the objective of improving organisational effectiveness, it is essential that organisation adopt a proactive and preventive approach to stress management.

Stress management is the technique of coping up with the perceived threat due to excessive pressures and demands placed upon one's mental, physical and emotional well-being, leading to adverse reaction.

Managing an over worked and stressed human resource have become a challenging and ever difficult task for today's managers. With a view to utilise the available human resource thus minimising costs and maximising profits, today both managers and their subordinates have to co-operate with work related stress. This stress if it goes to certain extent without being controlled can affect the person's family/social life, health, performance, etc., and changes the employee's whole attitude towards work – frustrating, de-motivating, and frightening him/her which in the long run damages both the organisation and the employee.

Organisational Stress Management Strategies

In addition to conducting stress management workshops, organisations also conduct off-site picnics, retreats, games, and interdepartmental competitions. Some companies also use a system of mentors and promote open communication to improve interactions and camaraderie at the workplace. Experts felt that organisations were resorting to creative methods to address the issue of stress at the workplace, but more action is required on this front, both in terms of assessment of the situation and implementation of concrete steps to tackle the problem.

According to Dr. Sanjay Bhattacharya, following strategies may be adopted for dealing with organisational stress:

1. Participative Decision Making Approach
2. Awareness and Management Approach
3. Employees Support Approach
4. Employee-Centred Commitment Approach.

Fig.10.4. Organisational Stress Management Strategies

1. Participative Decision Making Approach (PDMA)

By giving the employees a voice in decisions that directly affect their job performances, management can increase employee control and reduce this role stress. The use of common goals can reduce stress as well as provide motivation. Specific goals set in collaboration with staffs that are perceived as attainable clarify performance expectations. Additionally, goal feedback reduces uncertainties as to actual job performance. The result is less employee frustration, role ambiguity, and stress.

The organisation may:

- Promote a culture of consultation, participation, and open communication throughout the organisation.
- Develop a check list for managers to help identify tasks or structures which may create stress.
- Develop a program to promote good management, team-building, and goal setting skills for those with management and supervisory responsibilities.

2. Awareness and Management Approach (AMA)

The workshops/programs focusing on awareness, consequences, and right coping mechanism of stress helps to manage the stressful environment, effectively.

The organisation may:

- Raise the awareness of managers and staff about stress and its causes.

- Make courses available for all staff, on stress awareness and management so that they are better able to handle pressures they may encounter, and they are able to recognise stress when it occurs in themselves and others.
- Manage pressures which may affect employees by anticipating likely problems and taking actions to reduce the effects on them.
- Provide a range of stress management courses including sessions on time management, assertiveness, and dealing with difficult situations.

3. Employees Support Approach (ESA)

There is increasing evidence that social support – that is, collegial relationships with coworkers or supervisors can buffer the impact of stress.

The organisation may:

- Identify internal and external sources of assistance for employees with stress.
- Assist and advise employees who are stressed.
- Provide guidance for managers regarding modification of work for employees who are stressed, e.g., job redesign, reviewing work responsibilities, return to work arrangements after sickness, absence, etc.

4. Employee-Centred Commitment Approach (ECCA)

There is a need of having interaction of friends, families, or work colleagues for outlet of stress when stress levels become excessive. Therefore, expanding social support network, like retreats, celebrations, social get-togethers, etc., on regular intervals, can be a means for tension reduction and it may be a part of employee-centred commitment on part of the organisation.

The organisation may be committed to:

- Monitor levels of occurrence of stress and of sickness absence associated with stress.
- Develop a reporting procedure to provide feedback from managers and employees, occupational health, HR and staff development officials on effectiveness of the policy.
- Provide opportunities for employees to maintain and promote their health and well-being.

Organisational Development Intervention Stress Management (ODISM) – Model

Stress is what individuals experience when they feel they have difficulty coping with the pressures and demands placed upon them. Some pressures at work are inevitable. A total elimination of pressure is neither possible nor desirable but is important that any such pressure does not become work related stress. Pressures can arise from an individual's personal life as well as from work and people vary in their capacity and ability to cope with different types of pressure. Some individuals will recognise that their health is affected and will seek help and support; others will not recognise or acknowledge that they are stressed although it may be apparent to their manager and work colleagues.

Although in itself, stress is not an illness, there is evidence that stress can lead to mental and physical ill health.

The organisations need to be committed to implementing a stress management policy for all employees throughout the organisation. This includes improving the organisational environment through effective and sensitive management; enabling individuals to cope successfully with the demands and pressures of work, and providing support for employees whose health and well-being are affected by stress.

The term 'Organisational Development' is often used interchangeably with organisational effectiveness, especially when used as the name of a department or a part of the human resources function within an organisation. Organisational development is a growing field that is responsive to many new approaches including 'Positive Adult Development'.

The organisations need to develop educational strategy which focus on the whole culture of the organisation in order to bring about a planned change and stress management is one of the organisational development intervention strategies to build a cultural change. Stress and job performance go together. OD intervention technique helps to face challenges to meet the job requirements.

Organisational development intervention stress management model developed by Dr. Sanjay Bhattacharya (2010), provides a strategic model for the management of the organisation concerned with the negative effects, stress can have both on organisational performance and the quality of life of individuals at work.

OD involves organisational reflection, system improvement, planning, and self-analysis. If organisational development is to achieve the objective of improving organisational effectiveness, it is essential that companies adopt a proactive and preventive approach to stress management. Such an approach would reduce the costs of stress which result directly from organisational development and, additionally, the costs of previously existing stress factors such as high labour turnover, absenteeism, and reduce productivity.

Definition of Organisational Stress Management

'Organisational stress management is a method through which individuals are helped in the organisation to guide their interactions so that they may relate themselves to others and experience growth opportunities in accordance with their needs and opportunities to cope up with the personal and environmental stress factors to the end of organisational development'.

Sanjay Bhattacharya, Ph.D.

Analysis of Definition

1. Organisational stress management is a method – **made up of:** knowledge or understanding of techniques/skills/strategies/approaches, etc.
2. Through which individuals – **including:** individuals in the organisational setting.

3. Are helped in the organisation to guide their interactions – **through:** relationship based on acceptance, individualisation, helping to determine objectives, stimulation, and guidance of organisational process, and capacity building.
4. So that they may relate themselves to others and experience growth opportunities in accordance with their needs and opportunities to cope up with the personal and environmental stress factors – **such as:** participation, belongingness, determination, enabling to take responsibilities, achievement, self-motivation, adjustment with others.
5. To the end of organisational development – **objectives like:** change in behaviour of individuals and organisation in terms of democratic goals of cultural building.

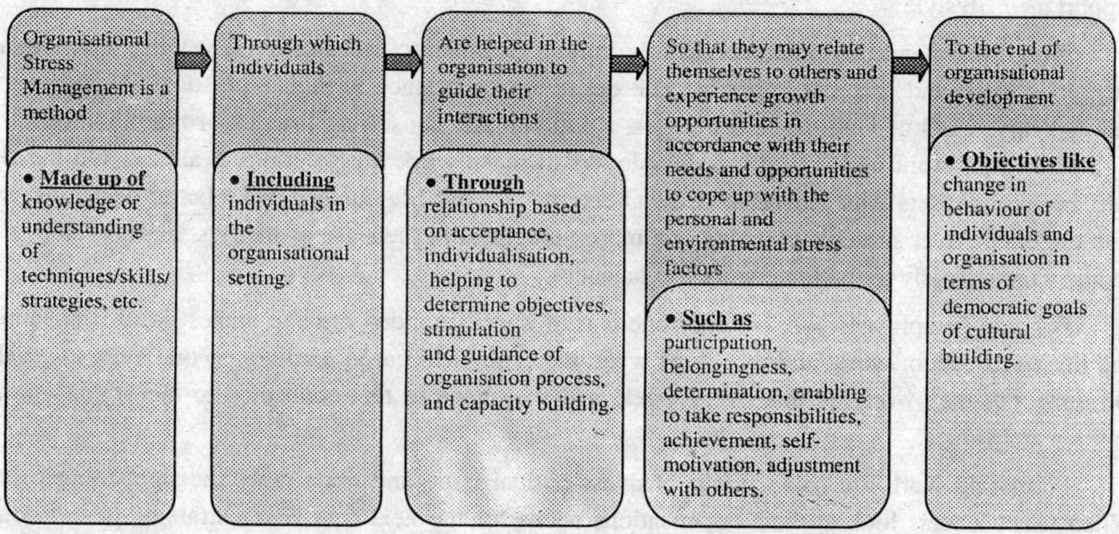

Fig.10.5. Organisational Development Intervention Stress Management (ODISM) Model – by *Sanjay Bhattacharya (2010)*

Organisational development, according to Richard Beckhard, is a planned organization – wide effort, managed from the top, to increase organisational effectiveness and health, through interventions in the organisation's 'processes', using behavioural science knowledge. According to Warren Bennis, organisational development is a complex strategy intended to change the beliefs, attitudes, values, and structure of organisations so that they can better adapt to new technologies, markets, and challenges. Warner Burke emphasises that OD is not just 'anything done to better an organisation' it is a particular kind of change process designed to bring about a particular kind of end result. Organisations which develop this philosophy, through the adoption of the practical action model, will be able to reduce the cost of stress substantially.

Work Life Balance

If an organisation wants to be positioned to meet its customers' needs and have talent in the right position for future growth, it must develop an inclusive culture with tolerant, accepting and encouraging attitudes around work life balance.

Employees have high expectations for work and life, and as they enter the workforce, employers must evolve, using tools such as social media and work life programs to recruit, manage, motivate and retain these workforce additions. Work life balance is not a new idea. Most employees require their work to have meaning and enjoyment. They want to believe in the companies they work for, rather than attach significance to a job as a way to define their lives; their jobs are usually just a means to support their lifestyle.

Work life balance is about successfully joining two distinct sides of ourselves in a harmonious way. It is work and life, not either/or. The definition of balance is highly personal. According to Elliott-Yeary, CEO of Optimance Strategies, a national HR consulting firm, is of the opinion that – high performers want and expect their employers to make work life solutions available. On the flip side, business leaders who pursue their own versions of work life balance make better decisions, can be more effective at strategic planning and more thoughtful in their use of metrics. Further, steps can be taken immediately to facilitate work life balance.

For many employees, work is only one part of a well-rounded life and makes significant family and life sacrifices for work, and they don't want that. They will put in a 60-hour work week to get the job done, but they won't do that every week, and they have to feel connected to the organisation's mission and values.

Promoting work-life balance is a business-critical issue and not simply the right thing to do. When talent leaders look at their organisations needs for the next five years, strategic plans should contain a list of the necessary skills for each critical role, and sustainable business results depend on attracting and retaining top talent. There are lots of good reasons to offer the workforce work life flexibility. For instance, it builds morale as well as helps retention and recruitment. According to the study – 'When the demands of personal and family life come up against rigidity, workers often feel compelled to work around these formal bounds, thus allowing them opportunities to attend to emergencies, crises and unexpected family and personal matters'.

Many employees fundamentally feel it is important to hurry up and accomplish things, enjoy experiences and relish life, because tomorrow is uncertain. Savvy leaders know that leveraging work life programs increases engagement, and engaged employees are more creative, productive, motivated and happy. This leads to longer tenure, which results in lower turnover and increased profits. Talent leaders will have to ask employees, what they need to be fully engaged.

Employees who are asked what they want from their jobs will offer a list of things: meaning, desire for a role that allows them to make a difference or that provides challenging projects and duties, promotes flexibility and of course, balance with respect to work life options. Companies that offer options to meet employees' work life balance can reap significant return on investment such as – fewer attendance problems, increased loyalty, reduced turnover, less time to fill open positions, fewer on-the-job accidents, minimise organisational stress, etc. What employees may not say but definitely expect is that they want to like the people they work with – including their boss – and they want to feel appreciated.

According to Resultance Inc. a generational consulting firm, there are several simple, actionable steps talent leaders can take to engage and motivate employees using the ROCK STAR acronym:

1. Reachable – Goals should fit the role and job description and allow the employee to be challenged.
2. Opportunity – Offer chances to work on new projects, or in new divisions or groups.
3. Challenging – Challenge employees' skills and abilities to enable them to reach new levels within the company.
4. Knowledge – Offer opportunities to be mentored.
5. Skills – On a regular basis assess the skills required for a job and determine what training is required to develop additional skills and abilities.
6. Tasks – What new tasks can be given to employees who want to increase their learning?
7. Acknowledgement – When employees go above and beyond, they want to be acknowledged and respected for their contributions.
8. Relevant – Work should be relevant and congruent to the company's mission and values.

If organisations offer employees opportunities to increase their level of responsibility, growth and development, recognition for achievement, and most of all balance, they will attract top talent, which will improve the bottom line. Talent leaders who have this awareness will retain and capitalise on a highly effective workforce by embracing workplace balance and avoid any organisational stress.

HR has evolved into a strategic function responsible as a key differentiator for corporate growth and well-being. Present day HR focuses on organisations attention to truly managing the human capital to develop and manage its productivity in sync with the corporate goals. A new kind of HR professional is emerging to manage this transformed function in line with organisational strategy and business model.

Review Discussions

1. Explain stress. What are its consequences?
2. What are various factors of stress?
3. What do you understand by organisational stress management?
4. Describe various organisational stress management strategies.
5. Explain Sanjay Bhattacharya's Organisational Development Intervention Stress Management model.
6. Explain work life balance.

♣♣♣♣♣♣

CHAPTER 11
LEARNING ORGANISATION

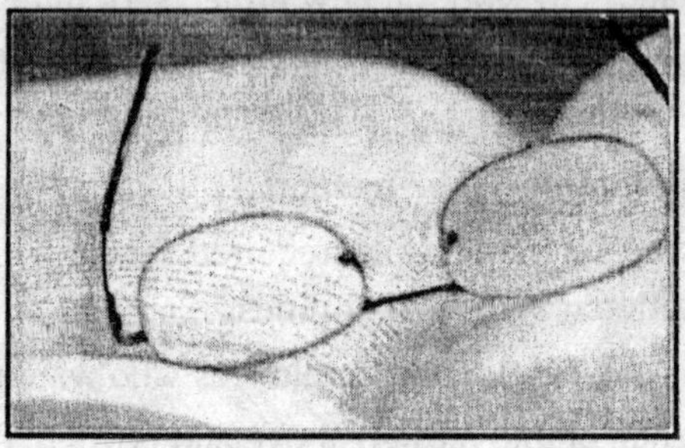

After studying this chapter, you should be able to:

- Comprehend learning organisation.
- Recognise the need of learning organisation.
- Discern to create a learning organisation.
- Be acquainted with the benefits of learning organisation.
- Be familiar with the levels of learning.
- Be aware of learning models.
- Be familiar with terms of organisational learning and learning organisation.
- Make out obstacles of learning organisation.

Introduction

To most learning professionals, the fact that individuals learn differently is seen as a challenge. However, it is possible for learning organisations not only to engage workers in the various mediums they prefer but also to leverage different learning styles for competitive advantage, all while maintaining cost-effective design and delivery.

Learning executives today face growing pressure to deliver effective learning experiences cost-effectively. If you are trying to develop a rapid, factory approach to learning delivery, the intricacies of individual learning styles are likely to be overlooked or tabled for a later day. Yet think for a moment of the hidden business costs when learning departments design courses without sufficient attention to the manner in which their employees as individuals optimally learn. Research suggests that much of what learning departments develop today washes over many employees like rain on a waterproof jacket. In other words, a great deal of corporate learning is either a waste of money or delivering only a small portion of the potential return on investment.

What is Learning?

Learning is the acquisition and development of memories and behaviours, including skills, knowledge, understanding, values, and wisdom. It is the product of experience and the goal of education.

What is Organisation?

An organisation is a social arrangement which pursues collective goals that controls its own performance, and has a boundary separating it from its environment, e.g., company, corporation, firm, enterprise, authority or institution, or part or combination thereof, whether incorporated or not, public or private.

Definition of Learning Organisation

Organisations that learn and encourage learning among its people promote exchange of information between employees, hence creating a more knowledgeable workforce. This produces a very flexible organisation where people will accept and adapt to new ideas and changes through a shared vision.

'A learning organisation is one in which people at all levels (individually and collectively), are continually increasing their capacity to produce results they really care about.'

Background

The learning organisation is a concept that is becoming an increasingly widespread philosophy in modern companies, from the largest multinationals to the smallest ventures. What is achieved by this philosophy depends considerably on one's interpretation of it and commitment to it.

The importance of learning was put forward by King Solomon as – 'Instruct a wise man and he will be wiser still; teach a righteous man and he will add to his learning'. Proverbs 9: 9 - Bible.

Chinese Philosopher, Confucius (551-479 BC) believed that everyone should benefit from learning.

'Without learning, the wise become foolish; by learning, the foolish become wise.'

'Learn as if you could never have enough of learning, as if you might miss something.'

Need of Learning Organisation

An organisation that performs badly is easily recognisable. It can be spotted when:

1. The employees seem unmotivated or uninterested in their work.
2. The workforce lacks the skill and knowledge to adjust to new jobs.
3. There is no one to come up with ideas.
4. The workforce simply follows orders.
5. The teams argue constantly and lack real productivity.
6. The teams lack communication between each other.

If any of these points sound familiar, there is a need of a learning organisation.

Creating a Learning Organisation

Learning is the key competency required by any organisation that wants to survive and thrive in the knowledge economy. Market championships keep asking learning questions, keep learning how to do things better, and keep spreading that knowledge throughout their organisation. Learning provides the catalyst and the intellectual resource to create a sustainable competitive advantage. Learning organisations obtain competitive advantage from continuous learning, both individual and collective. In organisations with a well established knowledge management system, learning by the people within an organisation becomes learning by the organisation itself.

A learning and development initiative facilitate real change in a workforce and requires deliberate follow-up and follow-through. Important aspects of creating a learning organisation are discussed as follows:

1. The Building Blocks
2. Implementation of Strategies
3. The Golden Rules
4. People Behaviour

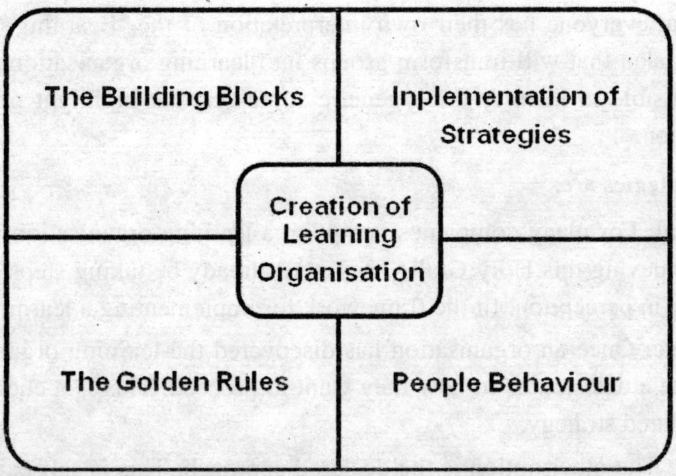

Fig.11.1. Creating a Learning Organisation

1. The Building Blocks

Before a learning organisation can be implemented, a sole foundation can be made by taking into account the following:

(i) Awareness: Organisation must be aware that learning is necessary before they can develop into a learning organisation. This must be take place at all levels, not just the management level.

(ii) Environment: Centralised, mechanistic structures do not create a good environment. Individuals do not have a comprehensive picture of the whole organisation and its goals. This causes political and narrow systems to be set up which stifle the learning process.

(iii) Leadership: Leaders should foster the systems thinking concept and encourage learning to help both the individual and organisation in learning. It is the leader's responsibility to help restructure the individual views of team-members.

(iv) Empowerment: The focus of control shifts from managers to workers. This is where the term empowerment is introduced. The workers become responsible for their actions; but the managers do not lose their involvement. They still need to encourage, enthuse and coordinate the workers.

(v) Learning: Organisations can learn to achieve these aims in learning labs. These are small-scale models of real-life settings where management teams learn how to learn together through simulation games. They need to find out what failure is like so that they can learn from their mistakes in the future.

2. Implementation of Strategies

Any organisation that wants to implement a learning organisation philosophy requires an overall strategy with clear, well defined goals. Once these have been established, the tools needed to facilitate the strategy must be identified.

It is clear that everyone has their own interpretation of the 'Learning Organisation' idea, so to produce an action plan that will transform groups into learning organisations might seem impossible. However, it is possible to identify three generic strategies that highlight possible routes to develop learning organisation.

The three strategies are:

(i) **Accidental:** For many companies, adopting a learning organisation philosophy is the second step to achieving this Holy Grail. They may already be taking steps to achieve their business goals that, in perception, fit the framework for implementing a learning organisation.

(ii) **Subversive:** Once an organisation has discovered the learning organisation philosophy, they must make a decision as to how they want to proceed. This is a choice between a subversive and a declared strategy.

(iii) **Declared:** The other option is the declared approach. This is self-explanatory. The principles of learning organisations are adopted as part of the company ethos, become company 'speak' and are manifest openly in all company initiatives.

3. The Golden Rules

The golden rules of learning organisation are as follows:

(i) Thrive on Change

This includes:

- Not to be scared
- Learning organisations feed on change
- Go all the way (no half-way house)
- Committed and focused
- Know objectives and plan

(ii) Encourage Experimentation

It is to be assumed that:

- Experimentation is a necessary risk
- Individual input is to be rewarded
- People need to be encouraged throughout the organisation

(iii) Communicate Success and Failure

This is to be done through:

- Reviews.
- Assessments (continuously by others as well as by self).

(iv) Facilitate learning from the Surrounding Environment

It is done by:

- Finding internal and external source of information.
- Learning from experience of other organisations (open your eyes).
- Above all discussing customer/stakeholder needs.

(v) Facilitate Learning from Employees

This may be through:

- Encouraging participation and experimentation.
- Investing in training multi-skilling (getting most from employees) and building morale.
- Empowering responsibility.
- Removal of hierarchy.

(vi) Reward Learning

This is needed because:

- Everybody wants their work to be appreciated to boost their morale.
- Everybody wants to be acknowledges when they exceed the set benchmarks for performance appraisal.

(vii) A Proper Selfishness

This is setting of:

- Well- defined and clear goals and objectives.
- Hints on clarifying objectives.

(viii) A Sense of Caring

This includes:

- Care for the individual.
- Finding ways of implementing this care.

4. People Behaviour

In learning organisation there are some behaviours that have to be encouraged and some behaviours that have to be discouraged.

Behaviour to Encourage

There are five disciplines (As described by Peter Senge) which are essential to a learning organisation and should be encouraged at all times. These are:

- Team Learning
- Shared Visions
- Mental Models

- Personal Mastery
- Systems Thinking

Behaviour to Discourage

An organisation which is not a learning one also displays behaviours however these should definitely not be encouraged. Rosabeth Moss Kantar studied a range of large American corporations and came up with rules for stifling initiative:

- Regard any new idea from below with suspicion because it is new and because it is from below.
- Make decisions to reorganise or change policies in secret and spring them on people unexpectedly (that also keeps people on their toes).

Benefits of Learning Organisation

The goal of learning organisation is to create a learning environment in which proven interactive methods are used that ensure learning is not only retained but achieved individually based on each participant' s learning style. The learning organisation works well because individuals, group, and the organisation as a whole tend to be competent and successful. Promoting a learning organisational culture is essential to challenges faced by all agencies discussed as follows-

1. The people develop: Learning can be delivered with a better return on investment by understanding the learning styles of especially critical workforces within any organisation. People's learning styles are not fixed for all time, and they may evolve as we do. They are also teachable. One can encourage the styles needed to succeed by developing learning programs or assigning people to tasks that require them to develop those styles. The people of a learning organisation develop because:

- Motivation level becomes high.
- The workforce become more flexible
- People are more creative
- Social interaction is improved.

2. Teams and group work well: A good interface can be created, allowing people to seek experiences almost spontaneously based on their own preference. This helps in:

- Knowledge sharing.
- Interdependency.

3. The organisation benefits: The concept of learning and thinking styles comes up often in our discussions of how we effectively communicate with our people. An awareness that people learn and think in different ways can be used to create more effective corporate communications for the benefit of the organisation. This can be observed by:

- Break down of traditional communication barriers.
- Improved stakeholder relations.

- Better information resources.
- Innovation and creativity.

Levels of Learning

A learning organisation involves the development of higher levels of knowledge and skill. A four level learning model of learning involves:

Level 1: Learning facts, knowledge, processes and procedures. Applies to known situation where changes are minor.

Level 2: Learning new job skills that are transferable to another situation. Applies to new situations where existing responses need to be changed. Bringing in outside expertise is a useful tool here.

Level 3: Learning to adapt. Applies to more dynamic situations where the solutions need developing. Experimentation and deriving lessons from success and failure is the mode of learning here.

Level 4: Learning to learn. It is about innovation and creativity; designing the future rather than merely adapting to it. This is where assumptions are challenged and knowledge is reframed.

Further more this learning concept can be applied at three levels – to the learning of individuals, of teams, and of organisations. Organisations that achieve learning to Level 4 will 'reinvent not just their organisation but their industry'.

Learning Models

The philosophy underpinning the learning organisation concept, is that learning is an essential ingredients if organisations are to survive; that learning at operational, policy, and strategic levels needs to be conscious, continuous, and integrated; and that management is responsible for creating an emotional climate in which all staff can learn continuously. Some of the important learning models are discussed as follows:

1. M. Pedler al Model

According to Pedler, 'Change should not happen just for the sake of change, but should be well thought out'. He stresses learning as a simplification and symbolic rather than concrete. It starts with strategy, ends with creation of learning opportunities and bubbling.

The learning company has 11 characteristics as mentioned below:

1. Adopt a learning approach to strategy.
2. Participative policymaking.
3. Informating (Information Systems).
4. Formative accounting valuing, self-responsibility, appraisal, targeting, resourcing, and review.
5. Internal exchange (client-server relationships).
6. Reward flexibility.

7. Roles and flexible, matrix structures.
8. Boundary workers as intelligence agents.
9. Company-to-company learning.
10. Learning climate.
11. Self-development opportunities for all.

2. Kolb Experiential Learning Cycle

A four-stage cyclical theory of learning originated by David A. Kolb known as Kolb's experiential learning theory is a holistic perspective that combines experience, perception, cognition, and behaviour.

Key terms in this learning model are: Learning cycles, learning styles, concrete experience, reflective observation, abstract conceptualisation, active experimentation.

Building upon earlier work by John Dewey and Kurt Levin, American educational theorist David A. Kolb believes 'learning is the process whereby knowledge is created through the transformation of experience' (1984, p. 38). The theory presents a cyclical model of learning, consisting of four stages shown below. One may begin at any stage, but must follow each other in the sequence:

- Concrete experience (or 'DO')
- Reflective observation (or 'OBSERVE')
- Abstract conceptualisation (or 'THINK')
- Active experimentation (or 'PLAN')

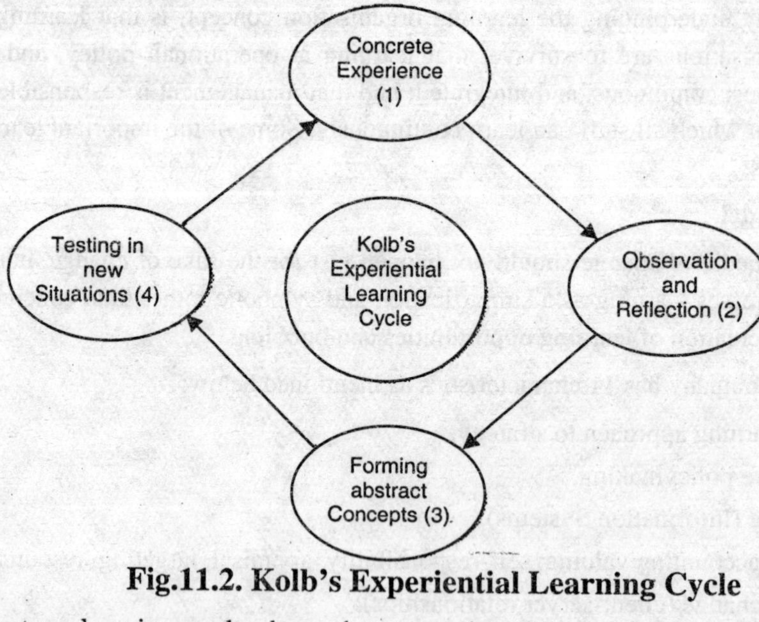

Fig.11.2. Kolb's Experiential Learning Cycle

Kolb's four-stage learning cycle shows how experience is translated through reflection into concepts, which in turn are used as guides for active experimentation and the choice of new experiences. The first stage, concrete experience (CE), is where the learner actively experiences an activity such as a lab session or field work. The second stage, reflective observation (RO), is when the learner consciously reflects back on that experience. The third stage, abstract conceptualisation (AC), is where the learner attempts to conceptualise a theory or model of what is observed. The fourth stage, active experimentation (AE), is where the learner is trying to plan how to test a model or theory or plan for a forthcoming experience.

Kolb identified four learning styles which correspond to these stages. The styles highlight conditions under which learners learn better. These styles are:

- Assimilators, who learn better when presented with sound logical theories to consider
- Convergers, who learn better when provided with practical applications of concepts and theories
- Accommodators, who learn better when provided with 'hands-on' experiences
- Divergers, who learn better when allowed to observe and collect a wide range of information.

3. Peter Senge's Five Disciplines Model

There are five disciplines (As described by Peter Senge) which are essential to a learning organisation and should be encouraged at all times.

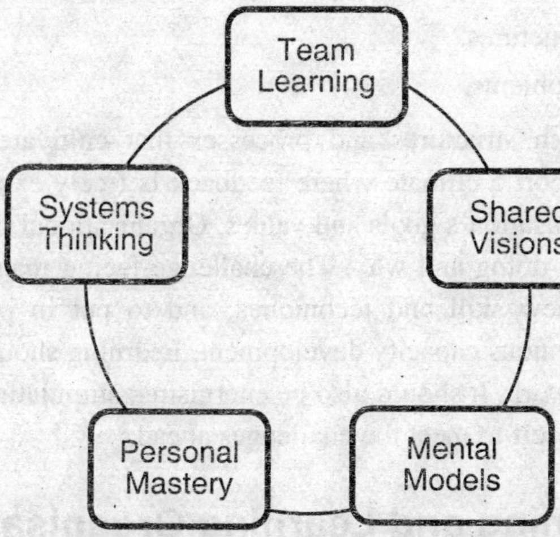

Fig.11.3. Peter Senge's Five Disciplines

Five Disciplines are expanded as follows:

(i) Team Learning

Through:

- Dialogue, discussion, and group relationships.
- Accelerating organisational learning through Synergy 2+2=5

(ii) Shared Vision

Through:

- Use instincts, intuition by sharing personal vision.
- Pictures of the future.

(iii) Mental Models

Through:

- Changing ingrained assumptions about influencing factors.

(iv) Personal Mastery

Through:

- Personal competence and vision.
- Developing patience to look at reality objectively.

(v) Systems Thinking

Through:

- Mind shift and understanding change processes.
- 'Feedback' to reinforce/counteract action.
- Recognise recurring structures.
- Remove root causes/problems.

Organisations can establish structures and processes that cultivate continuous learning. For example, management can support a climate where feedback is freely exchanged. Employees have a clear, shared vision of the organisation's goals and values. Organisational members get time to inquire and reflect about what they are doing and why. The challenge facing managers today is to make the effort needed to learn some new skill and techniques, and to put in processes that engage their workforce in programs of continuous capacity development. Learning should be integrated into doing, as part and parcel of everyday work. It should also be energising, stimulating, and fun, getting the best out of everybody, including oneself to meet the challenges ahead.

Organisational Learning and Learning Organisation

Organisational learning is concerned with how learning is concerned with how learning takes place in organisations. It focuses on collective learning but takes into account the proposition that organisations do not perform actions that produce the learning it is individual members of the organisation who behave in ways that lead to it, although organisations can create conditions which facilitate such learning. Organisational learning is concerned with the development of new knowledge or insights that have the potential to influence behaviour. It takes place within the wide institutional context of interorganisational relationships and refers broadly to an organisation's acquisition of understanding, know-how, techniques, and practices of any kind and by any means. Organisational learning examines how in this context individual and team learning can be translated into an organisational resource and is therefore linked to processes of knowledge management. Organisational learning could be defined as a process of coordinated systems change, with mechanisms built in for individuals and group to access, build and use organisational memory, structure, and culture to develop long-term organisational capacity. Organisational learning outcomes contribute to the development of a firm's resource based capability. This is in accordance with one of the basic principles of human resource management, namely that it is necessary to invest in people in order to develop the intellectual capital required by the organisation and thus increase its stock of knowledge and skills. Human capital theory indicates that – 'The knowledge and skills employees have which comes from education and training, including the training that experience brings generate productive capital'. It is equally important that the organisational learning focus should be on developing 'organisational capability'. This means paying attention to the intricate and often unnoticed or hidden learning that takes place and influences what occurs within the organisation. 'Hidden learning' is acquired and developed in the normal course of work by people acting as individuals and importantly as groups.

The essence of organisational learning is the organisation's ability to use the amazing mental capacity of all its members to create the kind of processes that will improve its own – Nancy Dixon, (1994). The learning organisation is often associated with that of organisational learning, has been defined as one 'that is able to discover what is effective by reframing its own experiences and learning from that process'. It is organisation where people continually expand their capacity to create the results they truly desire, where new and expansive patterns of thinking are nurtured, where collective aspiration is set free, and where people are continually learning to learn together.

Obstacles of Learning Organisation

There are some of the most common obstacles to becoming learning organisation as follows:

1. Operational/firefighting preoccupation – not creating time to sit back and think strategically.
2. To focused on systems and process (e.g., ISO 9000) to exclusion of other factors (bureaucratic vs. thinking).
3. Reluctance to train (or invest in training), other than for obvious immediate needs.
4. Too many hidden personal agendas.
5. Too top-down driven, oversight supervision resulting in lack of empowerment.
6. Product is intangible.
7. Lack of learning culture.
8. Hurdles due to traditional hierarchical structures.
9. Resistance to change on an individual level.
10. Lack of internal knowledge sharing at organisational level.

A learning organisation is an organisation skilled at creating, acquiring, and transferring knowledge and at modifying its behaviour to reflect new knowledge and insights. Without accompanying changes in the way that work gets done, only the potential for improvement exists.

Learning organisations translate new knowledge into new ways of behaving. In a learning organisation, manager and staff encourage work-related learning, the exchange of information between employees to create new ideas and knowledge, and continuous improvement. Staff test experiences and use those experiences to improve the organisation. Flexibility becomes a core value of the organisation as staff accepts and adapts new ideas and seeks ways to enhance products and services. In a learning organisation, people are appreciated for their skills, values, and work. Staff opinions are sought and are treated with respect. Exchanging information and sharing ideas and experiences throughout the organisation is encouraged. People learn new skills they can apply to their jobs. They use their skills to enhance services and improve the organisation. There are more opportunities for staff to be creative, to learn from mistakes, to take risks, and to reach new levels of expertise. In a learning organisation, learning takes place at the individual, group, and organisational levels. The perfect learning organisation is not an attainable goal; it is merely a desirable concept: there is no correct implementation of the learning organisation. Every company can continuously adapt and adjust and some will be better learning organisations than others, but every one of them has something new to learn.

Finally it should be mentioned that the learning organisation is just a means to a business goal, created to improve productivity and most importantly profit. Relatively how long this philosophy will remain fashionable is unknown. What is certain is that for any company in today's global marketplace continuous change and adaptation is the only way to survive.

Review Discussions

1. Explain learning organisation. What are the levels of learning?
2. What are the obstacles of a learning organisation?
3. What are the needs of learning organisation and how is it created?
4. Explain the interrelationships between organisational learning and learning organisation.
5. Discuss followings models of learning organisation:
   (i) M.Pedler.
   (ii) Kolb Experiential Cycle, and.
   (iii) Peter Senge's Five Discipline.

♣♣♣♣♣♣

CHAPTER 12

SWOT ANALYSIS

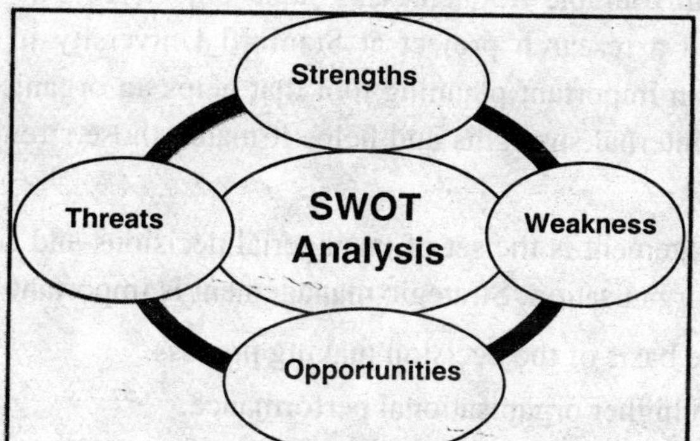

After studying this chapter, you should be able to:

- Understand SWOT analysis and strategic management process.
- Understand tool of strategic management.
- Know strategic use of SWOT.

Introduction

SWOT analysis is a methodology of examining potential strategies derived from the synthesis of organisational strengths, weaknesses, opportunities and threats (SWOT). The partnering of the different elements and the extensive data collected as a result of the analysis can serve as a spark for round table discussions and refinement of current strategies or generation of new strategies.

SWOT analysis is a strategic planning tool used to evaluate the strengths, weaknesses, opportunities, and threats involved in a project or in a business venture. It involves specifying the objective of the business venture or project and identifying the internal and external factors that are favourable and unfavourable to achieving that objective. The technique is credited to Albert Humphrey, who led a research project at Stanford University in the 1960s and 1970s using data. SWOT analysis is an important planning tool that helps an organisation identify, in a systematic and organised way, its internal strengths and helps it match those strengths with the best opportunities in the environment.

Strategic management is the set of managerial decisions and actions that determines the long run performance of an organisation. Strategic management is important because:

1. It forms the basis of the decision making process.
2. It results in higher organisational performance.
3. It requires that managers examine and adapt to business environmental changes.
4. It coordinates diverse organisational units, helping them focus on organisational goals.

SWOT basically stands for Strength, Weakness, Opportunity and Threat.

The analysis is meant to evaluate both the internal and external health of an organisation in any industry. The analysis enables any company to understand its competitive strength *vis-à-vis* the other entities in an industry.

SWOT represents:

- ***S***trengths
- ***W***eaknesses
- ***O***pportunities
- ***T***hreats

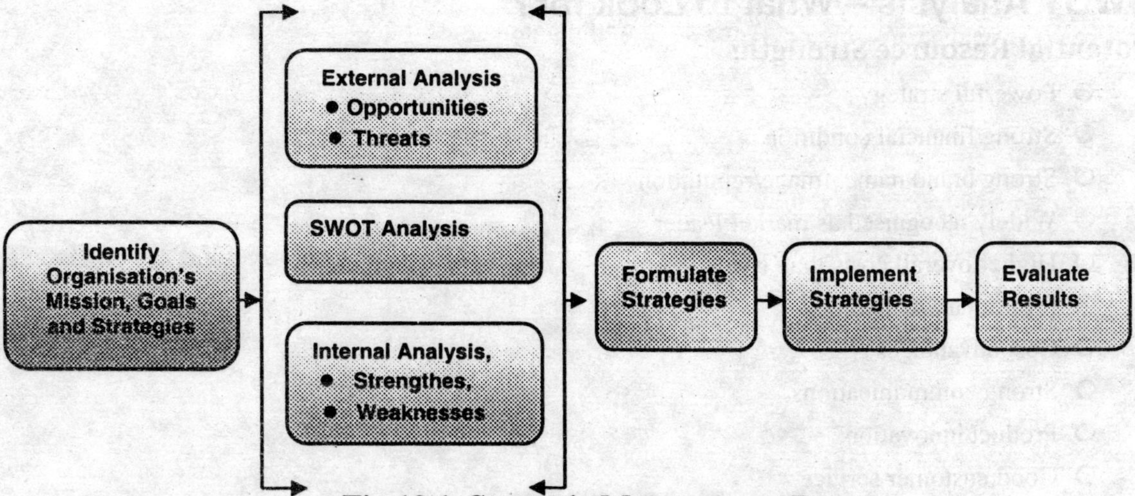

Fig.12.1. Strategic Management Process

As part of the development of strategies and plans to it enable the organisation to achieve its objectives. For an organisation's strategy to be well conceived, it must be matched to both:

- Taking advantage of its internal strengths while defending against its weaknesses
- Identifying the best market opportunities and minimising external threats to its well-being.

Resource strengths and competitive capabilities are competitive assets – Resource strength is something when a firm does well or a characteristic that enhances its competitiveness. It relates to:

- Valuable competencies or know-how.
- Valuable physical assets.
- Valuable human assets.
- Valuable intangible assets – e.g., 'Image'.
- Important competitive capabilities.
- An attribute that places an organisation in a position of competitive advantage.
- Alliances with capable partners.

Resource weaknesses and deficiencies are competitive liabilities – Resource weakness is something a firm lacks, does poorly, or a condition placing it at a disadvantage. It relate to:

- Deficiencies in know-how or expertise or competencies.
- Lack of important physical, organisational, or intangible assets
- Missing capabilities in key areas.

SWOT Analysis – What to Look for?

Potential Resource Strengths

- Powerful strategy
- Strong financial condition
- Strong brand name, image/reputation
- Widely recognised as market leader
- Higher overall costs than rivals
- Proprietary technology
- Cost advantages
- Strong communications
- Product innovation
- Good customer service
- Better product quality
- Alliances or Joint ventures

Potential Resource Weaknesses

- No clear strategic direction
- Obsolete facilities
- Weak balance sheet excess debt
- Missing some key skills/competencies
- Internal operating problems
- Falling behind in Research and Development (R&D)
- Weak marketing and communications skills
- Too narrow product-line.

Potential Resource Opportunities

- Serving additional 'customer' groups
- Expanding to new geographic areas
- Expanding product-line
- Transferring skills to new products or services
- Vertical integration
- Take market share from rivals
- Alliances or Acquisitions
- Openings to exploit new
- Technologies
- Openings to extend brand
- Name/image

Potential Resource Threats

- Entry of potent new competitors
- Substitute products or services
- Slowing market growth
- Adverse shifts in political or
- Economic conditions
- Costly new regulations
- Growing leverage of customers or suppliers
- Reduced buyer needs for product or services
- Demographic changes

Tool for Strategy Formulation

SWOT is basically a two by two matrix.

- Strengths and Weaknesses are within the control of the organisation.
- Opportunities and Threats are something that is beyond the scope of the organisation. The organisation does not have any control on these parameters.
- The political, economic, social, competitive, and techno-legal environments are some factors that can offer either opportunity or pose a threat for an organisation.

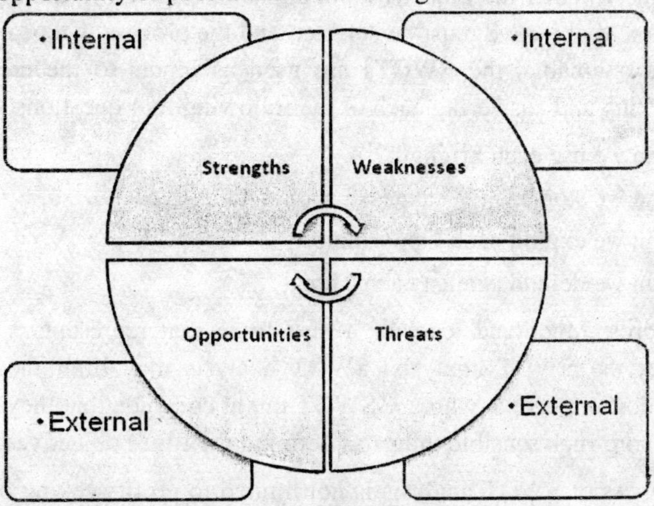

Fig.12.2. SWOT Analysis

Strengths – Opportunities (SO) Strategies – Use strengths to take advantage of opportunities

Weaknesses – Opportunities (WO) Strategies – Overcome weaknesses to take advantage of opportunities

Strengths – Threats (ST) Strategies – Use strengths to avoid threats

Weaknesses – Threats (WT) Strategies – Minimise weaknesses and avoid threats.

Strategic Use of SWOT

SWOTs must be oriented to an objective. If SWOT analysis does not start with defining a desired end state or objective, it runs the risk of being useless. A SWOT analysis may be incorporated into the strategic planning model. If a clear objective has been identified, SWOT analysis can be used to help in the pursuit of that objective. In this case, SWOTs are:

Strengths: Attributes of the organisation that are helpful to achieving the objective.

Weaknesses: Attributes of the organisation those are harmful to achieving the objective.

Opportunities: External conditions those are helpful to achieving the objective.

Threats: external conditions that is harmful to achieving the objective.

Identification of SWOTs is essential because subsequent steps in the process of planning for achievement of the selected objective are to be derived from the SWOTs. First, the decision makers have to determine whether the objective is attainable, as given in the SWOTs. If the objective is not attainable a different objective must be selected and the process is repeated. If, on the other hand, the objective seems attainable, the SWOTs are used as inputs to the creative generation of possible strategies, by asking and answering each of the following four questions, many times:

- How can we use each Strength?
- How can we stop each Weakness?
- How can we exploit each Opportunity?
- How can we defend against each Threat?

Ideally a cross-functional team or a task force that represents a broad range of perspectives should carry-out the SWOT analysis. SWOT analysis may limit the strategies considered in the evaluation. In addition, people who use SWOT might conclude that they have done an adequate job of planning and ignore such sensible things as defining the firm's objectives.

The usefulness of SWOT analysis is not limited to profit-seeking organisations. SWOT analysis may be used in any decision making situation when a desired end-state (objective) has been defined. Examples include: non-profit organisations, governmental units, and individuals. SWOT analysis may also be used in pre-crisis planning and preventive-crisis management. The importance of individual SWOTs will be revealed by the value of the strategies it generates. A SWOT item that produces valuable strategies is important. A SWOT item that generates no strategies is not important. SWOT analysis may limit the strategies considered in the evaluation. People who use SWOT might conclude that they have done an adequate job of planning and ignore such sensible things as defining the firm's objectives. The aim of any SWOT analysis is to identify the key internal and external factors that are important to achieving the objective.

SWOT analysis groups key pieces of information into two main categories – internal and external, which are important to achieve objectives.

Internal factors are strengths and weaknesses internal to the organisation. The internal factors may be viewed as strengths or weaknesses depending upon their impact on the organisation's objectives. External factors are opportunities and threats presented by the external environment. The external factors may include macroeconomic matters, technological change, legislation, and socio-cultural changes, as well as changes in the marketplace or competitive position.

SWOT analysis is just one method of categorisation and has its own weaknesses. For example, it may tend to persuade companies to compile lists rather than think about what is actually important in achieving objectives. It also presents the resulting lists uncritically and without clear prioritisation so that, for example, weak opportunities may appear to balance strong threats.

Conducting a SWOT analysis before defining and agreeing upon an objective (a desired end state) is to be avoided. SWOTs should not exist in the abstract. They can exist only with reference to an objective. If the desired end-state is not openly defined and agreed upon, the participants may have different end-states in mind and the results will be ineffective. Opportunities external to the company are often confused with strengths internal to the company. They need to be kept separated. SWOTs are sometimes confused with possible strategies. SWOTs are descriptions of conditions, while possible strategies define actions. This error is made especially with reference to opportunity analysis. To avoid this error, it may be useful to think of opportunities as 'auspicious conditions'.

A SWOT carried out on a **Human Resource Department** may look like this:

Strengths

- Developed techniques for dealing with major areas of HR, job evaluation, psychometric testing, and basic training.

Weaknesses

- Reactive rather than proactive; needs to be asked rather than developing unsolicited ideas.

Opportunities

- New management team, wanting to improve overall organisational effectiveness through organisational development and cultural management programs.

Threats

- HR contribution not recognised by top management who by-pass it by employing external-consultants.

A SWOT carried out on a **Marketing Department** may look like this:

In SWOT, strengths and weaknesses are internal factors.

Strengths

- Specialist marketing expertise.
- A new, innovative product or service.
- Location of business.
- Quality processes and procedures.
- Any other aspect of business that adds value to product or service.

Weaknesses

- Lack of marketing expertise.
- Undifferentiated products or services, (i.e., in relation to your competitors).
- Location of business.
- Poor quality goods or services.
- Damaged reputation.

In SWOT, opportunities and threats are external factors.

Opportunities

- A developing market such as the internet.
- Mergers, joint ventures or strategic alliances.
- Moving into new market segments that offer improved profits.
- A new international market.
- A market vacated by an ineffective competitor.

Threats

- A new competitor in home market.
- Price wars with competitors.
- A competitor has a new, innovative product or service.
- Competitors have superior access to channels of distribution.
- Taxation is introduced on your product or service.

SWOT analysis Template: Many listed criteria can apply to other quadrants, and the examples are not exhaustive. We may identify and use any other criteria that are appropriate to the situation.

Criteria examples	Strengths	Weaknesses	Criteria examples
Advantages of proposition? Capabilities? Competitive advantages? USP's (unique selling points)? Resources, Assets, People? Experience, knowledge, data? Financial reserves, likely returns? Marketing – reach, distribution, awareness? Innovative aspects? Location and geographical? Price, value, quality? Accreditations, qualifications, certifications? Processes, systems, IT, communications? Cultural, attitudinal, behavioural? Management cover, succession? Philosophy and values?			Disadvantages of proposition? Gaps in capabilities? Lack of competitive strength? Reputation, presence and reach? Financials? Own known vulnerabilities? Timescales, deadlines and pressures? Cash flow, start-up cash-drain? Continuity, supply chain robustness? Effects on core activities, distraction? Reliability of data, plan predictability? Morale, commitment, leadership? Accreditations, etc.? Processes and systems, etc.? Management cover, succession?
Criteria examples	**Opportunities**	**Threats**	**Criteria examples**
Market developments? Competitors' vulnerabilities? Industry or lifestyle trends? Technology development and innovation? Global influences? New markets, vertical, horizontal? Niche target markets? Geographical, export, import? New Unique Selling Perspectives (USPs)? Tactics: e.g., surprise, major contracts? Business and product development? Information and research? Partnerships, agencies, distribution? Volumes, production, economies? Seasonal, weather, fashion influences?			Political effects? Legislative effects? Environmental effects? IT developments? Competitor intentions – various? Market demand? New technologies, services, ideas? Vital contracts and partners? Sustaining internal capabilities? Obstacles faced? Insurmountable weaknesses? Loss of key staff? Sustainable financial backing? Economy – home, abroad? Seasonality, weather effects?

SWOT analysis can be very subjective hence we may not rely on SWOT too much. Two people rarely come-up with the same final version of SWOT. TOWS analysis is extremely similar. It simply looks at the negative factors first in order to turn them into positive factors. So, we may use SWOT as guide and not a prescription. We need to be realistic about the strengths and weaknesses of the organisation while conducting SWOT analysis. SWOT analysis should distinguish between where the organisation is today, and where it could be in the future. SWOT should always be specific, short, simple, and avoid complexity and over analysis. SWOT is subjective and once key issues have been identified with SWOT analysis, they feed into objectives.

Review Discussions

1. Explain SWOT analysis. What is its relevance in strategic management?
2. Describe the process of strategic management?
3. 'SWOT analysis is a tool for strategy formulation.' Explain this statement?
4. Discuss the strategic use of SWOT?

♣♣♣♣♣♣

CASE STUDIES

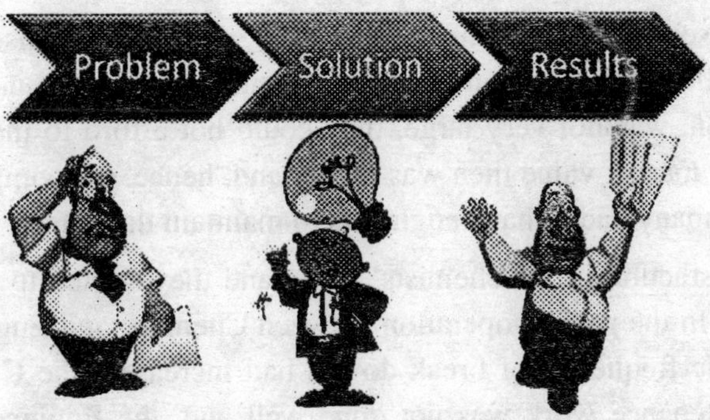

CASE: 1

SALARY REVISION

ABC Company is manufacturing chemicals for textile, paints, and rubber industries – both organic and inorganic. From its inception, the grade for the Chemists who were operating the various plants and the engineers who were maintaining them were same. About two or three years ago, the company noticed that these Engineers were leaving one after one; even the new recruits did not stay more than a few months. Investigations showed that the engineers were getting better offers. The company therefore decided to get new engineers, at higher grades.

This created an ambiguity between the salaries of the Chemists with eight to ten years experience and the Engineers who had two or three years' practical experience after their graduation.

The Chemists represented to the company that their grades should also be revised. Management explained to them that theirs being a comparatively small concern, and as the profit margin for the products, due competition, was not very large, they could not afford to increase everybody's salary. However, the Engineers' market value then was higher and, hence, the company is forced to pay extra salary to them, if the company had to have engineers to maintain the plant.

This created dissatisfaction in the chemists' ranks and they started to take no additional interest or initiative in the work. In the past, cooperation between Chemists and Engineers had been excellent; now it was noted that the frequency of break downs had increased: the Chemist began blaming the Engineers that the maintenance work was not done well and, the Engineers started saying that the operating people were not taking enough care during day-to-day operations. The increased break down had also reduced production and, hence, the total profits of the management.

Because the two groups are not pulling together, some of the Engineers are leaving the organisation as they feel frustrated because, inspite of their working had to cope with the increased frequency of break downs, the plant is not able to produce the output at the normal level, maintained in the past, and occasionally, the management also show their attitude to them that the new engineers are not maintaining the plant, as was being down by the older Engineers, who have since left the organisation for better jobs, elsewhere.

Questions

Analyse the above case and answer the following issues:

1. Is it natural for the company to give more to new Engineers because of the market conditions?
2. Is it natural for the Chemists to feel frustrated by this discrimination?
3. If both the reactions are natural, whose responsibility primarily it is to take care of the situations?

4. The management explained that the concern was small and there was competition and they could not afford to increase everybody's salary. Was there the issue of increase of everybody's salary or comparable position?

♣♣♣♣♣♣

CASE: 2
FORMATION OF THE UNION

The best test and the acid test of sound policy in industrial relations, said the General Manager, Astra Corporation, 'is our ability to make a union unnecessary in this organisation. I say that', he continued, 'not because of any personal objection to unions. If I were an employee of most organisations, I think, I would belong to a union, even if I had to organise it. Unions never appear unless management is negligent. Employees join unions because management has somehow overlooked their interests and needs.'

Six months after this statement to his associates, the GM was presented with a demand for elections among the employees of Astra. Shortly after, the local office of Central Trade Union Congress was certified as their bargaining agent. The GM immediately asks resignation of Industrial Relations Director and his staff. The new IR Director was asked to get rid of the union within twelve months.

Questions

1. Summaries the points you would make in agreeing or challenging the manager's viewpoint.
2. How would you regard the test to be applied to the new Industrial Relations Director?
3. What should be the course of action for Industrial Relations Director to get rid of unions?

♣♣♣♣♣♣

CASE: 3

PAY PACKAGE: SENIORS V/S. JUNIORS

Hi-Tech Electronics Limited was established in 1978 in Faridabad. It produces and markets all types of electronic goods. It has been one among the top five companies as for the level of technology and one among the top three companies regarding marketing young of the products. The company's policies and practices concerning human resource management are top in the country. The company's salary administration policies and practices were taken as guidelines not only by the other companies but also by various wage boards and pay commissions in the country. But this company has been struggling a lot because of a minor problem relating to administration of salary-benefits. The problem is stated hereunder:

The company employed nearly 400 young graduates and postgraduate engineers, just three years back. These employees formed the cream of the company's present human resource. Of course, the older generation of the company's employees also formed the cream of the company's human resources while they were young. The older employees occupied higher positions in all the departments, including human resources department. The company's salary policy and benefits policies were formulated five years back mainly on the basis of the older employees' desire. As such, salaries are fixed at very low level compared to other similar industries and the benefit schemes include an exhaustive list of benefits, including all types of retirement benefits. The cost of retirement benefits would be nearly 25 per cent of the cost of the present staff of the company.

The young employees demand the management to pay immediately whatever it can pay rather than providing extensive fringe benefits. According to them, the pay-packet motivates them much more than benefits which they get mostly in kind. But the older employees view that fringe benefits benefit much more than currency, which taxes them heavily. The company asked the Human Resources Manager to settle the issue.

Questions:

1. What is the crucial issue in this case?
2. If you are the HR Manager of the company, whom do you satisfy?
3. Is the company's basic benefit program in need of change? Suggest the basis.

♣♣♣♣♣♣

CASE: 4
LEADERSHIP STYLE – AFTER PROMOTION

Speed Engineering Company was a multi-location engineering company. It had manufacturing facilities at Hyderabad, Delhi, and Indore. The company adopted budgetary system.

Mr. Manohar was transferred to Indore unit as Plant Manager. He joined the company about ten years back as Trainee Engineer and became an Assistant Plant Manager at the Hyderabad unit. Mr. Manohar is very ambitious and is a bit autocratic. He believes in exercising his authority and control to carry-out his instructions. He has been a high achiever. He got quick promotions in the company.

Immediately after joining Indore unit as plant manager, Manohar made preliminary study of the plant and issued instructions to all departments to reduce their expenses by 5 per cent. A fortnight later, he instructed all departments to increase production by 10 per cent. He also instructed all supervisors to strictly follow the budget. He introduced several new reports and watched the operations very closely. He suspended two supervisors in the second month for not meeting the budget-targets.

With all his efforts, the unit was very much on the right track and within six months exceeded the new budget figures by 8 per cent. On setting the plant right, he was called back to the Hyderabad unit as plant manager where a vacancy had arisen. However, shortly after he left for Hyderabad, the productivity at Indore unit fell below the earlier level and the budget was again in trouble.

Questions

1. Analyse the type of organisational climate created by Manohar at Indore unit.
2. Why was there a drop in productivity at the unit after Manohar left?

♣♣♣♣♣♣

CASE: 5
LEADERSHIP AND WORK BEHAVIOUR

The Madhusudhan Company was located in a medium-sized industrial city in Maharashtra. The company employed a labour force of 250 workers in production of some simple chemicals for which there was a considerable industrial demand. The permanent labour force was divided into five groups, each under the direction of a foreman. Supervising the entire labour force was a general superintendent. Assigned directly out of the general superintendent's office, was an 'Extra Group' which was assigned daily by the superintendent's assistant to the departments needing temporary replacements or extra workers. Sometimes, the entire extra group would be assigned to one department. The extra group was composed of the newest common labourers in the company. This pool of common labour permitted considerable flexibility of shifting workers to the department having temporary increased workload. The pool arrangement also permitted greater flexibility in the size of total labour force, since, if layoffs were necessary, the members of the extra group were laid off first.

Govida Valia, a 24 years of age, was a newly-hired member of the extra group. He related the following experience, which took place during his sixth week on the job.

'One day, I was assigned with another labour to work in the by-products division under Jaspal, one of the five foremen. The job was loading salt, which was piled in a warehouse. The usual method of loading resulted in a wagon of salt being turned out in a day. The weekly quota called for loading two wagons, which took two days. Well, I saw how inefficient this method was. So, I adopted a new method that helped us turnout two loaded cars that day. When the foremen came around and saw what I had done, I could see that he was pleased.'

However, not once during that day did he come up and say, 'O.K.', men, take a break since you're way ahead of schedule.

As far as I am concerned, little things like that mean a lot, and I know that the rest of the man would have appreciated it, too. Infact, as far as I remember, Jaspal or any other foreman never did pat us on the back of doing a good job.

A week later, I was told to work in another department. The group there had a friendly person named Narayana – we always had something to say to each other after first time. I worked in the department in the same group with him. He was an older person who had been with the company for quite a while.

On this particular day, Narayana walked up to me and said, 'I hear you are one of Jaspal's men'. (Jaspal was the by-products division foreman). I passed a few remarks about how it was working under Jaspal.

Then he says, 'I know how you loaded that salt wagon out there'.

In a friendly manner he continued, 'Why do you have to load two wagons instead of one? What do you think would happen if one of our older men was expected to do that in the future'?

I was widely embarrassed because I knew there was no need to load salt that fast because it was not coming in that fast. I realised that, may be, Narayana was right. Narayana also added during this conversation that the company didn't appreciate this hard work, anyway.

Well, after this happened. I recalled other comments about my working too hard. Infact, on my first day of work, I was put with another new employee to remove mud. We worked a little while and then my companion said, 'Go slow, Govind, we want to have a job to do, don't we'?

Questions

1. Analyse the motivating factors, which are operating in Madhusudhan Company.
2. Analyse the behaviour of the foremen of Madhusudhan Company.
3. What will be Govind Valia's work behaviour in future? Why?
4. How would you go about doing an appraisal of job efficiency at Madhusudhan Company?

♣♣♣♣♣♣♣

CASE: 6
SELECTION, APPRAISAL, AND TRAINING

Turner Industries, a family-operated carpeting manufacturer, was started 49 years ago just outside Jackson Mississippi. Today, the company is the third largest producer of carpeting in the United States. With revenue of over $1 billion, Turner employs over 6,000 workers at this now-massive facility.

Five years ago, Turner developed an 'Employee Initiative' program to instill commitment to customer satisfaction throughout the company. The company's employees play a vital role in these programs. A flat organisational structure gives employees, working in a self-managed team, a significant authori and autonomy. Production work teams can undertake training, schedule work, and determine individual performance objectives. Any production process can be halted if an employee believes that quality is suffering or safety is jeopardised.

Teams formed the core of Turner's quality improvement effort. The company formed 25 'Proactive Teams' to address specific manufacturing and production challenges and in addition, selected teamwork on ways to enhance the relationship between Turner and its suppliers . The teams, in general, responded to customers' comments, work on developing new products, and create activities that bring employees together in social situations (sporting activities, picnics, and fund-raising efforts for employee supported charities). With diverse opportunities to affect the company, the teams demonstrated fundamental commitment to customer satisfaction – even creating marketing opportunities that generate satisfaction – even creating marketing opportunities that generate additional revenue.

Management and motivating of workforce require special care on the part of Turner's management. Training and recognition is the key. In a single year, the company invested $ 1,600 per employee in training. Recognition comes in the form of participation in teams, leadership opportunities, and interaction with top management.

Turner's effort at improving its management and human resource practices have allowed it to reduce the number of managers; lower its overall defection rate; and increase quality, efficiency, and customers satisfaction. Avenues have increased significantly over the last four years. As a result of focus on employees' needs, Turner has own over 20 quality awards and was voted the outstanding employer in the south in a regional competition. The company has been written about in the 'Top 200 Employers' in the US and its efforts to involve employees in determining the firm's direction have been very successful, enhancing customer satisfaction and improving business performance.

Questions

1. As a human resource manager, what employee characteristics might be used in the selection of team-members? Also identify a suitable selection process.
2. How might performance appraisal be done? Can team-members be involved in the review of other members? Why or why not?
3. Identify training needs of Turner. Do you believe a company can spend too much money training employees? Why or why not?

CASE: 7
FOREIGN BUSINESS PARTNER

When California-based Dalton & Dalton (D&D) was contracted by a large conglomerate in Taiwan, the President of D&D was quite surprised. For two years, D&D had been looking for an overseas conglomerate that would be interested in building and selling its high-tech medical equipment under a licensing agreement.

The Taiwanese conglomerate has proposed to D&D that the two companies enter into a joint venture type of licensing agreement. The ways in which the business deal will work are the following:

1. The Taiwanese will set up manufacturing facilities and create a marketing group to sell D&D high-tech medical equipment.
2. D&D will train 25 manufacturing and 25 salespeople from the conglomerate so that the latter understands how to make and sell this equipment. This training will take place in the States.
3. D&D will have the right to send people to the manufacturing facility to ensure that the equipment is built according to the specifications and will also have the right to travel with the salespeople to ensure that the equipment is being sold properly.

The arrangement sounds fine to the president of D&D. However, before she agrees to anything, she wants to get more information on how to do business with Taiwanese.

'If we are going to enter into a business venture with the foreign company, I think, we owe it to ourselves to know something about their culture and customs. I'd like to know how to interact effectively with these people and to get an idea about the types of problems we might have in communicating with them'.

Questions

1. If you were advising the president, what type of information would you suggest to be gathered?
2. What type of culture-related problems is there that could result in misunderstanding between the two parties?
3. Suggest an outline of the training programs to be conducted in this context.

♣♣♣♣♣♣

CASE: 8
EGO AND TEAMWORK

Govind was a landed agriculturist who never went to school but had a business brain. He made sure that his two sons went to college and graduated as engineers from the prestigious institution, IIT at Kharagpur. As was pre-planned, the elder son, Raj then went to do the master's in Metallurgy from Jaipur University while the younger son Brij went to BITS, Pilani to gain a master's in Mechanical Engineering. There came the realisation of a dream. With a loan from Punjab & Sind Bank, Govind set up his factory and handed it over to his sons. The registered office of the company was in Howrah, where two sons as Directors sat with their father, who was the Chairman of the company. They appointed Dr. Rajan as General Manager (Production) to manage the plant.

Falling health forced Govind to retire and settle down in his palatial villa in Alipore. He decided to devote the rest of his life to learning to read and enjoying music. Raja and his brother, Brij, fell away from their old father who had set up the wire and rod mill in Sibpur, West Bengal, in 1953. Whereas Raja was Director (Production), Brij was the Director (Research and Development). In addition, Raja looked after the Human Resources Management while Brij looked after the Marketing and Sales. Their young cousin, Jagdish, who had just returned from Boston with an MBA, was appointed as General Manager (Finance). Between the three of them, they managed to bring the company from INR 2 crore sales turnover in 1996 to INR 10 crore in 1976 and INR 25 crore in 1986.

There came a major expansion, funded by prime financial institutions. They set up a state-of-the-art rolling mill in1987 at Rishra with the active cooperation from M/s. Duncan Brothers in South Africa and appointed Parnab Roy as General Manager (Projects). An overall investment of ₹ 50 crore was envisaged and the mill would be operable in April 1989. But with the changing Central Government in India and the turbulence in South Africa, the project got delayed. Phase I of the project was at last commissioned in 1993 and phase II got under way. Originally, phase II ought to have been completed in 1992. The total capital outlay had crossed INR 90 crore mark already. The financial institutions had started putting pressure on the directors to complete the project in quick time.

It was common knowledge that each of the three general managers took every opportunity to show the others in poor light. Each was competent in his own field of operations, but was a poor team-player, since the ego came in the way of his soliciting advice and cooperation in every other way. The General Manager (Production) blamed the General Manager (Projects) for the delay in commissioning the new mill. The General Manager (Projects) blamed the General Manager (Finance) for not releasing funds and facilitating payments to suppliers in time. The General Manager (Finance) blamed the other two for not giving him adequate notice of requirements and withholding vital information from him as a result of which letters of credit remained unopened, shipments were delayed, demurrage costs were rising and the company earned a bad name in the market.

In 1994, the plant had a series of shutdowns since raw material availability was erratic and the import duties were sky-rocketing. It was suspected that the materials-accounting was in poor shape and production managers were high-handed when it came to removing items from the stores for which the poor stores clerk dared not ask back-up documentation. The directors decided to appoint a Senior Manager (Commercial) reporting to them, directly. This was seen as an affront by their young cousin as well as by the General Manager (Production).The General Manager (Projects) seemed unconcerned.

Suddenly, in April 1995, production came to a standstill since raw material was just not available to feed the factory. Acrimony between the three general managers rose to a feverish pitch and fingers were being pointed at the new Senior Manager (Commercial). The Senior Manager (Commercial) had all along complained that he was not getting the cooperation required to function effectively.

All the three general managers were very efficient, strong willed and technically competent, but they had an ego problem and were neither prepared to consult their colleagues, delegate authority nor divulge their plans openly. Their desire to show their colleagues in poor light was overwhelming. Counseling these general managers had been of no avail and they were literally holding the directors and the company to ransom, it seemed.

Questions

1. What, according to you, is the major problem?
2. If you are appointed as an expert to study the system and report, how would you report?
3. What is the ethical issue involved in this case?

♣♣♣♣♣♣

CASE: 9
STRESS MANAGEMENT

When Mahesh joined the Indian Bank in1985, he had one clear goal to prove his potentiality. He did prove that and has been promoted five times since his entry into the bank. Compared to others, his progress has been the fastest. Currently, his job demands that Mahesh should work 10 hours a day with practically no holiday. At least, two days in a week Mahesh is required to travel.

Peers and subordinates at the bank have appreciation for Mahesh. They don't grudge the success achieved by Mahesh, though there are some who wish they too had been promoted as well.

The post of a general manager fell vacant. One should work as GM a couple of years if he were to climb up to the top of the ladder. Mahesh applied for the post along with others in the bank. The chairman has assured Mahesh that the post would be his.

A sudden development took place, which almost wrecked Mahesh's chances. The bank has the practice of subjecting all its executives to medical check-up, once a year. The medical reports go straight to the chairman who would initiate remedial measures, where necessary. Though Mahesh was only 35, he had to undergo the test.

The chairman of the bank received a copy of Mahesh's medical examination results, along with a note from the doctor. The note explained that Mahesh was seriously overworked and recommended that he be given an immediate four weeks' vacation. The doctor also recommended that Mahesh must take physical exercise, everyday. The note warned that if Mahesh did not care for the advice, he would be in for heart trouble in another six months.

After reading the doctor's note the chairman sat back in his chair and started brooding over the situation. Three issues were the uppermost in his mind.

1. How would Mahesh take this news?
2. How many others would have similar fitness problems?
3. Since the environment in the bank helps create problem, what could he do to alleviate it?

The idea of holding a stress-management program flashed in his mind and suddenly, he instructed his secretary to set up a meeting with the Doctor and some key members at the earliest.

Questions

1. If the news is broken to Mahesh, how would he react?
2. What would you recommend, if you were to give advice to the chairman on this matter?

CASE: 10
VISION

Robert J. Eaton has big shoes to fill. In July 1993 he took the post of Chairman at Chryster Corp. that had previously been held by 'Mr. Charisma', Lee Iacocca had taken over the top spot at Chryster in 1980, when the company was on the verge of bankruptcy. In only a few short years, Iacocca had turned Chryster into a money-making machine.

Iacocca's style was bold and visionary. He developed several grand strategies for Chryster. To get the company immediately profitable, he created a basic compact model – the K car – and used its platform to create a host of new cars including the incredibly successful minivan. To fill the need of subcompacts, he began importing cars from Japan and putting Chryster Corp, nameplates on them.

But that was then and this is now. Robert Eaton has joined an impressive group of chief executives who no longer buy the notion that leaders need to provide grand visions or long-term strategies for their companies. In its place, they are emphasising the short-term bottom line.

'Internally, we don't use the word – vision', says Eaton. 'I believe in quantifiable short-term results – things we can all relate to – as opposed to some esoteric thing no one can quantify.'

That view is also being articulated by CEOs at Apple Computer, IBM, Aetna Life & Casualty, and General Motors. When asked for his recipe for an IBM comeback, the recently appointed chairman, Louis V. Gerstner, said, 'The last thing IBM needs right now is a vision'.

It appears that, at least among some leaders, grand visions are out of fashion. They're concentrating on the nuts and bolts of running their businesses.

Questions

1. Isn't this short-term focus likely to hurt their companies in the longer-term?
2. What's the purpose of a grand vision? What takes its place if a company's leader doesn't provide it?
3. Don't organisations need radical new ideas to win in the marketplace?
4. Eaton says his goal for Chryster is, 'getting a little bit better every single day'. Is that a viable goal for a real 'leader'?

♣♣♣♣♣♣

CASE: 11

MICROSOFT'S WORKAHOLIC CULTURE

In the old days it was so simple. Dad went to work and Mom stayed home and cared for the kids as we know, those traditional roles are now the exception. Today, Mom is likely to hold a full-time job outside the home Dad is likely a play a major role in doing household chores and raising the children. But have organisational policies changed to reflect these new roles? In a number of companies, the answer seems to be 'no'. Ironically, today's organisational policies may better reflect the needs of working mothers than the needs of fathers who want to balance family and work responsibilities. There are risks for fathers who choose 'the daddy track'.

Take the case of Jeff Coulter. Jeff had a sales job with Microsoft, a company known for expecting long hours from its employees. This is illustrated by the story of a Microsoft Programer who ran into the company's CEO, Bill Gates, one evening when the former was leaving for home. It was 8 p.m. Gates asked the employee where he was going. 'Home', he replied. 'I,ve been here for twelve hours'. 'Oh', responded Gates, 'only working half day'? Microsoft's culture embraces a relentless work ethic. 'Complaining about how hard you work at Microsoft', says one Manager 'is like complaining about the weather in Seattle'.

Coulter put in 50-hours workweeks at Microsoft. But, in order to get his work completed and get home in time for dinner, he would come in early. His coworkers and boss, who came in after he did in the mornings, only noticed that Coulter was leaving at 5 or 5:30 each evening. Coulter was eventually fired. The company said it was for inadequate performance. Coulter thinks otherwise. He says Microsoft discriminated against him because of his family status.

The following experts from Coulter's boss were secretly recorded by him during conversations with her – 'Microsoft hires everybody who's killing themselves is, competing with other people who are killing themselves and it is like survival of the fittest. You picked a company where it's a disadvantage to be married. It's a disadvantage to have any other priority other than work.' Microsoft's position is that these comments were taken out of context. Coulter, meanwhile, continues to believe his family cost him his job.

Questions

1. Is it unrealistic for a company like Microsoft to expect employees to put their careers ahead of their families? Do you think organisations need to change in response to changing family roles and values?
2. Working long hours is a widely recognised part of Microsoft's culture. Do you think Microsoft needs to change its culture to meet the needs of family-oriented employees like Jeff Coulter, or do you think workers like Jeff need to change to fit into Microsoft's culture?

3. Is there a double standard where organisations provide flex-time, child care, and other family-friendly options to reduce career-family conflict for women while men put their careers at risk if they want to spend time with their family?

♣♣♣♣♣♣

CASE: 12

CAREER DEVELOPMENT AS A PERSONAL RESPONSIBILITY

Assisting individuals with their career development plans and planning can be a powerful tool for integrating organisational and individual goals. But the managerial challenge is to design a program that will enable individuals to plan their careers with realistic information about career path opportunities that exist within a particular organisation. At the most basic level individuals must know and understand how their goals fit with those of their supervisors and work groups. In the absence of such information, individuals cannot find their places in the organisation and consequently, will never be able to make optimal to it.

One R&D organisation implemented a career development program in one of its divisions. The management of the division initially perceived the program to be an attempt to get non-supervisory employees to take responsibility for their own career development. Eventually, however, the program was to improve and provided not only opportunities for individual growth, but also a way for supervisors to support employee's career goals and to disseminate organisational goals and objectives.

Another initial focus of the programe was to improve peer relations among the non-supervisory personnel. Managers and supervisors perceived poor peer relations to be a problem, but it was later discovered that the nonsupervisory personnel did not see the same problem was the unfair way that supervisors assigned jobs and distributed rewards. Non-supervisory employees perceived the problem to be poor employee-supervisor relations, not peer relations. The program then became a catalyst for managing employee-supervisor relations because effective career development can succeed only in workplaces that employees believe to be free of arbitrary job and reward assignments.

These changes in management's expectations for what a career development program can accomplish were the result of how the program was designed. Rather than imposing the program, management designed the program only after involving managers, supervisors, and non-supervisory personnel in a needs-assessment phase. It was during this phase that it became obvious that an individual's career goals and strategies can be developed only with participation of the individual's supervisor who can represent the organisation's goals and strategies. The information obtained in the design phase enabled management to think in terms of a program that could go beyond the usual expectations for a career development program. But what would be the features of the program?

The division's management decided on a workshop to include a series of related activities was to accomplish certain objectives in the context of the entire program. The workshop's first activity was the division leader's presentation of the division's mission, goals, and overall strategy. The presentation outlined current and future major projects and anticipated job requirements as well as the division's philosophy of career development. Prior to attending the workshop, participants had received from their supervisors answers to some questions, including – What are the major goals for the work group and how I support you to meet those goals? What do you see as the major results for my job in the next 12 months? How can you support me to achieve those results? What are my major competencies? What, in your view, is an outstanding employee?

The workshop activity included group discussion of the division leader's presentation and the responses of supervisors to the key questions. The participants completed a variety of self-assessment inventories to help them discern values. The participants took all this information as important input in the development of their own 'Individual Development Plans' (IDP).

The IDP identifies what each individual can and should do to achieve career aspirations. It identifies development needs for performance improvement and job competency and specific actions to take to improve any deficiencies. It also identifies the assistance required of the supervisor and other division-controlled support such as job assignments, training, and information. The IDP also identifies all the obstacles that must be overcome if the individual is to accomplish the plan. Completing the IDP was the last activity of the workshop and all other activities led up to this important exercise. Following the workshop, individuals discussed their IDPs with their supervisors.

Through the participation of all key individuals throughout the organisation, the career development workshop became more than a career planning exercise. The workshop can be used as an important strategy for integrating organisational and individual goals. In addition it can serve as an important activity for identifying and managing key work-related problems that can stifle not only an organisation's purposes, but an individual aspect as well.

Questions

1. Explain how the R&D unit integrated the unit's objectives with its employees' objectives through the career development program.
2. What can you identify as potential sources of conflict among employees and their supervisors who participate in this kind of program?
3. In what ways could the IDP concept be used in this context of classrooms, students, and teachers?

♣♣♣♣♣♣

CASE: 13
SAN DIEGO ZOO'S TEAM APPROACH

Employees at the San Diego Zoo used to have very narrow and very well defined job responsibilities. Keepers did the keeping and gardeners did the gardening. Employees in construction and maintenance constructed and maintained. This system worked as long as there were clearly defined boundaries between animal exhibits, public areas, and horticultural displays.

Four years ago the zoo began to develop bioclimatic zones, in which plants and animals are grouped together in ageless enclosures that resemble their native habitats. Instead of viewing the exhibits from afar, visitors now walk into and become part of these zones in what the zoo calls an immersion experience. Bioclimatic zones, such as the humid, 3.5-acre Tiger River exhibit, not only provide a healthier environment for plants and animals, they provide a better way to educate visitors about conservation issues and to increase their enjoyment of the zoo experience.

Because the zones themselves are more interdependent – plants are there to be eaten, not just admired – the employees who manage them must work together more easily. This is why, instead of maintaining the new exhibits with employees from traditional functional areas, the zoo has assigned self-directed, multidisciplinary teams to manage the bioclimatic zones.

Tiger River, for example, is run by a seven-member team of Mammal and Bird Specialists, Horticulturalists, and maintenance and construction workers. The team tracks its own budget, and members are jointly responsible for the display. Before, the gardener may not have cared about trash on the ground because that was the groundskeeper's job. But today, the horticulturist may spend a morning cleaning the paths, helping the bird keeper chase down some geese, and answering questions from curious visitors without ever looking at the plants.

Tiger River team-members received extensive cross-training, and together they analysed the work required, set goals for themselves, and gradually built a sense of mutual responsibility and ownership for the exhibit. The move to self-directed teams met with problems and some resistance, but the process is now paying off. Zoo attendance is up, despite the depressed southern California economy. Workers compensation claims are down and employees report a much higher quality of work-life. As one team-member explained, 'Until I was cross-trained and became responsible for a whole area, I had little regard for other job classifications. Tiger River has taught me to respect and help others for the benefit of the entire zoological society. This, in turn, gave me pride, which enriched my work'.

Self-directed teams like those implemented at the San Diego Zoo are getting a lot of attention these days. In a survey conducted by Development Dimensions International(DDI), a human resources consulting firm in Pittsburgh, 27 per cent of respondents reported that their organisations currently use self-directed teams, and half of those individuals predicted that the majority of their workforce will be organised in teams within the next five years.

This interest is self-directed teams is nothing short of phenomenal, since it's such a new concept. The same DDI survey revealed that most respondents have two years or less experience with self-directed teams. As corporate executives and small-business owners alike embrace the total quality movement, they're finding that self-directed teams represent potentially one of the most productive forms of employee involvement.

Self-directed teams require an enormous amount of thought and planning, and no organisation should implement them without understanding what self-directed teams are and aren't the same functional department who join together to foster team spirit. Self-directed teams also aren't cross-functional groups of employees who come together to solve a particular problem and then return to their regular jobs. Neither of these two approaches represents self-direction because it doesn't change the way the organisation is structured or the way work gets done.

The adoption of self-directed teams not only requires changing the attitudes of people; it requires changing the organisational structure, information patterns, rewards and compensation systems, and the whole concept of career paths. With self-directed teams, employees require a lot of training in team skills. They need cross-training in different functions, and they require much greater business training so that they can understand the impact of their actions on the entire organisation.

Questions

1. Should leaders at the San Diego Zoo have feared the loss of power when the self-directed teams were established? Why?
2. Was the San Diego Zoo move to self-directed teams automatically self-directing?
3. Why is the management of change so much a part of the transition to self-directed teams?

♣♣♣♣♣♣

CASE: 14
THE FIRST-LEVEL SUPERVISORS

A few years ago, the top executives of a well-managed Government Company decided to organise an early management program for first level supervisors. This company had long been in the forefront of management education and was quite ready to listen to the advice of management specialists concerning this subject. They surveyed their own experience only to find that many young people, professionally trained, were leaving the company for private employment, where the rewards were thought to be greater. This left the company with something less than the best qualified candidates for supervision; it also left it with a notably older group of supervisors.

A career development program was carefully worked out. The development of the candidates comprised of :

1. A week of formal supervisory training;
2. Assignments to an establishment supervisor who would act as a teacher and guide, advising the candidate on a course of reading and enrolment in college courses wherever available, discussing the theory and practice of management with the candidate and evaluating his or her progress;
3. Work on task-force assignments as available and appropriate. Frequently, candidates were appointed to supervisory positions before they finished their programs; if not, they would either stay within the program until assigned or resign from it to resume a technical career.

Several advantages emerged from this program. The candidates were pleased that their careers were a matter of interest and concern to the higher level executives; candidates could more easily bring themselves to the attention of their supervisors; the company was provided with a group of youthful candidates for supervision. The brain-drain from the company almost stopped. Gradually, more vigour in management levels became evident and young men and women could establish a broader base of experience from which to decide whether they really wanted to be managers. Certain disadvantages also became apparent. Many good candidates failed to apply for the program because they were not sure of their own career objectives, they did not want to move away from the places where they were originally domiciled or they felt too busy to undergo the training described. Some complained of inadequate counseling, and many who failed to apply were later disgruntled when they found themselves no longer among the candidates for supervisory appointments. The company is now in a mood to reassess its experience with the program.

Questions

1. Is this a good training programme? Are there any missing elements?
2. If you were asked to suggest improvements, what would you say?

♣♣♣♣♣♣♣

CASE: 15
RELEVANCE OF THEORETICAL CONCEPTS

As a part of the company's management development programme, a group of managers from various functional areas have devoted several class sessions to the study of motivation theory and the relevance of such knowledge to the manager's responsibility for directing and controlling the operations of his organisational unit.

One of the participants in the program is Ashish Chopra, who has been a supervisor in the production department for about a year. During the discussion session, Ashish Chopra made the following observation:

'Motivation theory makes sense in general, but there is really no opportunity for me to apply these concepts in my job situation. After all, our shop employees are unionised and have job security and wage scales that are negotiated and are not under my control. The study of motivation concepts has given me some ideas about how to get my sons to do their chores and their home-work, but it has not given me anything I can use on the job. Furthermore, in a working situation we are all dealing with adults, and it seems to me this reward and punishment thing smacks of personal manipulation that just won't go over with people.

Questions

1. Analyse the case showing your acquaintance with the various theories of motivation.
2. How far Ashish Chopra justified in his comments?
3. Offer practical suggestions to apply motivational concepts in job situations.

♣♣♣♣♣♣

BIBLIOGRAPHY

- Hellriegel, D., Slocum, J., and Woodman, R. (1998). Organisational Behaviour.
- Belbin, R., Meredith (1981), Management Teams – Why they succeed or fail?
- Belbin, R., Meredith Team – Roles at Work.
- Denison, D. (1990), Corporate Culture and Organisational Effectiveness.
- Patterson, M., Warr, P., and West, M. (2004). Organisational Climate and Company Productivity: The role of the employee affect and employee level. *Journal of Occupational and Organisational Psychology.*
- Schneider, B. (1990). Organisational Climate and Culture.
- Potosky, D., and Ramakrishna, H. (2001). Goal orientation, self-efficacy, Organisational climate, and job performance. Academy of Management.
- Ekvall, G. (1996). Organisational climate for creativity and innovation. *European Journal of Work and Organisational Psychology.*
- Hansen, G., Wernerfelt B. (1989). Determinants of firm performance: The relative importance of economic and Organisational factors. *Strategic Management Journal.*
- Thompson, M. (1996) in Ashkanasy, N., Wilderom, C., and Peterson, M. (2000). Handbook of Organisational Culture and Climate.
- Sharma, R.K., Organisation and Management: New Delhi: Kalyani Publishers, 1998.
- Wendell, I. French, Cecil, H., Bell. Organisation Development. Sixth Edition, Pearson Education (Singapore) Pvt. Ltd. Indian Branch New Delhi, India.
- Ahuja, K.K; Personnel Management, Need for Organisational Development, Third Revised Edition: 1999, Dhanpat Rai & Co. (P) Ltd. 1982, New Delhi, India.
- Singh, B.P., and Chhabra T.N., Personnel Management and Industrial Relation, Third Edition: 1999, Dhanpat Rai & Co. (P) Ltd. 1982, New, Delhi, India.
- Roa and Narayan: Organisational Theory and Behaviour, Steps in OD.
- Paul, Hersey, and Kenneth, H. Blanchard. Management of Organisational Behaviour, Job Enrichment. Utilizing Resources, 4th Edition. Prentice-Hall of India Private Limited, New Delhi, 1986.
- Flippo, Edwin, B: Personnel Management, Type of Organisational Structure, Library of congress cataloguing in publication Data, McGraw-Hill Book Co., Singapore; 1984.
- Robert, Bacal: Communicating with your boss, Conflict 911 online publications, 2007.
- Robert, Bacal: Defusing Hostile People, part 1 and 2, Conflict 911 online publications, 2007.
- Robert, Bacal: Five habits of effective conflict resolvers, Conflict 911 online publications, 2007.
- Barley, S.R., and D.B. Knight: 'Towards a Cultural Theory of Stress Complaints'. Research in Organisational Behaviour, Vol.14 (Greenwich, CT: JAI Press, 1992) pp.1- 48.

- Iron Son, G.H.: 'Job Stress and Health', Job Satisfaction (New York: Lexington Books, 1992) pp.219-39.
- Trent, J.T., A.L. Smith, and D.L. Wood, Telecommuting: 'Stress and Social Support', Psychological Reports (June 1994, pp.1312-14.
- Jagadish, S.B., and Readdy, A.N. Venkatesh: (Modi Hosp, Gulbarga) Study of level of stress among health professionals – A Management Perspective. *Journal of Community Guidance and Research, 2000,* 17 (3), 24 - 248.
- Dess and Miller: Strategic Management, McGraw-Hill, 1993.
- Narayanan, Lakshmi, Menon, Shanker, and Spector, Paul. (U South Florida, Sarasota) A cross-cultural comparison of job stressors and reactions among employees holding comparable jobs in two countries. *International Journal of Stress Management, 1999,* 6 (3), pp. 197 - 212.
- Saini, Anjali, and Das, Ira. (DEI, Agra) Teachers' Stress in personal and occupational life. *Indian Journal of Psychometry and Education, 1999,* 30(2), pp. 115-118.
- Gaur, Shubhra Prateek, and Dhawan, Nisha. (U. Delhi, Delhi) Work-related Stress and Adaptation Pattern Among Women Professionals. Psychological Studies, 2000, 45 (162), pp. 58-64.
- Pattanayak, B., Sarangi, Arpita, and Mishra, P.K. (IIM, Indore) Role stress in work life management in public sector. Social Science International, 2000, 16(1-2), pp. 52-65.
- Allen, A. Louis: Management and Organisation, New Delhi: Kalyani Publishers, 1976.
- Asthana, G. P. Management: New Delhi: Shiva Lal Agrawal & Company, 1974.
- Chabra, N. T: Principle and Practice of Management, New Delhi: Educational Technical Publishers, 1999.
- Gupta, R. S., Sharma, B. D. Principle and Practice of Management, New Delhi: Kalyani Publishers, 1997.
- Chatterjee S. S. An Introduction to Management, Lucknow: World Publishers Ltd., 1988.
- Koontz, Harold, Donnell, O. Cyril. Management a System and Contingency, New York: McGraw-Hill Ltd., 1976.
- Sharma, R. K., Gupta, S. K. Organisation and Management, New Delhi: Kalyani Publishers, 1998.
- Saksena, S. C: Business Administration and Management, New Delhi: Kalyani Publishers, 1973.
- Tripathi, P. C., Reddy, P. Principles of Management, New Delhi: T.M.H.P.C.L., 1991.
- Terry, R. Georage. Principles of Management, Allahabad: Educational Technical Publishers, 1989.
- Weihrich, Heinz. Management a Global Perspective, New Delhi: International Educations, 1994.

- Kaushal, H. Case Study Solutions – Human Resource Development, New Delhi: MacMillan India Ltd., 2004.
- Robbins, Stephen P. Organisational Behaviour, Seventh Edition-1996, Prentice-Hall of India Private Limited, New Delhi.
- Kondalkar, V.G. Organisational Behaviour, New Age International (P) Ltd., Publisher, New Delhi, 2007.
- Luthans, Fred. Organisational Behaviour, McGraw-Hills, International Edition, 1995.
- Thomas K.A. Conflict and Negotiations Process in Organisations, Handbook of Industrial and Organisational Psychology, 2nd Edition, Vol. 3 Palo Alto, Consulting Psychologist Press, 1992.
- Austin, David, L. Conflict: A More Professional Approach, Vol-21, July 1976.
- Schein, Edgar, H. Organisational Psychology, Eagle Wood Cliff, NJ, Prentice-Hall Inc, 1966.
- Baron, R.A. Behaviour in Organisations, understanding and managing the human side of work, Alyn and Baon, 1983.
- Hersey, P., and Balnchard. Management of Organisational Behaviour: Utilising Human Resources, Prentice-Hall of India, New Delhi, 1977.
- Coch, L., and J.R.P. French, Jr. Overcoming Resistance to Change, Rinehart and Winston, Inc, New York, 1952.
- Wendell, L. French and Cecil, H. Bell, Jr. Organisational Development, Prentice-Hall, 5th Edition, 1996.
- Peter, M. Senge. The fifth discipline – The Art and Practice of Learning Organisation, Doubleday/Currency, New York, 1990.
- Davis, K. Human Behaviour at Work, Tata McGraw-Hill, New Delhi, 1977.
- Comeron, M. Ford and Dennis, A. Gioia: Creative Actions in Organisations, Sage Publications, 1995.
- Pareek, Udai. Making Organisational Role Effective, Tata McGraw-Hill Publishing Co. Ltd., New Delhi.
- French, W.L. and Bell, C.H. Organisational Development, Prentice-Hall, New Delhi, 1980.
- Chakraborthy, S.K. Management by Objectives, MacMillan & Co., New Delhi, 1976.
- Bower, G.H. and Hilgard, E.J. Theories of Learning, Englewood Cliffs, NJ, Prentice-Hall, 1975.
- Beckhard, Rochard. Organisational Development, Strategies and Models, Reading Addison Wesley, 1969.
- Linkert, Renisis. Human Organisation – Its Management and Values, New York, McGraw-Hill, 1967.
- Donnelly, J. H. Jr. Gibson, J. L. and Ivancevich, J. M. Fundamentals of Management, Irwin/ McGraw-Hill, 1998.

- Aldag, Ramon, J. and Brief, Arthur, P. Managing Organisational Behaviour, St. Paul, West Publishing Co., 1981.
- Drucker, Peter, F. Management – Tasks, Responsibilities and Practices, London, William Heinemann Ltd., 1974.
- Humble, John W. Management by Objectives, London, Industrial Education and Research Foundation,1967.
- Bhattacharya, Sanjay. Organisational Development Intervention Stress Management Model, Vol. 13, No.2 August, 2010 *Business Manager- Magazine,* Alwa, Rajasthan, (India).
- Linikert, Rensis, L. The Human Organisations, New York, McGraw-Hill Book Co., Inc, 1967.
- Ordiorne, Geaorge, S. Management by Objectives, New York, Pitman, 1956.
- Singh, B.P., and Chhabra, T.N. Organisational Theory and Behaviour, Dhanpat Rai & Co., New Delhi, 1998.
- Thelen, H. Dynamics of Groups at Work, Chicago, University of Chicago, 1963.
- Vroom, Victor, H. Work and Motivation, New York, John Wiley and Sons, Inc., 1964.
- William, J. Cliftou, Dubrin, Andrew, J., and Sisk, Henry, L. Management and Organisation, Cincinnati, Western Publishing Co., 1985.
- Breach, E.F.L. Principles and Practice of Management, Longmans, Green & Co., London, 1965.
- Fayol, Henri. General and Industrial Management, Sir Isaac Pitman & Sons Ltd., London, 1968.
- French, W.L. and Hellreigal, Don. Personnel Management and Organisational Development, Houghton Mifflin Co., Boston, 1971.
- Harrel, Thomas, W. Industrial Psychology, Oxford & IBH Publishing Co., London, 1964.
- Koontz, Harold, and Weihrich, Heinz, Management, McGraw-Hill, Tokyo,1993.
- Miner, J.B. Personnel Psychology, McGraw-Hill Book Co., New York, 1969.
- Monappa, A. and Saiyadain, M.S., Personnel Management, Tata McGraw-Hill, New Delhi, 1979.
- Mooney, James. The Principles of Organisation, Harper and Brothers, New York, 1947.
- Rao, T.V. The HRD Missionary, Oxford & IBH, New Delhi, 1990.
- Taylor, F.W. Scientific Management, Harper and Brother, New York, 1947.
- Tiffin, J. and Mc Mormick, E.J. Industrial Psychology, Prentice-Hall of India, New Delhi, 1971.
- Torgersen, Weinstock. Management – An Integrated Approach, Prentice-Hall of India, 1971.
- Yorder, Dale. Personnel Management and Industrial Relations, Prentice-Hall of India, New Delhi, 1974.